Modern Language Association of America

Research and Scholarship in Composition

*Lil Brannon, Anne Ruggles Gere, Dixie Goswami, Susan Hilligoss,
C. H. Knoblauch, Geneva Smitherman-Donaldson, and Art Young,*
Series Editors

1. Anne Herrington and Charles Moran, eds. *Writing, Teaching, and
   Learning in the Disciplines.* 1992.

Writing, Teaching, and Learning in the Disciplines

Edited by
Anne Herrington and Charles Moran

The Modern Language Association of America
New York   1992

© 1992 by The Modern Language Association of America

Library of Congress Cataloging-in-Publication Data

Writing, teaching, and learning in the disciplines / edited by Anne
   Herrington and Charles Moran.
         p.   cm. — (Research and scholarship in composition ; 1)
   Includes bibliographical references (p.) and index.
   ISBN 0-87352-577-9   ISBN 0-87352-578-7 (pbk.)
      1. Language arts—Correlation with content subjects.   2. English
   language—Rhetoric—Study and teaching.   3. Interdisciplinary
   approach in education.   I. Herrington, Anne, 1948–   . II. Moran,
   Charles, 1936–   .   III. Series.
   LB1576.W76   1992
   428'.007—dc20   92-8756

Published by The Modern Language Association of America
10 Astor Place, New York, New York 10003-6981

Contents

Preface to the Series

The Research and Scholarship in Composition series, developed with the support of the Modern Language Association's Publications Committee, responds to the recent growth of interest in composition and to the remarkable number of publications now devoted to it. We intend the series to provide a carefully coordinated overview of the varied theoretical schools, educational philosophies, institutional groupings, classroom situations, and pedagogical practices that collectively constitute the major areas of inquiry in the field of composition studies.

Each volume combines theory, research, and practice in order to clarify theoretical issues, synthesize research and scholarship, and improve the quality of writing instruction. Further, each volume reviews the most significant issues in a particular area of composition research and instruction; reflects on ways research and teaching inform each other; views composition studies in the larger context of literary, literacy, and cultural studies; and draws conclusions from various scholarly perspectives about what has been done and what yet needs to be done in the field.

We hope this series will serve a wide audience of teachers, scholars, and students who are interested in the teaching of writing, research in composition, and the connections among composition, literature, and other areas of study. These volumes should act as a lively orientation to the field for students and nonspecialists and provide experienced teachers and scholars with useful overviews of research on important questions, with insightful reflections about teaching, and with thoughtful analyses about future developments in composition studies. Each book is a spirited conversation in which you are cordially invited to join.

Series Editors

Preface to the Volume

Writing in the disciplines is an extraordinary field. It is at its deepest level a teachers' movement, one that has flourished, remarkably, in an educational system that values not teaching but research. At its best, it considers not just teaching but *learning* and thus sees student, teacher, and discipline as an interrelated system. It flourishes in faculty workshops and professional conferences, where teachers excitedly talk with one another about ways in which writing connects with their teaching and with their students' learning. And it flourishes in research in which scholars seek to understand discourse practices both within and across disciplinary and professional groups and classrooms. As practiced in teaching and research, writing in the disciplines is an enterprise in which there is great energy, much activity, and the potential for educational reform.

Writing in the disciplines is a large and various territory, one that has been settled but not yet fully mapped. The several names that have arisen to designate this territory—*writing in the disciplines, writing across the curriculum, writing in the content areas, language for learning*—reflect its various sites—in Britain and the United States, in schools at all levels, from elementary through postsecondary. Under its different names, writing in the disciplines has been a powerful force in American and British education. Proof of the movement's power in higher education in the United States is to be found in the surveys by Susan McLeod and others, who have found writing-in-the-disciplines programs established or projected in more than one-third of the institutions surveyed. Further proof is the number of books and articles published on various aspects of writing in the disciplines—including the decision of the Modern Language Association to support and publish this volume.

In this book we hope to provide the outlines of a map of this territory, focusing on the region of higher education in the United States. The essays that follow address questions that provide the coordinates for the topographical detail: What social, intellectual, and poltical forces have shaped this field? What inquiries define the field as a research area? How does the new field relate to the discipline of English and to the other academic disciplines in which it operates? What motives do teachers have in using writing in their classes? What are the outcomes of particular ways of bringing writing into disciplinary teaching? What issues of teaching and learning does writing in the disciplines bring to the foreground? What is, or should be, the relation between the writing we ask students to do in our classes and the discourse practices and values of disciplinary and professional communities?

We have grouped the essays into sections using these questions as guides. Each section opens with an introduction that highlights the issues and approaches of the essays within that section. The collection starts with two essays, one from England and one from the United States, that together provide a historical perspective on the writing-in-the-disciplines movement. The second section begins with two theoretical perspectives on the relationship between writing, learning, and disciplinary knowledge and discourse: the first emphasizes a general theory of teaching; the second, rhetorical studies of disciplinary discourses. The two essays that conclude this section, both based on empirical studies, demonstrate the importance of bridging these two approaches and the difficulty we encounter in trying to do so. The third section focuses directly on teaching and the aims of using writing in classrooms, bringing us the voices and perspectives of five teachers— one also a WAC program director. In the fourth section the emphasis shifts from teachers' reflections to empirical studies of the functions of writing in specific classrooms. The fifth section steps back from the classroom a bit to examine and critique the values—both the ideological and epistemological assumptions—embedded in the language of disciplinary discourse. The book closes with a consideration of the prospects for writing in the disciplines. This chapter represents our own views as they have been shaped by our editorial work with the contributors to this collection and by our own experience as early settlers in this territory we call writing in the disciplines.

Taken together, the chapters do not represent any single view, nor do they advocate a single methodology. We take the field as we find it: various, energetic, dynamic, and subject to change. This diversity, in our view, is a sign that writing in the disciplines is a healthy, vital enterprise. As we work within a context of diverse, contesting points of view, we are challenged to reflect on, and revise, our own views. This openness to alternatives has been characteristic of writing-in-the-disciplines research and pedagogy. It has made possible the adaptation and flexibility—both in our sense of "discipline" and in our sense of appropriate pedagogy—that James Britton sees as fundamental to our work as scholars and teachers. It is our hope that these essays will encourage and further our collective work, as we strive to understand how writing may connect with our teaching, our scholarship, and our students' learning.

Our work together as coeditors of this book has been consonant with our work in writing in the disciplines: the final product is the result of collective endeavor. We want, therefore, to acknowledge our collaborators in this venture. First on our list is Art Young, the contact editor for this volume in the series. Art has helped us at every stage of the process, from the submission of the proposal to the final editing. We acknowledge as well the skill, industry, and patience of our authors, who have generously responded to our editorial queries and suggestions. Finally, we express appreciation for the careful work of our MLA editor, Adrienne Marie Ward. Her thorough readings of the manuscript have contributed greatly to the accuracy and integrity of the book.

AH and CM

PART I

Historical Perspectives

Introduction

Movements such as writing in the disciplines have histories: at some point they were not; at another point they were; and somehow there was a progress from not-being to being. Nancy Martin and David R. Russell undertake to follow this progress and, further, to understand the many forces—both in the United Kingdom and in the United States—that collaborated to bring writing in the disciplines to its present situation in American postsecondary education.

The two histories are extraordinarily different yet intimately related. Martin's narrative, however objective-seeming at times, is the story told by one who lived the events she chronicles. For her, writing in the disciplines is a British phenomenon, one that took place in the 1960s in the world of what we in America would call "elementary" education. Important figures in this development are Martin herself and James Britton, whose essay "Theories of the Disciplines and a Learning Theory" follows Russell's in this volume. A crucial moment for Martin and her colleagues was the discovery, in the early 1960s, of the work of Lev Vygotsky, A. R. Luria, and F. Yudovich. From this intersection came the conviction that language and learning were intimately connected—that one could not somehow separate language from the rest of life, or of school, and teach it as a discrete entity. From this discovery came an awareness that "we knew almost nothing specific about the ways students encountered and used language throughout the school day." This led to collaboration with teachers in classroom-based research projects—not just in English but in all school subjects.

For Russell, the American history begins with John Dewey and his belief that teaching must take what the student already knows and build on that. As in England, the "skills" approach to the teaching of writing was both the incumbent and the opposition. But in the United States the countermovement was short-lived and fragmentary until the 1970s. An impetus and occasion for change was, in Russell's view, the Anglo-American Conference on the Teaching of English—the Dartmouth Seminar, as it is more often known—that in 1966 brought

3

together such British and American theorists and educators as Douglas Barnes, Britton, and Harold Rosen from the United Kingdom, and Wayne Booth, James Moffett, and Albert Kitzhaber from the United States. Almost ten years later, writing-in-the-disciplines programs began to arise in American colleges and universities, led by people like Elaine Maimon and Toby Fulwiler.

We asked the two historians to read each others' essays and comment. Russell notes that the British and American movements, radically disparate, owe their differences to the social and institutional forces that shaped them:

> The social and institutional nature of language across the curriculum/writing across the curriculum emerges in both essays. First, different national traditions, educational systems, and the place of literacy and its teaching in the societies shape LAC/WAC in different ways. . . . Second, the LAC/WAC movement in both nations depended on the formation of professional communities (NATE/CCCC) and communities of researchers within these larger communities. . . . And these researchers drew on a wide variety of research from many disciplines and nations. And progressive education movements in the early part of the century ultimately underlie both. Third, specialization has both created the need for LAC/WAC and posed great challenges. For example, the division between literary and literacy instruction (reception and production of texts, reading and writing) has been a bane in both nations. Fourth, in both nations, LAC/WAC has been deeply affected by the wider society—through funding and governmental support (and interference) and through wider political shifts in the society.

Martin, after reading Russell's essay, adds to our understanding of the difference between the British and American histories:

> David Russell refers only to *writing* across the curriculum, never to *language* across the curriculum. Presumably writing is the informing concept in relation to the growing demands for higher education in America? He writes, "The rapid growth of WAC in higher education was . . . a response to the demands for writing instruction created by increasing student enrollment, particularly of previously excluded groups." So WAC in America looks to be a response to the expansion of higher education and the corresponding demands for *adequate standards of written language*.

England had its literacy crisis with the raising of the school age to 16 years, but the pressures were not on *writing* but on what educational content could be offered to satisfy the new clientele of school students. It was thought that a good proportion of English—in all its aspects—would be needed.

And Martin points to what she sees as another important difference:

> David writes that in the United States "the widespread ferment in discussions of writing and learning did not produce a single movement with an overarching philosophy or organizational structure." I think that the movement in the United Kingdom *did* produce an overarching philosophy. As my essay tries to make clear, the movement in the United Kingdom began as "language across the curriculum" and very rapidly became modified to be "language and learning" or "language for learning." It thus represented a big shift in the concept of subject English. No longer did we see practice in talking and writing *to improve language* but to improve *learning*. So there was a new focus on processes of learning. I am inclined to think that the movements in the United States and the United Kingdom are still after different things.

On balance, Martin may be right here. Yet, as Russell makes clear, writing in the disciplines in America is not a single phenomenon. One of the many strands in the American WAC movement is the work of British educators and writers—among them Martin herself.

Both historians conclude their essays by estimating the viability of the writing-in-the-disciplines movement. Will it persist? endure? Russell, responding to Martin's essay, finds it "interesting that both of us are pessimistic about the potential of WAC to restore, as Nancy Martin puts it, 'the vanishing commonality of the different subjects.' . . . But I am optimistic (though very cautious) about WAC's ultimate success in American postsecondary education."

Language across the Curriculum: Where It Began and What It Promises

Nancy Martin

The author, now retired, taught at the University of London's Institute of Education. *I was formerly director of the British Schools Council Writing-across-the-Curriculum project and a member of James Britton's writing research team, which produced* The Development of Writing Abilities (11–18). *I am interested in the broader prospects for research offered by teamwork and collaboration at various levels. I have taught in a number of universities in North America. My publications include* Case Studies from Government High Schools in Western Australia, Writing and Learning across the Curriculum (11–16) *and* The Word for Teaching Is Learning *(joint ed.).*

When the history of British education in the twentieth century comes to be reassessed at sufficient distance from the banging of the politicians' drums, the 1960s will be seen for what they were: watershed years during which the social and intellectual stirrings arising from postwar changes began to take shape in public life and institutions.

Some of these events had profound effects on education. If we want to understand the force and continuing influence of the changes that the 1960s brought to birth—including the writing across the curriculum movement—we need to know something of the history of these events. Further, this history allows us to attempt an explanation of how it was that writing across the curriculum (or language across the curriculum, as it is more generally called in England) became in the United Kingdom a movement that began and continues in the secondary and primary schools, in sharp contrast to the American movement, which has been largely a postsecondary phenomenon, as David R. Russell demonstrates in his essay in this volume.

6

A Historical Overview

It would seem that the ideas inherent in writing across the curriculum gain ground in practice where writing is part of the paradigm of English teaching—that is, a subject of instruction, with its accepted mores, texts, procedures, and standards. In the United Kingdom written composition is a major part of the substance of secondary education and conforms to the paradigm. A written examination in English (including an essay) is compulsory for students at age sixteen, and, at eighteen, a written examination is widely a part of university entrance. After that, any instruction in writing is a matter for individual tutors in their various disciplines—to do something about, or not, as they wish. In the United States, on the contrary, freshman composition in the first stage of tertiary education is well-nigh universal. This is where the instruction takes place and where the paradigm operates.

How did it happen that composition came to occupy a major part in the teaching of English in the schools in the United Kingdom but not in the United States? With regard to the United Kingdom, the answer, in part, may lie in the traditional pedagogy of the classics. Up to the turn of the century (1900) and considerably later in many schools, English was taught at all levels as if it were Latin. Of course, at the elementary level, reading and writing and grammar were taught in pursuit of literacy, though grammar was called "English" and meant "grammar," just as elementary Latin had meant "grammar." An example from the "English Schedules" for 1900, issued by the Board of Education for Standard 4 (ten-year-olds) suggests what was expected:

> *Reading* To read a passage from a reading book or history of England.
>
> *Writing* Eight lines of poetry or prose, slowly read once, then dictated.
>
> *English* Parsing easy sentences, and showing by examples the use of each of the parts of speech.   (Shayer 4)

At the secondary level the classics teachers who became the teachers of English (when English crept into the curriculum) transferred their procedures, learned in the teaching of Latin, to English. Thus literary study became allusion hunting, grammar, figure-of-speech spotting, and paraphrasing, and "composition became the imitation of models and the mastering of complicated sets of rules" (Shayer 6–7). David Shayer says, " 'Imitation' was not simply an isolated classroom exercise, but a whole way of thinking that was taken for granted by a great many, if not the vast majority, of teachers until 1920 and beyond. Briefly, the pupil . . . is always expected to imitate, copy, or reproduce" (10).

What is extraordinary about the development of subject English in these years is that composition, in spite of its alien treatment, retained its position as a major part of the English curriculum throughout secondary education. Perhaps it needs to be remembered that composition, including verse composition, was the crown of a successful education (prestigious prizes were awarded in the universities for verse and prose compositions in Greek and Latin) and probably more time was spent on it than any other part of the English curriculum. Barren as much of this teaching must have been, the tenacity of the tradition was such that "writing" was, and is, an important feature in the timetable, plans, and curriculum of English departments.

In the early years of the century, a campaign was begun to separate English from the domination of classics and to establish English as a subject in its own right with its own content and its own specialist teachers. An important part of this campaign was the inauguration in 1906 of the English Association, whose explicit aim was to promote "English as a subject in its own right with its own place in the curriculum and to counter the stultifying and conservative influence of the classical tradition" (Ball 55). Since classics, modern languages, and other subjects had supporting associations, the English Association came into being with this same aim of support for the mother tongue in education.

It was, however, a difficult campaign to pursue. Education in the different ethnic regions of the United Kingdom had taken different directions. In England there was no infrastructure to work through, no recognized discipline of English in universities, no corpus of studies, no body of graduate teachers to move the campaign through the secondary schools with their associated public opinion. So in spite of the efforts of the English Association and a very gradually more liberal approach by government to public elementary education, change was extremely slow, though clear beginnings were made in the literature programs in prestigious private girls' schools; the prestigious private boys' schools were bastions of the classics for years more.

After the First World War English was admitted as an academic study at Oxford and Cambridge; and for fifty years before this, English had been making some progress as a university discipline in London and the new provincial university colleges. But these studies were philological and historical and remained so until well into the twentieth century. The idea that the study of English literature could be a university discipline took a long time to emerge. Although some administrators and educators were asserting at the turn of the century that the study of English literature should be the central subject in our schools—and Matthew Arnold had fought for the humanizing effect of great literature in the 1860s and had advocated its importance in counteracting the "commercial theory" of the educators framing the regulations of the Board of Education—nevertheless the English universities could not for many years be persuaded that English literature could offer adequate levels of academic study except in terms of history or textual editing.

In Scotland, however, the eighteenth-century literary renaissance set a different direction for public taste and education. Series of public lectures on rhetoric and belles lettres in Edinburgh from 1751 on, and somewhat later at Glasgow University, set the scene for an interest in contemporary as well as classical European literature. In 1762 a Regius Professor of Rhetoric and Belles Lettres was created at Edinburgh University. "The cultivation of literary study by the educated classes had become fashionable and there was an obvious desire to see this study given university status" (Lothian xxiii). Associated with this public interest was the increasing influence of the literary critical quarterlies, the *Edinburgh Review* and *Blackwoods*, in the first part of the nineteenth century. These traditions persisted in Scotland, and Scottish education remained in many ways different from education in England, Wales, and Northern Ireland.

When, subsequently, literary criticism developed throughout the United Kingdom as the main thrust of university education in literature, it inevitably became also the direction of literature work in secondary schools as well. But since other English work with younger students necessarily focused on literacy, the only continuity between English in the schools and English in the universities was to be found at the top end of the secondary schools. This gap served to cut English teachers off from the professional support at university level that was available, for instance, to teachers of mathematics or science.

The tenacity of the tradition of writing in British preuniversity education must be attributed, in part, to the progressive movement in the early part of the twentieth century. The beginnings of this movement in England tended to be among teachers in private schools for young children—Caldwell Cook, for instance, of the Perse preparatory school (under fourteen years old) in Cambridge, and Susan Isaacs of the Malting House School (pupils two to ten years old), whose publications became widely known. There were, of course, other writers and teachers in these years, 1915–30, who asserted the importance of fantasy and imaginative play and expression—including painting. But action is more effective than rhetoric: in the five years between 1912 (first Perse Playbook) and 1917, Caldwell Cook published five other Playbooks containing, as well as his introduction, the stories, plays, sketches, and poems written by his pupils. Later these were published by Heffer of Cambridge as anthologies in their own right. Cook's own book, *The Play Way*, came out in 1917, a forerunner by many years of the drama-in-education movement of the 1960s.

The movement for freedom in writing can further be attributed to the influence of the New Education Fellowship and its journal, the *New Era*, both of which were linked to similar movements on the Continent. The innovators associated with this movement believed in the creative and independent character of learning and wanted to make room for creativity in more traditional classrooms. Artists, writers, painters, and some parents had discovered children's art. Exhibitions were held that startled the adult world. Franz Cizek of Vienna, for instance, arranged an exhibit of children's art in London in the 1930s. Cizek had obtained striking and original paintings and drawings from children by allowing them complete freedom to create. People began to ask, "If children can paint as well as we now see they can, could they not express their visions of reality with similar vigor and beauty in writing?"

Influenced by the Society for Education through Art, English teachers—and the newly founded London Association for the Teaching of English—began to value what children wrote as meaningful accounts of their experience. This understanding was extended to children's talk—no longer just chatter, but an aspect of learning. These ideas were the basis of the evidence presented to the Plowden Committee in its survey of primary education in England. The committee's 1966 report strongly influenced the directions of state primary education (Central Advisory Council). No swing of fashion, this, but some eighty years of effort in the same direction.

Language and Learning: A Case Study of Intellectual Innovation

Stephen Ball distinguishes between "conditions of change" and "relations of change." The former—the "conditions"—are themselves shifts in the economic and social conditions of schooling that "allow, inhibit, or provide for changes in the process and content of school knowledge." The latter—the "relations"—are those "activities and strategies which actually initiate change" (13). A major part of the activities and strategies that initiated the changes in the concept of subject English (exemplified in the language-across-the-curriculum movement) lay in the communication networks operating among teachers of English. These networks included subject associations, conferences, research projects, university and in-service courses, and formal and informal discussions of influential ideas and practices. The operation of these networks is exemplified in the case study that follows.

Activities and Networks That Initiated Change

Dates are markers that help to logicalize the flux of memory. At its most skeletal, this narrative is carried on a few highly significant dates in the 1960s: dates of conferences, dates of book publication, dates of research funding. But just as there is nothing in the skeleton of *Homo sapiens* to explain humankind's capacity to speak, so the significance of these conferences and publications has to be seen in the context of the volcanic climate of the 1960s and in the history of the postwar decades preceding them.

The events I speak of were the products of intense intellectual activity. Together with the conditions of change in the 1960s, they profoundly affected views of education then and since. They shifted attention from teaching to learning, to the role of teachers and to the role of language in learning. In the narrative I use the pronoun *we* to refer to any or all of us working on the projects referred to, and sometimes to the research team working on writing abilities.

In 1947 the London Association for the Teaching of English was founded from the English department of the University of London's Institute of Education; the national association was established sixteen years later. LATE aimed to be a forum for London teachers of English and to find focal points of cooperative work between the university English departments and their student teachers, together with teachers in the London schools. Most of the work described here would not have been possible without this cooperation.

The objectives of the new association, set down in the records with the utmost simplicity, are educational research; administrative and practical work, such as campaigns; exchange of views and experiences; and authoritative lectures (and books). We worked through study groups, meeting separately, and when a study was ready, it was either presented to the association at a general meeting, published in some way, or reported in the educational press. These operations were coordinated—and to some extent initiated—by a secretary of studies. James Britton occupied that position for the first five years.

In the immediate postwar years there was a sense that everything was starting afresh, that we needed to reexamine the old and try out the new. In this climate classroom inquiry and, later, small funded studies formed a large part of our activities and set a mode of work that persisted till the recession of the 1980s.

In the 1950s the idea of a common school was growing; the Education Act of 1944 had established secondary education for all to the age of fifteen, but within a tripartite system of selection for three types of school—grammar schools for the best, technical schools for the next best, and secondary modern for the rest. London already had plans for large common schools, and when a Labor government was elected, the development of comprehensive schools went ahead. This restructuring of the educational system produced an outburst of problems, plans, questions, and experiments, but through this welter of practical problems, the research dimension persisted. Our ideas in the 1950s were deeply influenced by Jean Piaget's theoretical work on learning, as well as by his studies of the intellectual development of young children. There were also the language acquisition studies of other psychologists and linguists—Roger Brown, William Labov, David McNeil, Margaret Donaldson, and Jerome Bruner. As English teachers, we sought a pedagogy that had its roots in language development and would also be contained within a philosophical framework of humane learning theory. We read Piaget's *Play, Dreams and Imitation in Childhood* with a sense of being on the edge of discovery, and even more so as we explored his descriptions of egocentric speech and its occurence and role in children's behavior (see his *Language and Thought of the Child*).

The phenomenon of egocentric speech became a kind of pivot for our developing language theories. We saw social speech as language for others and egocentric speech as language for oneself—and we saw the origin of writing in the latter. With the first edition of Lev Vygotsky's *Thought and Language* (written in 1928 and translated and first published in English in 1962) came a copy of the correspondence between Vygotsky and Piaget about the origins and destination of egocentric speech. We were curious about and interested in the occasions and functions of nonsocial speech (egocentric, presleep "spiels" by young children) and also in social speech in all its multifarious situations; and we were interested in the solitary, or nonsocial, aspects of writing as well as in the social role of discourse and the writer's sense of audience. We found that the Russians had been pursuing studies of the relation between speech and mental development for three decades. Most of this work was not available in English at the time, but we came across a small book by A. R. Luria and F. Yudovich called *Speech and the Development of Mental Processes in the Child*. Luria was a leading Soviet psychologist; his book is an account of five-year-old twins with a slight speech impairment and a history of general backwardness. It records the methods used to overcome their speech difficulties. In it we read, with something akin to shock, the overwhelming, detailed evidence that in developing their speech, Luria had lifted the children out of their backwardness to reach the level of the other children in their age group.

It was all there in this 110-page book: records of observations, classifications of words, analyses, tables of changes in structures. Significantly, the first chapter is called "The Role of Speech in the Formation of Mental Processes: An Outline of the Problem," while last chapters are titled "Improvements in Play Activity" and "Improvements in Intellectual Operations." The patient, cumulative observations track the growing maturity of the twins as their speech capacities improved.

After encountering this work, we undertook observations of our own and set up a study group to observe and record different kinds of speech according to Luria's functional categories: synpraxic speech (speech integrated with action), narrative speech, and planning speech. We were able to make physically recorded observations, but until tape recorders became widespread, what we could do was limited. With the work of Piaget, Vygotsky, and Luria as both guide and stimulus, we developed the outline of a coherent theory of language in relation to mental development, a theory that became the foundation of our courses at the University of London's Institute of Education. This theory was the intellectual seedbed from which our further work grew.

At this point we divide the narrative of the evolution of our understanding of the relation between learning and language. Two parallel operations were developed in the late 1960s that carried this work to the point where publication became urgent. One stemmed from the work of teachers within the networks of communication set up by LATE; the other was a research unit located at the University of London's Institute of Education and funded to work with teachers in some sixty schools to explore the development of writing abilities at the secondary level. Members of the English department at the Institute of Education played a leading part in the two operations, both of which were oriented toward learning in a general sense rather than toward improving language.

First, then, to continue the language and learning case study. Further work from LATE centered on the role of talk, especially in learning situations. We at the institute cooperated with other members of LATE who were teaching in primary and secondary schools, and with them developed hypotheses about talk and set up study groups to record and analyze tapes and transcripts from many different situations. The association's aims (research, campaigns, and publications) and its procedures (group study and classroom experiment) established patterns of cooperative inquiry rooted in classroom observation and experiment, while its summer conferences were designed to open up new areas of work and explore new theoretical ideas.

In 1967, LATE decided to hold its summer conference on *talk*. It had become obvious that our study could not be confined to the talk that went on in English lessons; all the language encounters of the school day had become our field of study. Thus, although it was as yet unnamed, "language in the curriculum" had become our focus.

We found we knew almost nothing specific about the ways students encountered and used language throughout the school day. For our scrutiny we needed all the help we could get from teachers of subjects other than English. In preparation for the conference, we drew up the following questions:

- What are the different kinds of talk used by children and young people?
- What are their different functions?
- How does the size and the nature of the group affect the quality of the talk?
- How do different kinds of talk develop in the school years?

We also recorded school conversations and talk situations to use at the conference to help us answer these questions.

The 1968 LATE conference took us into yet deeper waters. We had in the intervening year spent much time trying to determine whether there was such a register as the language of education. We discussed problems of impersonal language. Harold Rosen launched an attack on the alienating effect of such language on young learners. The Writing Research Unit (see below) contributed its work on the nature and role of expressive language. This conference broadened our ongoing inquiry into spoken language to see how far the outlines of our work and thought on talk could be extended to other kinds of language. We therefore asked another set of questions about *writing* parallel to those we had asked about talk in 1967:

- How much writing and of what kinds do pupils ordinarily do in and out of school?
- What kinds of writing do teachers expect of pupils in different contexts, and why?

- How does the nature of the writing task affect what the pupils write and how they write it?
- How do different kinds of writing develop in the school years?

A second purpose of the 1968 conference was to discuss and amend a draft of a statement about language that could be circulated to schools for discussion by teachers of subjects other than English. This draft statement, or "manifesto," as we sometimes called it, was just over three pages long and consisted of three parts. First was a statement of the problem: students' difficulties with written language—a main source of their learning. Part 2, "The Background," dealt with aspects of language development, from the specific to the general, from the personal to the impersonal, and asserted the importance of personal experience and personal language as the basis of learning. Part 3, "What Might Be Done," formed the main body of the document and was really a brief blueprint for language in school. An excerpt here may indicate the direction of the attitude and the thinking: "Children talking in small groups are taking a more active part in all their work. Tentative and inexplicit talk in small groups is the bridge from partial understanding to confident, meaningful statement" (Barnes, Britton, and Rosen 126). The draft received interested comment, especially from one head of English, who thought it would take twenty years for teachers to realize that it was as much about learning as it was about language. We tried to find a slogan that might stick in memory. "Future thinking depends on present talking" was one that did not stick. In the event, it was "language across the curriculum" that did take, but it emerged later.

The chief outcome of the two conferences was the decision to publish a book that would contain the manifesto and to precede it with visible talk in the form of transcripts in a variety of subject lessons and in long out-of-class conversations. We also agreed that the book should contain commentaries on the transcripts by Douglas Barnes and James Britton in order to stress, to scholars and the general public, the importance of talk in learning in all subjects. *Language, the Learner and School* was published by Penguin Education in 1969. It stayed in print for twenty years and sold one hundred thousand copies during that time.

Publication of the book in 1969 and the subsequent history of the work can be seen as the launch of language across the curriculum. There was, however, the parallel operation of the Writing Research Unit at the University of London, referred to above. Whereas the inquiries of the London teachers were directed primarily toward the nature and role of talk in learning, the work of the Writing Research Unit was designed to explore the development of *writing* abilities at the secondary level. By the time this research was published (Britton, Burgess, Martin, McLeod, and Rosen 1975), together with the complementary report of the Writing Development Project (1975), the beginnings of a research literature concerned with both spoken and written language across the curriculum were available in the United Kingdom and, quite rapidly, worldwide.

Conditions of Change in the 1960s

The changes in public apprehension of the significance of the mother tongue in learning took place in a period of intellectual and social turmoil; views of language were radically altered by the work—in particular—of Noam Chomsky, Vygotsky, and Bruner. In the optimistic climate of the 1960s, every new direction seemed worth pursuing, and the explorations were assisted by the institutions that sprang up to channel and stabilize experiments in curriculum, organization, and pedagogy.

The first of these new institutions was the National Association for the Teaching of English (NATE). Before NATE, English teachers had loosely organized themselves through a number of local associations. Now, in 1963, the same conditions of change that would result in the formation of the Schools Council led to the foundation of NATE. The existence of the association meant more and wider channels for dissemination of ideas and more help for teachers in an era of upheaval. It expressed as well the growing professionalism of English teachers who were acquiring the intention and capacity to develop the directions in curriculum and pedagogy that they thought best.

NATE was a partner in the Anglo-American conference of English specialists at Dartmouth College in 1966. The association asked the British educator John Dixon to write a book for the teaching profession and Herbert Muller, an American historian, to write one for the general public. It is hard to assess the real importance of this conference. Those who attended regard it as seminal. Because it gave rise to a series of international conferences on English, the Dartmouth conference promoted the spread of ideas and research, but probably its most influential outcome was John Dixon's book *Growth through English* and the realization in practice of the conference's view of English teaching. Participants in the month-long seminar explored most aspects of English teaching, including various whole-view models. The conference rejected the "skills" model and the "literary heritage" model in favor of a "language and personal growth" model. Students' learning and development were seen as depending on their *using* language to make sense of personal experience, real or imagined. The book thus contributed to the dissemination of the idea that language is an educator, a model that had profound implications for the operation of classrooms and for the definition of the teacher's role in the classroom community.

For our history, the most important of the new institutions was the Schools Council for Curriculum and Examination, established in 1965. This was a unique program set up to support experimental curricula and new models for conducting examinations. Never before in Britain had money been available for such wide-ranging school-based research. The council, an independent body of teachers and teachers' representatives, together with members of the local education authorities, worked through committees for the different subjects that set targets for attention and produced numerous publications. The council's major impact was in its substantial funding for curriculum research and experimentation planned and carried out by teachers in schools and colleges. For over a decade it sponsored a great many projects that varied in scope and duration and spanned the curriculum. Representative examples include Humanities for the Young School-Leaver, Mathematics in the Primary Schools, Education for a Multi-Cultural Society, and Arts and the Adolescent. There were at least seven initial English-language projects, two of the major ones being Development of Writing Abilities in the Secondary School (1966–71), under the direction of Britton, and Writing across the Secondary Curriculum (1971–76), under my direction.

It is always difficult to determine the point at which a research project can be said to have begun. In our case, the work of the Writing Research Unit had been preceded by much preliminary thinking and discussion under the creative leadership of Britton, whose interest in the philosophy of language was given scope by the work on language then undertaken in other disciplines, most notably in psychology, linguistics, and anthropology. The direction of this writing research was set by two papers Britton gave at the Dartmouth conference and to the faculty of the Institute of Education at the University of London. These papers formed the basis of his book *Language and Learning* and provided the theoretical framework for both subsequent research and the ongoing classroom inquiries initiated by LATE. A major aspect of Britton's theory is the distinction between literary and nonliterary discourse, between two kinds of language-using behavior. When we use language as participants, we use it "to get things done" (*Language* 125); we are "participating in the world's affairs" (101). As spectators, we use language to contemplate, re-create, and celebrate what has happened to us or to other people—or what might conceivably happen or have happened. In doing so, we enrich and embroider our versions of experience, fill in the gaps, extend frontiers, and iron out inconsistencies (see *Language*, ch. 3; "Viewpoints"). Britton's purpose was to find common ground between much of the writing students do in school and the literature they read. He goes on to suggest that "the distinction that matters is not whether the events recounted are true or fictional, but whether we recount them (or listen to them) as spectators or participants: and whenever we play the role of spectator of human affairs, I suggest we are in the position of literature" ("Literature" 37).

This distinction between the two uses of language enabled us to survey the kinds and amount of school writing and talk as a whole, in relation to the different disciplines, and to estimate the extent to which new kinds of abilities—abilities that allowed students to undertake different kinds of writing—were being developed in the school years. The particular value of *Language and Learning* was that, in addition to its innovative thinking about the uses of language, it made accessible to the general public a great deal of research on language and learning from disciplines outside English and hitherto available only in the specialist publications of these fields. The book has been in print, at the time of this writing, for twenty-one years.

The Development of Writing Abilities, 11–18

The writing research project The Development of Writing Abilities, 11 to 18, which Britton led and which incorporated so much of his preliminary thinking and writing, was designed as a study of "how the written language of young children becomes differentiated, during the years eleven to eighteen, into kinds of written discourse appropriate to different purposes" (Britton, Burgess, Martin, McLeod, and Rosen 50). In a 1966 briefing paper, we had described our working assumption in these words: "Our experience suggests that there is likely to be a hierarchy of kinds of writing shaped by the thinking problems which the writer confronts" (53). Starting with a survey of the kinds of writing found in the various school subjects, the team developed a theoretical model of the processes of adult writing and used this model to gauge the extent of students' approximation to the adult model, in terms of function and of the writer's sense of audience.

We found that as students moved up the school from age eleven to age seventeen, their writing became increasingly directed toward an audience of the teacher in the role of examiner or assessor, and that the function of writing became increasingly informational (we called it *transactional*). Further, while there was a small amount of expressive and poetic (literary) writing in most subjects in year 1 (age eleven), by year 3 (age thirteen), these kinds of writing had disappeared except in English and religious education. It thus seemed that examination pressures—increasing as the students went up the school—narrowed the writing as to both function and audience. In year 7 (age seventeen), when reflective and speculative writing might have been expected to be at its optimum, there was little but recapitulated information. Results similar to ours were obtained when the survey was repeated in New Jersey, Toronto, and Tasmania, using our two-dimensional model of audience and function categories.

Hard on the heels of the Development of Writing Abilities project came the Writing across the Secondary Curriculum project. It was designed to take the findings of the writing research project into schools as widely as possible in order to inquire from teachers of all subjects what use they made of spoken or written language in their lessons. In describing the findings, we had theoretical points to make about the role of language in learning, and practical things to report about the narrowing effect of examination pressures on students' school writing. The results of our analyses and reports of visits to schools provoked far-reaching discussion with teachers of different disciplines—particularly science—about the value of talk and writing in their classes. One of the outcomes was the exploratory and innovative work in various subjects sparked by the study. We incorporated much of this in a newsletter for exchange among cooperating and associated schools widely scattered through the United Kingdom.

The publication of *The Development of Writing Abilities (11–18)* in 1975, following Britton's *Language and Learning* in 1970, established the academic credibility of the new directions for work related to language. A year later, the report of the project *Writing and Learning across the Curriculum, 11–16*, by Nancy Martin, Pat D'Arcy, Bryan Newton, and Robert Parker, made theoretical aspects of the role of language in education more widely accessible. The Schools Council's publications in the field of language in the curriculum established the new approach sufficiently for it to figure significantly in *A Language for Life*, the report of the Bullock Committee (Dept. of Education and Science) commissioned by Margaret Thatcher, then secretary of state for education. Charged "to inquire into the teaching in the schools of reading and the other uses of English," the committee made language across the curriculum the subject of a full chapter in the report. In fact, although the report covers all aspects of English in education, two central themes lie at the heart of it: reading, and language across the curriculum. The report states clearly that schools should address the problem of language development in all subjects across the curriculum, not primarily to improve language, but to facilitate learning. Following the report's publication in 1975, hundreds of schools, both primary and secondary, set up working parties to devise a policy for language across the curriculum.

These policies are not much in evidence today. It is as if the available energy and imagination needed for planning and implementing policies related to language have been sucked away into the insatiable maw of the national curriculum. It is possible, too, that the ideas were accepted too quickly and have not been worked through in thought and action. Certainly the important general idea, that we organize our perceptions of the world and our thinking about it through language, has not been adequately assimilated. What has been accepted instead is a focus on the improvement of language rather than a policy for learning. However, it is possible that the ideas about language and learning that sustained the movement are working in various ways to make language across the national curriculum a significant aspect of the new order.

Inevitably the presentation of so many different events, proceedings, and ideas results in a piecemeal impression of the history and development of language across the curriculum in the United Kingdom. Of course, much of the thinking, talking, writing, and doing *is* piecemeal, but the intellectual pursuit of an informing theory is traceable through all these activities. The shaping and articulating of the theory can be observed as the community of English educators worked on it over the years. Foremost in this community has been Britton. From an even broader conceptual framework than the questions he was asking about the relation of language to learning were the questions he posed about the nature of art and literature as forms of knowing. Such inquiries challenged many then-current assumptions about the teaching of both language and literature and provided a rationale for English that includes language across the curriculum. Britton's conception locates the value of language work not in language development as such but in the contribution of language to the formation of mind.

Clearly, language across the curriculum belongs to the rationale of all subjects, not as an alternative technique for teaching but as a growing understanding of the nature of learning. This shift in focus from teaching to learning is rooted in the common concern that teachers have for learning, and it therefore provides a commonality of aim and a field for discussion that can offset the isolation arising from the specialist structure of secondary schools. Furthermore, the importance of language forms a part of all the statements of attainment in the national curriculum, and the unplanned effect of more opportunities to use language at all levels may bring its own changes. They might include alterations in class structure, in student-teacher relations, and in the extent of collaborative work.

At the higher levels of tertiary education and research, the various specialisms become increasingly esoteric. It would seem, therefore, that language across the curriculum at these levels is not seen to serve the interests of the specialist or the specialism. However, while advances in the disciplines take people further away from understanding each others' worlds, there is a direction in teaching, as distinct from research, that is by its nature a shared one. This is an interest in the processes of learning and in the ways in which teaching may be accommodated to these processes once we know more about them. This, and not the vanishing commonality of the different subjects, is the promise of language across the curriculum.

American Origins of the Writing-across-the-Curriculum Movement

David R. Russell

The author is assistant professor of English at Iowa State University.
I began studying the history of writing instruction outside general composition courses in 1985. Looking at patterns of literacy in sixteenth-century England, I realized that most other nations never developed postsecondary composition courses. How had mass education in the United States produced this anomaly? The writing-across-the-curriculum movement was well launched by 1985, and the idea that writing could be taught and learned effectively only with the cooperation of faculty members in all fields seemed so obvious that I wondered why it hadn't been tried earlier. It had, in many places, though never for very long.

Writing has been an issue in American secondary and higher education since written papers and examinations came into wide use in the 1870s, eventually driving out formal recitation and oral examination.[1] Significantly, that shift coincided with the rise of academic disciplines and the reorganization of secondary and higher education by disciplines, each with its own text-based discourse conventions to carry on its professional work and select, evaluate, and credential students. But from the first "literacy crisis," in the 1870s—precipitated by the new discipline-specific writing requirements and the entry of students from previously excluded groups into the nascent mass education system— the academic disciplines have taken little direct interest in writing, either by consciously investigating their own conventions of scholarly writing or by teaching their students those conventions in a deliberate, systematic way—despite a century-long tradition of complaints by faculty members and other professionals about the poor writing of students (Daniels; Greenbaum). Given the traditional separation of writing instruction from postelementary pedagogy in the American mass education system, the birth and unprecedented growth of the writing-across-the-curriculum movement in the last decade and a half is surprising. But the WAC movement has deep, though rarely exposed, roots in the recurring debates over approaches to writing and to pedagogy—especially in the American tradition of progressive education.

From its birth in the late nineteenth century, progressive education has wrestled with the conflict within industrial society between pressure to increase specialization of knowledge and of professional work (upholding disciplinary standards) and pressure to integrate more fully an ever-widening number of citizens into intellectually meaningful activity within mass society (promoting social equity). Language, particularly the written language that organized and facilitated the differentiation and rationalization of industrial society, lay at the very center of the conflict between disciplinary standards and social equity, exclusion and access. But the role written knowledge plays in preparing students for (or excluding them from) disciplinary communities was rarely addressed systematically, either by the disciplines and the professional interests they represented or by progressive education, which itself became professionalized in education departments and public school bureaucracies. Rhetoric departments died out, writing instruction was marginalized, and the issues of student writing remained largely submerged, reappearing only when the conflicts between disciplinary standards and social equity, exclusion and access, became most visible—usually when previously excluded groups pressed for entry into higher education and thus into professional roles.

Faculty members and administrators have long agreed that every teacher should teach writing (a cliché as old as mass education), but since the turn of the century, the American education system has placed the responsibility for teaching writing outside the disciplines, including, to a large extent, the discipline of "English" or literary study (Berlin 32–57; Stewart; Piché). Writing came to be seen not in broad rhetorical terms, as a central function of the emerging disciplines, but in two reductive (and conflicting) ways, neither of which engaged the intellectual activity of disciplines. Writing was thought of, on the one hand, as a set of elementary transcription skills unrelated to disciplinary activity ("talking with the pen instead of the tongue," as the 1892 Harvard Committee on Composition and Rhetoric put it) or, on the other hand, as a belletristic art, the product of genius or inspiration rather than of the mundane social and professional activity of the disciplines (Russell, "Romantics"). In the great middle lay most of the writing done by students and professionals, academic or "real-world." But this writing was largely dismissed by the sciences, with their positivist orientation, and by the humanities, with their belletristic orientation, as an arhetorical, unproblematic recording of thought or speech, unworthy of serious intellectual attention, beneath systematic consideration in the inquiry and teaching of the disciplines.

Since the 1870s, writing instruction in America has largely been separate from other instruction and has been relegated to lower levels: to first-year composition courses taught primarily by junior, temporary, or graduate student instructors; to one relatively small component of the secondary English curriculum (composition units); or even to the primary schools. Instead of being an integral part of teaching and learning, writing instruction has gradually been confined to the margins of postelementary mass education, an adjunct to the "real" work of the disciplines and thus of secondary and higher education.[2] And in the disciplines, the organizing units of postelementary education, writing was thus able to remain largely transparent, unexamined. The discursive practices of each academic field are so embedded in the texture of its disciplinary activity that they have not, until very recently, become an object of study or teaching within the disciplines. The American Historical Association, for example, has rarely devoted its attention to the question of how students learn to write (or write to learn) history, apart from occasional mentions in its reports on secondary instruction (e.g., Beard 227). Even the MLA, the professional association representing scholarship in written texts and the discipline most often considered responsible for teaching composition, disbanded its pedagogical section—the section devoted to writing instruction—as early as 1903 and rarely concerned itself with questions of writing instruction (much less of writing instruction in other disciplines) until the 1960s (Stewart; Applebee, *Tradition* 198–204).

Several essays in this volume suggest reasons for this lack of rhetorical self-consciousness within disciplines. As Charles Bazerman says, following Bruno Latour, the "overt teachings of a discipline . . . may ignore or even suppress knowledge of the contexts and forces in which the field operates and that shape the knowledge of the discipline." And as Judith A. Langer points out, even when faculty members conceive of their discipline's knowledge as a dynamic social and rhetorical process, they may continue to teach as if that knowledge were static and arhetorical. This transparency of writing has created a central contradiction in the American mass education system: its organizing principle—disciplinary specialization—recognizes no integral role for writing, and in many ways the disciplines have resisted the sharing of responsibility for writing instruction; yet schools and colleges are expected to teach students to write in ways sanctioned by the disciplines.

United States mass education has found ways of living with this contradiction. The 1870s literacy crisis led to the creation of that characteristically American institution, general composition courses, which effectively relieved faculty members outside of English and rhetoric departments of any direct responsibility for teaching writing (Douglas). Around the turn of the century, with yet another influx of students from previously excluded groups, institution-wide speaking and writing requirements were dropped, relieving teachers of the obligation to assign and evaluate extended writing (Wozniack). By the 1940s, American secondary and higher education had almost entirely given up externally graded written examinations, its last institutionally mandated site for writing in the disciplines, in favor of "new type" or "objective" tests (Kandel). As a result, the disciplines were no longer responsible for communally arriving at standards for student writing; the assigning and evaluating of even brief writing was almost entirely at the discretion of individual faculty members, who had few incentives from their institutions or from their disciplines to pursue these tasks.

But even before institution-wide writing requirements and external essay examinations faded, the mass education system had settled into a restrictive conception of school writing that allowed disciplines to live comfortably with the contradiction of writing as the responsibility of every discipline and of no discipline. Instead of viewing writing as a complex and continuously developing response to a specialized, text-based, discourse community, highly embedded in the differentiated practices of that community, educators came to see it as a set of generalizable, mechanical "skills" independent of disciplinary knowledge, learned once and for all at an early age. Writing skills could be taught separately from content, as a mere adjunct or service to a curriculum (in freshman composition, for example) or to a single course (in a research paper, for example). And because secondary and higher education is organized around specialized content, the generalized skills came to be subordinate. Moreover, this narrow conception of writing and learning fit well with the industrial model American schools adopted. Progress could be measured in the number of errors reduced per dollar invested, and students could be tracked and taught according to their "deficiencies." Thus, writing instruction past the elementary school was viewed as mere remediation of deficiencies in skill rather than as a means of fostering a continuously developing intellectual and social attainment intimately tied to disciplinary learning (Dixon 1–4; Rose; Piché; Russell, "Cooperation").

In the light of these narrow views of writing and learning, it is not surprising that all but a handful of the many cross-curricular efforts to improve student writing launched over the last hundred years merely asked general faculty members to correct students' mechanical and grammatical errors or, more commonly, to refer "deficient" students to a "remedial" program run by composition instructors.[3] Nor is it surprising that most efforts to improve student learning in the disciplines had little to say about the role that writing might play in pedagogy. The skills model of writing offered no intellectually interesting reason to connect the process of learning to write with one's students' (or one's own) intellectual or professional development—with the activities of a discipline, in other words.

Progressive Education and Its Discrediting

The few attempts progressive educators made to introduce a developmental model for writing instruction across the curriculum are important, however, for they form the backdrop of the current WAC movement. From the birth of progressive education, in the 1890s, some curricular reformers in that tradition have seen writing and speaking in developmental terms—a "growth," as Dewey's early colleague Fred Newton Scott put it (464)—and railed against the "remedial racket" (Porter G. Perrin's term [382]). Dewey himself considered language central to learning, a means of organizing experience in progressively more sophisticated and meaningful ways. Unlike "child-centered" progressives, such as Hughes Mearns, Dewey argued that students' use of language must lead systematically from the experience of the individual to the collective experience of the culture as represented by the organized disciplines. Education must begin with the student's experience, Dewey argued, but it cannot end there, as many of his child-centered followers assumed. "The next step," Dewey wrote in his most impassioned attack on the excesses of his followers, "is the progressive development of what is already experienced into a fuller and richer and also more organized form, a form that gradually approximates that in which subject matter is presented to the skilled, mature person" (148). New experience must be continually and consciously related to old experience—the individual's personal history, certainly, but also the culture's experience preserved in the organized knowledge of the disciplines. Language plays a central role in this "continuous spiral" of progressively wider and "thicker" engagement with the culture (53). "There must be some advance made in conscious articulation of facts and ideas," Dewey insisted, for there to be "connectedness in growth" (50). Thus curriculum and instruction—particularly beyond elemen-

tary school—must consciously and carefully weave together the interests of the learner with the structures and activities of the disciplines
through increasingly more sophisticated uses of language, balancing
in a range of discourse the personal and private experience of the
student and the public and impersonal knowledge of the community
(or, in the modern world, communi*ties* of disciplinary specialists). In
this view, progressive education must not be "child-centered" but
rather, to borrow James Britton's coinage, "adult- and child-centered,"
engaging the world of the learner with the world of the discipline the
teacher represents (*re-presents*) ("English Teaching" 204–05).

However, neither the disciplines, on the one hand, nor progressive
education, on the other hand, explored in any systematic way the role
of language in disciplinary learning to achieve such a balance. The
disciplines, at the most powerful and influential levels of their activity
(in research universities and professional organizations), concerned
themselves primarily with specialized, high-level teaching and research, turning their attention to secondary education and introductory courses only in times of crisis.[4] Progressive reformers in education
departments, isolated in their own embattled discipline, championed
child-centered teaching and radical curricular change in order to overcome the dominance of the disciplines, not to foster ongoing dialogue
with them (Cremin 183–85; for recent developments, see Clifford and
Guthrie). Largely ignoring Dewey's insistence on the importance of
disciplinary knowledge, progressive reformers attempted to transcend
disciplinary traditions through "correlation" of subject matter in core
courses organized around student experiences instead of around "fixed-
in-advance" knowledge (Weeks). Students' writing would grow out of
their experience and escape the confines of teacher-made assignments
requiring the usual academic conventions. For the most radical of the
child-centered progressives, unfettered freedom of expression became
an educational end in itself (a doctrine Dewey called "really stupid"
[Dewey et al. 37]). Predictably, administrators, parents, and disciplines
(including English) rejected "correlation" as unworkable, chaotic, or
downright subversive (this despite many successes) (Applebee, *Tradition* 122–23, 144–46; Aikin; Wright; Smith, Tyler, and the Evaluation
Staff). Correlation threatened to overthrow the disciplinary structure
that organized modern education (and modern knowledge) rather than
mediate between that structure and the experience of students.

In the years following World War II, progressive education was thor-
oughly discredited in the public eye, and experiments in cross-curricular
writing instruction returned to the familiar skills model, this time
with a new emphasis on practical "communications." At hundreds of

institutions, English and speech departments cooperated to train the newest influx of previously excluded students—returning GIs—in the "four skills," listening, reading, speaking, and writing. But the "communications movement," as it was called, rarely involved other departments; indeed, the communications approach offered no intellectually satisfying reason for departments to take an active role in language instruction, because it treated writing as a generalizable skill, unrelated to the specialized intellectual and professional activities of the disciplines (Berlin 92–107; Applebee, *Tradition* 156–60).

However, a handful of institutions actively involved faculty members in the disciplines, most notably the University of California at Berkeley in its Prose Improvement Committee (1947–64). This university-wide committee supervised the training of TAs from about a dozen disciplines in assessing and tutoring the writing assigned in large lecture courses. The committee explicitly rejected the skills model and adopted instead a specifically developmental perspective, which saw writing as central to disciplinary teaching and learning (Russell, "Writing across the Curriculum"). In the committee's final report before it disbanded (for lack of departments willing to use its services), the chair, Ralph Rader, wrote:

> When student writing is deficient, then, it is deficient . . . in ways having directly to do with the student's real control of the subject matter of his discipline and not in ways having to do with the special disciplines of English or Speech departments. To raise the level of student writing . . . would be in effect to raise the student's level of intellectual attainment in the subject matter itself. To say this is to indicate . . . the reason for the lack of response to the committee program: faculty are by and large satisfied with the intellectual attainment of their students. The Committee is suggesting, then . . . that the faculty should not be so easily satisfied.   (5)

Though such interdisciplinary efforts were rare, the communications movement did spur renewed interest in composition and rhetoric within English departments and, more important, gave rise to a professional association for writing teachers, the Conference on College Composition and Communication. CCCC provided a forum for discussion and research of issues outside the purview of the MLA (as then organized) and became the seedbed for the WAC movement and research into writing in the disciplines (Bird).

The 1960s: Language and Equity

Though the WAC movement did not appear in the United States until the mid-1970s, the fundamental institutional, social, and theoretical shifts that gave rise to the movement took shape in the 1960s. The decade left its greatest legacy for WAC through far-reaching changes in the structure and social role of mass education. Higher education began a vast building project. The number of institutions increased by more than one-fourth in the decade, and the number of students more than doubled, from 3.6 million in 1960 to 8 million in 1970 (Bureau 166). The expanded higher education system trained and credentialed students for new roles or roles that had traditionally required no post-secondary training. Institutional and disciplinary differentiation increased apace and, with it, linguistic differentiation. Academics began speaking of *interdisciplinarity* and sought ways of understanding the discipline-specific "discourse communities" that specialization created (King and Brownell; Sherif and Sherif).

Though the expansion in higher education allowed selective institutions to become even more selective and research-oriented (many such institutions dropped or reduced composition requirements), it also brought a host of students into higher education who had previously been excluded (R. Smith). But there were few institutional structures for dealing with the needs of these new students, including the need for writing instruction to help them enter specialized academic discourse communities. Moreover, the ratio of students to regular faculty members increased dramatically, as the system increasingly relied on graduate students or part-time teachers for instruction in composition and other fields (a result of the vastly expanded research mission of higher education under the influence of corporate and state funding) (Jenks and Riesman). Many faculty members felt that standards were declining, that the new students could not do "college-level" writing (presumably the writing that instructors assigned in the disciplines). In turn, many undergraduates felt alienated from the increasingly specialized teaching staff in the new "multiversities." Faculty members and students did not speak (or write) the same language, and there were few opportunities, formal or informal, to learn specialized discourses.

The social turmoil of the 1960s also highlighted the role of language in education. The campuses exploded in a rash of political upheavals. Racial desegregation forced secondary and higher education to address the problem of teaching long-excluded social groups who did not write the dominant form of English. In this highly charged political environment, educators had to confront volatile issues of language and access, language and learning, that had been largely submerged when higher education placed disciplinary standards over equity and access. The NCTE funded the Task Force on Teaching English to the Disadvantaged in 1964, and the federal government funded programs for teaching reading and writing to inner-city youth (Applebee, *Tradition* 225–28). The late 1960s also witnessed a small revival of child-centered progressive thought, which had been central to discussions of writing and pedagogy in the 1920s and 1930s. Writing teachers in the child-centered progressive tradition, such as Ken Macrorie (*Uptaught*) and Peter Elbow (*Writing without Teachers*), sought to overturn the skills model of composition, just as the broader "open classroom" movement and other late 1960s progressive reform efforts sought to overturn the industrial model of specialized education (see Kohl; Postman and Weingartner). However, progressive reformers in the 1960s, like their predecessors, did not systematically address the issue of writing pedagogy and disciplinarity.

In the wake of Sputnik, federal funds were appropriated for curricular reform along disciplinary lines. Disciplines, including English, again turned their attention to pedagogy and found in the theories of Jerome Bruner a rationale for discipline-centered secondary and undergraduate teaching. Bruner's emphasis on the structure of the disciplines was in one sense a corrective to the progressives' insistence on the experience of the student. But Bruner, no less than Dewey, conceived of education in developmental and transactional terms, though he relied more heavily on Continental theorists, mainly Piaget, rather than on the American progressive tradition. And like Dewey, Bruner emphasized inductive teaching (the "discovery" method), affective and intuitive factors in learning, and, significantly, the role of language in ordering experience (M. J. Smith). Unfortunately, pedagogical reformers in the disciplines focused on Bruner's notion of a "spiral curriculum," which would teach the central concepts of a discipline "in some intellectually honest form to any child at any stage of development," and paid less heed to his insights into the role of language and of inductive teaching in formulating such curricula (Bruner 13). The curriculum materials produced by research-oriented university instructors in the federally funded projects of the late 1950s and early 1960s were concerned primarily with *what* to teach and *when*, rather than *how* to teach it and *why*. The sciences, where funding was most generous, paid little attention to laboratory writing, though in some cases the typical "cookbook" lab manuals were expanded to include more white space for students to write (Hurd, *New Directions* 30). In

English, which in 1964 belatedly received federal funding, a national curriculum research effort, Project English, developed traditional skills-oriented composition curricula that lacked an integral relation not only to other disciplines but also to the other two parts of the English disciplinary "tripod": literature and language (though the student-oriented process approach of Wallace W. Douglas at the Northwestern University site and the materials for "disadvantaged" students at the Hunter College site were important exceptions) (Shugrue).

In 1966, just as the federally funded English projects were drawing to a close, the American English profession's confidence in its traditional pedagogy and disciplinary focus was deeply shaken by a month-long encounter with British colleagues at the Dartmouth Seminar, a meeting of some fifty educators jointly sponsored by the MLA, the NCTE, and the young British professional association the National Association for the Teaching of English. As one participant put it, the two delegations found they had "passed each other in mid-Atlantic" (Dixon 72). While American education since World War II had generally been moving away from the progressive tradition toward a pedagogy centered on disciplinary rigor, standard curricula, and standard "objective" evaluation, the British school reformers had been moving in the opposite direction, toward pedagogy centered on informal classroom *talk*, dramatics, and expressive writing. Echoing American progressives of the 1920s and 1930s, the British pedagogy stressed not structured disciplinary knowledge but experience-centered "awareness" leading to personal development, and adherents attacked standard examinations (in their tradition, as in earlier American practice, primarily essay tests) and hierarchical imposition of curriculum by disciplines (Dixon 81–83).

In a working paper, British researcher Harold Rosen raised the central question of what relation informal, personal writing bore to the more formal and impersonal writing required in the disciplines, a question Britain's Schools Council was just beginning to investigate (Dixon 87; Muller 106). But the Dartmouth Seminar did not take up the question of writing in the disciplines (indeed, none of its many working groups was specifically concerned with composition, though several groups dealt with it peripherally) (Muller 98). Discussions of "practical" writing in the disciplines went against the grain of the conference, with its concern for liberating students from "the System, the Machine" (160). A few participants felt that the conference overemphasized individual experience and personal development at the expense of public and disciplinary claims. As Herbert J. Muller wrote in his report on the seminar, "I think John Dewey, now much maligned in America, took a more comprehensive, balanced view of education, with a clearer eye to both practical and intellectual interests, and to individuality as something that can be fully developed only in and through community" (176). But even the conference's critics agreed that Dartmouth had effectively reopened the crucial theoretical and policy issues that the American antiprogressive emphasis had stifled, and several of the conference participants—James Britton, Douglas Barnes, Harold Rosen, and James Moffett, among others—would, in the coming decade, create and shape the WAC movement.

First Stirrings of WAC

During the 1960s, the interest in writing instruction evident in the 1950s communications movement coalesced into a revival of rhetoric as an academic discipline, giving institutions recognized experts who would design and implement curricular reforms in writing instruction (Berlin 120–28). Researchers in composition embraced native theorists such as Bruner and began to discover Continental and British theorists who would be central to WAC initiatives in the 1970s. Composition research acquired a new disciplinary rigor and produced studies of the rhetorical, cognitive, and social dimensions of writing, studies that in the mid-1970s would provide an intellectual basis for WAC (Berlin, ch. 7).

Though composition was still marginalized in English departments and in the wider institutions, the late 1960s stress on increased access invigorated efforts in the progressive tradition to initiate students into academic communities through language instruction. The City University of New York, for example, found it politically necessary to begin its open admissions policy five years ahead of schedule. At CUNY Mina Shaughnessy became interested in writing and access; she eventually rose to a deanship and pioneered the study of "basic writing," a highly influential developmental approach to teaching academic writing to students from previously excluded groups. Shaughnessy's research and curriculum reform brought respectability to an area that had been regarded as intellectually uninteresting and reshaped the remedial writing lab tradition along developmental lines (Lyons).

Across the river at Brooklyn College, Kenneth A. Bruffee began, in 1972, a program of undergraduate peer tutoring for students in all courses, through a writing lab staffed by undergraduates from many disciplines (Bruffee, "Brooklyn"). And across the continent in that same year, at California State at Dominguez Hills, a similar program was initiated to train undergraduate writing tutors assigned to particular courses in the disciplines (Sutton). Research conducted in the 1960s had shown that American college students suffered from "an indifference to ideas, and the irrelevance of their education to their associations and relationships with other students" (Clark and Trow 67, qtd. in Bruffee, "Brooklyn" 449). These peer tutoring programs and the continuing research by Bruffee and others explored the potential for using writing to link students' experience with their learning in a collaborative environment—an important theme of the future WAC movement.

Also in the early 1970s, in a few small private liberal arts colleges with selective admissions (Carleton, Central, Grinnell), writing programs sprang up that encouraged faculty from disciplines outside English to use writing in their courses. In the previous decade, selective colleges had been able to raise admissions standards and reduce or even eliminate composition courses, as the new or expanded institutions with lower standards enrolled the less well prepared students (Wilcox 94–102). But in the late 1960s and early 1970s, as pressure for widening access increased, private colleges began rethinking their admissions policies—and their writing programs. Again the "skills" orientation prevailed, with remedial labs a common model. But a few colleges organized cross-curricular programs to deal with rising enrollment of students whose writing the faculty considered inadequate. After its enrollment doubled within a few years, Carleton College, in Northfield, Minnesota, began a "college writing proficiency requirement" to show "formal recognition of the fact that teachers in departments other than English may assume the responsibility of judging a student's ability to read and write well" (Larsen 8). Students could satisfy the proficiency requirement by writing for courses in departments other than English. In 1974, under the leadership of Harriet W. Sheridan, Carleton offered faculty members a two-week conference on evaluating and using writing in their pedagogy. And instead of the usual remedial lab, Sheridan began a "writing fellows" program, which trained undergraduates to tutor their peers on writing assignments from courses in the disciplines.

At Central College in Pella, Iowa, a group of faculty members led by Barbara E. Fassler Walvoord began meeting in a week-long seminar, held once each semester, to discuss student writing. In 1975, Central received federal funding under a grant from HEW for "special services for economically disadvantaged students" to hire a full-time coordinator for a college-wide reading and writing program (which later included a peer tutoring program funded by Exxon). As at Carleton, the heart of the program was departmental responsibility for certifying majors as competent in reading, writing, and (in Central's case) oral communications, supported by workshops to help instructors in the disciplines foster and evaluate student writing (Walvoord; "Development").

The most important predecessor of the American WAC movement—certainly at the secondary level—was the Bay Area Writing Project (later the California and National Writing projects). In 1971, seven years after the demise of the Prose Improvement Committee, the University of California at Berkeley began another developmental program to improve college students' writing, this time by focusing on writing instruction in secondary schools. But instead of using the "top-down" approach of the federally sponsored curriculum reforms of the 1960s, with their prescribed "teacher-proof" materials and content-centered disciplinary emphasis, Berkeley adopted a collegial, interdisciplinary, "bottom-up" approach reminiscent of the Prose Improvement Committee, organized around workshops in which secondary teachers shared experiences, presented successful methods, and together investigated the roles writing could play in their classrooms, all the while writing a good deal themselves. The BAWP staff—usually from English, not education, departments—found opportunities to expose participants to writing research and theory without claiming to have definitive answers. The first workshops began in 1974 and were so popular that two years later the California Department of Education (with help from a federal grant for compensatory education) made the BAWP approach its statewide staff development model (causing some friction with education departments) (Clifford and Guthrie 317–18). Writing projects proliferated nationwide, with some sixteen sites in California and sixty-eight in other states by 1979 ("Bay Area").

Most of the participants were English teachers, though teachers from other disciplines also attended the workshops. But the project's developmental approach to writing as an integral part of learning (not a separate skill) transcended disciplinary boundaries. And more important, its collegial workshop environment, with faculty members discussing writing and learning (while writing themselves), helped free composition from the remedial stigma—and would become a hallmark of the WAC movement.

The Newest Literacy Crisis: A Movement Coalesces

These and other similar programs might have remained scattered experiments but for yet another national literacy crisis—this one in the mid-1970s—that produced the most dramatic institutional demand for writing instruction since the mass education system founded composition courses a century before. The public outcry was precipitated by alarmist press reports of declining writing ability, based (tenuously) on the results of the 1974 National Assessment of Educational Progress. The NAEP test of student writing, administered every five years, seemed to show that student writing had declined since the first administration in 1969. In fact, the results were inconclusive. The 1979 administration produced higher results than those from either 1969 or 1974 in many areas, and NAEP officials called for "caution in making global statements about writing." But in 1974, caution was the first casualty in a war on "illiteracy," laxness, and waste in schools and colleges. A *Newsweek* cover story, "Why Johnny Can't Write," concluded that, "willy-nilly, the U.S. educational system is spawning a generation of semi-literates" (58). Academics joined the chorus. NEH chair Ronald Berman saw in the NAEP evidence of "a massive regression toward the intellectually invertebrate" (qtd. in Daniels 138). The immediate target of the attacks was the supposed permissiveness of schools in the wake of the late 1960s reforms. But like similar literacy crises in the 1870s, 1910s, and late 1940s, the mid-1970s crisis coincided with widening access to previously excluded groups. And like its predecessors, the mid-1970s uproar led to a renewed emphasis on mechanical correctness and "skills"—now dubbed "back to the basics"—accompanied by the usual remedial drill that is America's almost reflexive response to a perceived lack of writing competence.

However, unlike the previous literacy crises, this one drew a more considered response in some quarters. America now had a corps of writing specialists to provide leadership, a resurgence of interdisciplinary interest in rhetoric, a growing body of research on writing, sources of public and private funding to support experiments, and a theoretical basis to allow for more than the usual remedial and cosmetic changes in response to the public outcry.

The British tradition of teaching, research, and curricular reform in language instruction, which had so challenged American English educators in 1966, proved to be the catalyst for the American WAC movement almost a decade later. American reformers borrowed the term "writing across the curriculum" from the British Schools Council research effort to map the ways language is used for learning, a project begun about the time of the Dartmouth Seminar and drawing to a close in 1975. But more important, Americans drew heavily on the British theoretical and research models rather than go directly to their own progressive tradition of language instruction (though of course there was much cross-fertilization). American reformers quickly adopted and adapted Britton's classification of discourse into transactional, expressive, and poetic functions, particularly his valorization of expressive discourse in pedagogy (echoing the American child-centered progressives' earlier emphasis on "creative expression"), and they borrowed British methods of qualitative research: a descriptive inquiry more philosophical than quantitative, attentive to the discourse of students and teachers, broadly humanistic, and free of the "educationist" perspective so suspect in American higher education.

The report of the Schools Council project, entitled *The Development of Writing Abilities (11–18)*, was published just as America was in the throes of its latest literacy crisis (Britton, Burgess, Martin, McLeod, and Rosen). A few influential secondary school reformers attempted to spread the theory and concept of WAC as a developmental alternative to the remedial skills orientation. But the main thrust of American reform was in higher education, unlike in Britain, where WAC reforms were (and largely are) at the secondary level. There were CCCC convention sessions on WAC in 1976 and 1977, led by program organizers such as Walvoord and Sheridan. Robert Parker and others organized an NEH summer institute at Rutgers in 1977 to bring the new theories and classroom practices to fifty college faculty members. Future leaders of the WAC movement such as Toby Fulwiler were exposed to the new British writing research. Perhaps more important, they saw illustrated in the teaching of Lee Odell, Dixie Goswami, and other institute instructors the collegial workshop method that was the hallmark of the Bay Area Writing Project faculty development model and of British research methods (a National Writing Project workshop was meeting down the hall from the NEH seminar).

That same year, Janet Emig, a Rutgers education professor whose work on the development of secondary students' writing was heavily influenced by the British approach, published a seminal essay, "Writing as a Mode of Learning," that wove together the British research, the Continental theories of Vygotsky, Luria, and Piaget, and American theorists such as Dewey, Bruner, and George Kelly. Emig's essay announced the central themes of the emerging WAC movement: that writing has "unique value for learning," not only in English but in all disciplines, and that it is "a central academic process" (127–28).

The Movement Gains Momentum

In the highly charged political atmosphere of the new literacy crisis, Elaine Maimon and Toby Fulwiler began widely influential programs at Beaver College (a small liberal arts college of eight hundred students) and Michigan Technological University (a public regional university of six thousand). Both were junior English faculty members with training in literature, not composition, who, in the long tradition of the marginalization of composition, had just been named composition directors. Maimon's dean called her in, confronted her with the *Newsweek* exposé, and charged her with the task of improving student writing. Inspired by the research and experimentation going on elsewhere (particularly the Carleton program), she began working with colleagues in other disciplines who were interested in improving pedagogy through writing—biologist Gail Hearn, for example, was working on an NSF-sponsored project to study ways to improve students' laboratory observations. They began collaborative teaching and research experiments and read widely in the new literature on writing and learning. Maimon and her colleagues eventually convinced the college's Educational Policy Committee to adopt a developmental strategy involving many faculty members instead of a marginalized remedial approach. With an NEH grant, in 1977 she launched the first of many faculty workshops on writing. These workshops treated writing (and teaching) as a serious intellectual and scholarly activity intimately related to disciplinary interests, not as a generalizable elementary skill (the first workshop was led by Sheridan, using Aristotle's *Rhetoric* as its central text). "The teaching of writing," as Maimon put it, "is scholarly not scullery" (5).

At a very different kind of institution, Michigan Tech, Fulwiler and his department chair, Art Young, responded to faculty calls for a junior-year examination on grammar and mechanics by creating a WAC program to involve technical and scientific, as well as humanities, faculty members in writing instruction. With a General Motors grant (ordinarily given to improve technical instruction), they conducted the first of their influential writing retreats for fifteen volunteer faculty members at a mountain lodge in northern Michigan. Fulwiler used Britton's theoretical formulation and the BAWP's workshop style to emphasize the uses of expressive language—often in journals or "learning logs." Young called the response to the first retreat "heartwarming if not epidemical" (5). And future retreats led by Michigan Tech faculty members at other institutions around the country made this "consciousness-raising" model of WAC one of the most prominent.

WAC soon spread to the new open admissions colleges and community colleges, to the expanding regional universities, and to major state universities and consortia of colleges and secondary schools. The national interest in literacy made WAC programs frequent beneficiaries of corporate and government funding. And WAC became popular among administrators in higher education, not only as a means of responding to the public demand for better student writing but also as a faculty development program and, in broader terms, as a means of encouraging a sense of academic community.

However, the widespread ferment in discussions of writing and learning did not produce a single movement with an overarching philosophy or organizational structure. As WAC programs proliferated in secondary schools, colleges, and universities around the country, they reflected the enormous structural variety of American postelementary education. Some programs were merely general composition courses that taught belletristic essays on subjects treated in other disciplines (e.g., Stephen Jay Gould and Loren Eiseley); others were tutoring programs or expanded writing labs; still others were organized around an institution-wide writing examination or a writing requirement satisfied by taking certain "writing-intensive" courses offered by several departments.

But the WAC programs had certain similarities. Though they were almost always organized by composition instructors from English departments, not by those from other disciplines, they were usually supervised by an interdisciplinary committee. WAC initiatives were (and largely are still) outside the regular departmental structure of academia—and therefore subject to the vagaries of personnel, funding, and priorities. They depended for their success on the individual commitment of faculty members (and individual administrators) in a grassroots pedagogical reform movement—not on the support of departments and disciplines (McLeod, *Strengthening*; Fulwiler and Young). As Fredrick Rudolph, a leading historian of American college curriculum, has said of interdisciplinary programs, "Unless handsomely funded and courageously defended, efforts to launch courses and programs outside the departmental structure [have] generally failed" (251). Yet by the early 1980s, scattered theories and experiments had become a national movement, with publications, conferences, and a growing number of programs. As with previous literacy crises, the one in the mid-1970s faded when pressures for widening access abated in the 1980s. Other movements across the curriculum took the spotlight— "core curriculum," "cultural literacy," "ethics across the curriculum," and so on. But unlike the ephemeral responses to various literacy crises of the past, the WAC movement carried on its slow work of reform, despite cuts in outside funding, competition from other educational movements, and reduced emphasis on expanding access to higher education. Indeed, a 1988 survey of all 2,735 institutions of higher education in the United States and Canada found that, of the 1,113 that replied, 427 (38 percent) had some WAC program, and 235 of these programs had been in existence for three years or more (McLeod, "Writing").

Progressive Pedagogy and the Disciplines

The rapid growth of WAC in higher education was in the deepest sense a response to the demands for writing instruction created by increasing enrollment, particularly of previously excluded groups, but those demands were not new and do not in themselves explain the unique structures American higher education evolved in the WAC movement or the movement's comparative longevity. Significantly, the late 1970s and early 1980s responses to the newest literacy crisis often went beyond the usual remedial correctives or administrative measures that had characterized WAC's many antecedents. The reasons for WAC's success are complex. The movement's strength and longevity (in comparison with earlier efforts to involve faculty members in improving students' writing) is the result, in part, of the fact that reformers found a new way to revive progressive alternatives to traditional pedagogy. They were able to face the issues of writing and specialization, which had lain submerged for a century, and evolve a broader version of progressive pedagogy, one that recognized the importance of disciplinary knowledge and structure for effecting reforms. Though WAC did not entirely change the ground of the argument over writing from "skills" to "development," it certainly staked out another, higher ground for discussions of writing, one that linked writing not only to learning and student development but also to the intellectual interests of specialists. Today it is possible to discuss writing in the disciplines as more than a favor to the English department or as a means of evaluating students' content knowledge. Unlike its predecessors, WAC (in its most common forms) did not attempt to substitute some overarching educational or philosophical program or a millennial hope of doing away with disciplinary boundaries and enshrining some version of "plain English," as reformers from both the left and the right had advocated for almost a century. Instead, WAC acknowledged differences among disciplines and tried to understand them, without trying to dismiss or transcend them.

Student-centered progressive education had in the 1960s reemerged as an option for faculty members outside education departments, but in the late 1970s the old battles between student-centered and discipline-centered teaching were broadened to consider the nature of education in a society organized by specialization—and by specialized written discourse. (Maimon called Dewey "the presiding ghost" in Beaver College's efforts to make writing an issue in the whole curriculum.) For Maimon, Fulwiler, and many other WAC proponents, the emphasis was not on writing improvement as an end in itself, or even (at least initially) as a means of improving communication. Rather, they stressed the power of writing to produce active, student- *and* teacher-centered learning. WAC was a tool for faculty development, for reforming pedagogy, though of course improved writing was an important benefit. For many college faculty members—unlike secondary teachers, who take education courses and attend faculty development meetings—WAC workshops provided their first opportunity to discuss pedagogy (much less writing) in an institutionally sponsored forum. And because the discussions centered on writing, an activity embedded in every disciplinary matrix, faculty members could bring to bear their resources as specialists, addressing the unique curricular and pedagogical problems of their disciplines. WAC programs produced a collegial environment out of which fruitful research as well as pedagogical and curricular reform grew. For example, the first book on WAC, C. Williams Griffin's *Teaching Writing in All Disciplines*, included essays by a physicist, F. D. Lee, and a finance professor, Dean Drenk.

The WAC movement of the 1970s, unlike its predecessors, was also able to draw on an emerging discipline of rhetoric and composition for its organizational and theoretical base, outside education departments and traditional literary study. In the 1970s, graduate study in rhetoric and composition began within English departments (some forty PhD programs existed by 1987); scholarly books, journals, and conferences proliferated (Chapman and Tate). After a century of marginalization, the study of writing could be viewed as a serious intellectual activity. The whole WAC enterprise was thus able to treat rhetoric and composition as a research area, a field worthy of serious intellectual activity, intimately related to disciplinary inquiry—an important source of credibility in American higher education, where research is often valued over teaching. There were conflicts, of course—over "jargon," "turf," pedagogical approach, and other issues. But for the faculty members participating in WAC programs, at least, writing could not so easily remain transparent, either in their pedagogy or in their own research (Fulwiler, "How Well"; Maimon).

WAC programs gave rise to research projects on rhetoric and argument in many disciplines and to cross-disciplinary comparative studies. And from the late 1970s, the WAC movement drew strength from research, in several disciplines, into the social and rhetorical nature of disciplinary inquiry and discourse, research carried on in such diverse fields as history, anthropology, and the sociology of science, as well as in linguistics, cognitive psychology, and literary theory (see McCloskey; Myers, "Social"; Broadhead and Freed; J. B. White; H. White; Yates; Fleck; Latour). By recognizing the disciplinary organization of knowledge (and thus of postelementary education), WAC has been able to appeal to faculty members from many departments, whose primary loyalty and interest lay in a discipline, not in a particular educational philosophy or institution. And by carrying on cooperative research with faculty members in many disciplines, progressive reformers today, unlike their forebears, at last have the means to explore the ways students and teachers can create that balance between the individual student's experience and the collective experience that a discipline and its teachers represent. Since the late 1970s in America, such cooperative research has sought to find those language experiences that engage students with disciplinary communities (see Jolliffe; McCarthy and Walvoord; see also Kaufer and Geisler; Herrington; Anderson et al.; Anson, "Classroom"; Berkenkotter, Huckin, and Ackerman).

These were great accomplishments: to reopen issues of pedagogy that had been largely unexplored for decades and to make visible those issues of writing and learning that had been largely transparent in the disciplines. But WAC thus far has only begun to explore those issues that lie behind its basic assumption: that language, learning, and teaching are inextricably linked. To understand the ways students (and teachers) learn through writing will be an unending project, for to arrive at such understanding means negotiating—and continually renegotiating—the relations between the many interests that have a stake in the ways language is used in education: students and faculty members, with their diverse backgrounds and goals; institutions on a huge spectrum and hierarchy; disciplines with various and sometimes competing professional interests; and, of course, social organizations of many kinds, which depend on postelementary institutions to educate (and often select) their members.

The WAC movement, like the tradition of progressive education it is ultimately a part of, was born out of a desire to make the mass education system more equitable and inclusive but, at the same time, more rational in its pursuit of disciplinary excellence and the differentiation of knowledge and work that drives modern (and postmodern) society. Thus the WAC movement, like its progressive antecedents, must negotiate the claims of both equity and disciplinary standards, social unity and social specialization. Through these negotiations it may be possible to realize the vision of Dewey: that curricula would be arrived at by means of open communication and rational engagement, not by fiat;

that new institutional structures would be created, new pedagogical traditions evolved, continually to balance the experience of the learner with the demands of the disciplines through discourse—of students, teachers, disciplines, and the wider culture.

NOTES

[1] This account draws heavily on my *Writing in the Academic Disciplines, 1870–1990: A Curricular History,* especially chapters 2 and 9.

[2] On the marginalization of composition in higher education, see, for example, Berlin 31 and Stewart. On composition in secondary schools, see Applebee, *Tradition* 32–34 and Piché.

[3] At the secondary level, these were called "hospitals" or, later, "labs" (both terms reflect the medical model on which remediation is based). At the college level, the most influential program was Harvard's Committee on the Use of English by Students (1915–50), which policed student writing with the aid of faculty members in the disciplines.

[4] Academia's reaction to Sputnik is only the most obvious instance. See, for example, the history of university involvement with secondary physics and chemistry courses (Hurd, *New Directions* 80–86).

PART II

Disciplinary and Predisciplinary Theory

Introduction

The authors in this section address an important issue for the field of writing in the disciplines: What should we emphasize in both research and teaching—disciplinary discourse and ways of knowing, or more general issues of teaching and learning that are assumed to transcend disciplines?

In the first two essays, James Britton and Charles Bazerman present differing answers to this question. Britton writes that "my hope for the enterprise of education lies not in the specialized knowledge developed within the disciplines, but in the power of what I have called predisciplinary theory, one that draws on psychology, sociology, and linguistics but is none of these, a theory that remains close to the observed phenomena of teaching and learning." According to Britton, as postsecondary educators, we should think more about "who knows what," and less about "what is known." At many universities, disciplinary research, and not teaching, has "academic esteem." Further, in government policy and in the popular mind there is a related "touch of Philistinism"—an assumption that education leads to employment, rather than to broader human development.

In contrast to Britton's call for a focus on general issues of learning and teaching, Bazerman stresses the need for careful rhetorical analysis of disciplinary discourses. Such analysis Bazerman sees as an addition to "English studies," a work to be appropriately undertaken by members of English departments as well as by faculty members in the disciplines. The explicit teaching of disciplinary discourse, he argues, "holds what is taught up for inspection. It provides the students with means to rethink the ends of the discourse and offers a wide array of means to carry the discourse in new directions." Bazerman makes clear that he is not arguing for indoctrinating students unreflectively into disciplinary ways. Indeed, his approach seems compatible with that articulated by Stephen M. Fishman, one of the interchange authors who, after reading Bazerman's chapter, wrote, "For me, disciplinary initiation means bringing a variety of languages together, clearing a safe space in which privileged and less privileged languages can be positioned and related."

Both Britton and Bazerman are advocating heightened critical awareness of our disciplinary discourses. Judith A. Langer makes the same case in her essay, although her focus is less on broad rhetorical issues and more specifically on the "features of argument and analysis that characterize academic learning in particular disciplines." Knowing the conventions of thought specific to a discipline, we will be better able to structure and respond to students' learning of a particular field. Yet in her study, Langer finds that teachers in a range of disciplines focus on their students' mastery of content and not on the thinking that was evidenced in their students' writing. Her study leads her to call for "communicative 'signs' that can be used to talk about the shapes of knowledge within a discipline," "overt conversational tools to help students think about planning, organizing, and presenting their ideas in discipline-specific ways." The bringing to awareness of discipline-specific modes of thinking and writing can result, in Langer's view, in better learning and teaching.

While Langer has studied the ways in which teachers talk about their teaching, Lee Odell looks at the criteria we bring to bear in the evaluation of writing. He finds that too often teachers take a formalist view of writing, making a distinction between writing and content that separates the evaluation of writing from students' understanding of the subject. Odell presents an alternative "epistemic" approach to evaluation that begins by identifying the ways of knowing that are valued for particular writing tasks. Essentially, like Bazerman, Odell is calling for a form of rhetorical analysis; however, unlike Bazerman, who would have us analyze the discourse practices of professionals, Odell wants us to analyze our students'. After reading Bazerman's and Langer's essays, Odell explains, "I think the rhetorical analysis should focus on student work as a way of helping students see what they need to do and as a way of requiring a teacher to identify and reflect on what he or she values." Like Langer, Odell finds that many teachers are "unlikely to be very reflective about the ways of knowing they value."

Theories of the Disciplines and a Learning Theory

James Britton

The author, now retired, was professor of education at the University of London's Institute of Education.

My interests have been in the uses of language, spoken, written, and read—or as the means of thinking—from the earliest stage of childhood to the recollections of old age. Daughters and granddaughters and generations of pupils have been my teachers. It has long seemed to me that grammatical studies and poetry somehow feed the same interest.

In considering writing in the disciplines as a movement in British education, I need to state at the outset my doubts about the value to us of the disciplines as they are presently constituted—or, at least, my hope that the disciplines, properly considered, are dynamic, movable entities, difficult, even impossible to pin down long enough for the process of definition to get usefully underway. I should say at the outset as well that my hope for the enterprise of education lies not in the specialized knowledge developed within the disciplines, but in the power of what I have called predisciplinary theory, one that draws on psychology, sociology, and linguistics but is none of these, a theory that remains close to the observed phenomena of teaching and learning. This is, I know, retrograde, for the motion in British university study and in American postsecondary education lies in the other direction, toward increasing specialization and the devaluation of teaching. In my view, the attention paid the disciplines would be much better paid to the processes of learning—to shift the emphasis, as I discuss later, from what is known to who knows what.

47

The Disciplines: Theories at Work

Susanne K. Langer, in her essay "The Growing Center of Knowledge," traces the stages by which our commonsense view of the world forms the starting point for a speculative and increasingly accurate conceptual notion of experience. In tracing this progress, she lays the foundation for a theory of disciplines. Understanding experience, Langer claims, consists in imagining its structure with the help of words or other symbols and, in the light of these general and usually tacit ideas, interpreting aspects of the world as we experience them. "All our experience—practical, ethical, or intellectual—," she writes, "is built upon an intuitively constructed logical scaffold known as common sense" (150). We are not, Langer believes, in the everyday business of questioning our commonsense views of experience. We hold these views rather as a kind of stable framework of expectations. But on occasion— and clearly the frequency of such occasions will vary tremendously from individual to individual—what might be called a breakdown of expectations will bring us to question the commonsense view we have previously taken for granted.

This "common sense" is not a fixed entity. A propensity to extend our knowledge by *generalizing*, applying what has been learned in one context to suggest a meaning to features in other contexts—which is itself sound enough as a strategy—will sometimes lead us into error. Imagination and careful observation, if we succeed in them, will suggest to us fresh circumstances—matters that go beyond the expectations derived by common sense. Moreover, such a discovery is itself likely to prove a link in a chain of logical conclusions affecting a widening area of our knowledge regarding our environment.

Langer points out that it is a typically human capacity to see one thing in terms of another, and in particular to interpret abstract phenomena by applying, as it were, a model. "Death is seen as an eternal sleep, youth and age as spring and winter, life as a flame consuming the candle that provides it" (154). Her essay goes on to examine some of the discrepancies that will result from the spontaneous commonsense solutions to the problems raised by our experiences. "It is really a rough and ready instrument that is prone to yield absurdities when its concepts are tested for all they imply. . . . The thinker, therefore, is confronted by the task of criticizing and correcting, perhaps even rejecting, the accepted images and tacit assumptions and of building a new, more abstract, more negotiable set of concepts" (159–60). The development of more abstract and more negotiable concepts—that is to say, concepts more open to adaptation and extension—constitutes the concern of my present essay.

George Kelly had strong views on the negotiability of our theoretical concepts. He began one of his articles with this statement: "This paper, throughout, deals with half-truths only. Nothing that it contains is, or is intended to be, wholly true. The theoretical statements propounded are no more than partially accurate constructions of events which, in turn, are no more than partially perceived" ("Behaviour" 257). Structural alternativism or what we might call "second-guessing"—progressive planning and the cultivation of the tentative—were key tenets of Kelly's approach and serve to remind us of the transforming effects, for example, of what Thomas S. Kuhn called a change of "paradigm," the substitution of a novel frame of reference for the one that had governed research to that point (176). But it is as well to remind ourselves at the same time of Michael Polanyi's complementary notion of the fiduciary nature of the theorist's beliefs, their steadfast grounding in lasting trust (*Personal* 294). The way the pieces fit together, each so to speak a confirmation of the principles by which they were seen to be distinctive, offers confirmation of the negotiability of the conception.

A very wide range of analytic and theoretical thinking spans the kind of activity indicated by Langer's refinement of commonsense categories and the so-called revolution that changes the framework within which scientists pursuing research in a particular discipline operate. I think these two kinds of activity—refinement and revolution—have in common the function of providing, as far as possible, rational terms of reference within which to seek the solution of a problem, whether one of behavior or of belief. The concept of a discipline, as it concerns me here, is likely to be arrived at by consistent, corporate, and cumulative activity at a highly abstract level.

A full and detailed study of the nature and distribution of academic disciplines has been produced by Tony Becher, professor of education at the University of Sussex. He gives the study the intriguing title *Academic Tribes and Territories*, a reflection of his view that the character of an academic discipline is a function both of the intellectual nature of the study pursued and of the personal, social, and institutional circumstances of the people engaged in it. The study is based on interviews with practitioners in twelve academic fields: of the pure sciences, biology, chemistry, physics; of applied sciences, mechanical engineering and pharmacy; of social sciences, economics and sociology; of the humanities, history and modern languages (including English); and academic law, geography, and mathematics. Becher elected

Table 1

	Reflective	Active
Abstract	Natural sciences Mathematics	Science-based professions, e.g., engineering
Concrete	Humanities Social sciences	Social professions, e.g., education, social work, law

to examine the disciplines as practiced at an advanced level in institutions of high prestige by experienced and successful professionals.

Surveying the scene in summary fashion, he suggests that "from the perspective of those engaged in its creation, knowledge would appear ... comparable with a badly made patchwork quilt, some of whose constituent scraps of material are only loosely tacked together, while others untidily overlap, and yet others seem inadvertently to have been omitted, leaving large and shapeless gaps in the fabric as a whole" (7). Attempting to bring precision into so diverse a theater of operations, Becher takes over a set of categories from previous research regarding scientific and artistic studies as representatives of abstract and concrete modes; he incorporates an additional feature, the active as opposed to the reflective, to distinguish practical applications from basic theory. The application of these distinctions to examples of disciplines is shown in table 1.

Considerations of academic prestige form a recurrent theme in Becher's book, and they culminate in what might be called a roll of honor of the disciplines: "Roughly speaking, hard knowledge domains are regarded more highly than soft ones, and pure than applied" (57). Hard knowledge domains are, of course, those that handle quantitative data, and soft knowledge domains are those that deal in qualitative distinctions. By these standards, the discipline of physics tops the list, and what might be classed as the humanities brings up the tail. Becher makes it clear from the beginning that, in elite colleges and universities, the educational role is not a factor in determining the academic esteem of a discipline. In describing the responses made in interviews with faculty members, he recorded:

> A limited number of respondents—particularly in the more vocationally oriented disciplines—did choose to talk about undergraduate courses and students, but the large majority preferred to focus on their activities as seekers after knowledge rather than as

communicators of it. The reason for this, it might be inferred, is that membership of the academic profession—at least in elite departments—is defined in terms of excellence in scholarship and originality in research, and not to any significant degree in terms of teaching ability. (3)

Such a judgment, I believe, indicates something of the failure of higher education echelons to endorse the purpose of education on the total front. We have been slow in Great Britain to assess the value of what is known in the light of who knows it. Reinforcing this failure on our part, a touch of philistinism at government levels has exacerbated the problem. One broadly comprehensive study, *Higher Education and the Preparation for Work* (Boys et al.), was carried out by specialists in higher education from the particular point of view of the preparation of students for their place in industry. A series of chapters deals with problems that arose in Britain when it was no longer possible to ignore the subsequent employment of students on the general grounds that academic qualifications had general value. No doubt, demands of the kind raised in the United States asking "how much for the dollar" coincided with the touch of high-placed philistinism I referred to above. At all events, it often seemed necessary for subject specialists in higher education to plan on the basis of suiting a subject to economic career openings. The higher education study attempts in each case to assess the causes of changes in curriculum: whether they reflect recent academic interests or external demands—including, in particular, employment opportunities.

It is time to declare my limited concern with such data: my experience and my theoretical concern began, many years ago, with attempts to understand the effects of schooling on language development in the secondary school; thence, with the observation of our own children and with the tackling, both at home and in schools, of the psychological and linguistical processes that contributed to development; and by now, in the context of a university department of education, with opportunities for study and research. I speak from operational experience, therefore, in two distinguishable areas: the disciplines that make up a school curriculum, from primary to secondary level; and the disciplines—linguistics and psychology, principally—that the craft of teaching draws on.

When, therefore, the higher education study goes into details regarding the teaching of electrical engineering, economics, and business studies, I am in no position to comment and would have no purpose in doing so. The subjects they elect to treat, however, include history,

English, and physics, and these are certainly part of my concern. The writers report that students of history have traditionally failed to make vocational use of their knowledge, but that limited changes in a number of institutions have attempted to bring the discipline into line with the demands of employment. Nevertheless, both with history and English faculties, the innovations made are more likely to reflect shifts in the interpretation of the subject than any reassessment of vocational requirements. New branches of study and warring academic factions have been particularly active in the English faculty and "have included linguistic theories, structuralism and 'post-structuralism,' marxist views about the creation of literature and its social function, and feminist criticism" (39). It does not appear that employment opportunities have brought about any of these changes: indeed, there seems to have been in the profession a wide acceptance of the notion that experience in an English department counted as a generally useful and marketable qualification.

Moreover, to take an elite view of the teaching of physics, it is still the general educational value of the subject that predominates; but as distinctions begin to be made between the "pure" knowledge versus the "applied," consultancies and research funds set up vocational emphases within the department. Academic research remains, however, high in prestige, continues to extend our knowledge, and provides a career structure both in university faculties and in industry. It is realistically anticipated that most graduates will obtain posts that employ their knowledge and skills in a professional capacity of some kind, in spite of the acknowledged difficulty of the work. New techniques continue, moreover, to provide new career openings. However, the maintenance of standards of work for higher education in physics is firmly in the hands of the community of physicists.

In a final chapter that attempts to set out the conclusions to be drawn from the complex study as a whole, the report finds that academic courses maintaining a broadly "liberal" view of higher education exist side by side in many subjects with those "whose prime objectives are to produce graduates able to apply knowledge to particular ends, who are effective people with the relevant knowledge and skills for specific areas of practice" (196).

It is useful to revert at this point to Becher's study. Becher makes some interesting comparisons and contrasts between the disciplines. He notes that causal connections are more easily established in the natural world than in disciplines that treat human characteristics. Here, judgment and persuasion must be taken into account, and the whole notion of *intention*, which plays no role in scientific and mathematical interactions, may be crucial to an understanding. Becher poses the question of whether disciplines represent a worldwide consensus and believes that, subject to such variations in a society as may result from the nature of its educational system, they justify the claim that they possess strong family likenesses. It is, he believes, through the medium of language—the nature of the discourse that carries their meanings—that differences between disciplines will principally emerge. Thus "the professional language and literature of a disciplinary group play a key role in establishing its cultural identity" (23). The identity may take the form of a particular symbolism, as in mathematics or parts of work in physics, or it may involve the use of specialized terms not in frequent general use, as is the case in many reports in biology, the social sciences, and, of course, in history and English, "those disciplines which pride themselves on not being 'jargon-ridden,' since the communication here none the less creates what linguists would call its own register—a particular set of favoured terms, sentence structures and logical syntax—which it is not easy for an outsider to imitate" (24).

Fresh problems arising within a discipline will sometimes demand new allies, new methods, differing from those in use in general within the discipline, and, with them, new uses of language. Becher has referred to these areas of concern as *specialisms* and notes that some theorists would prefer to see academic studies as loose clusters of specialisms rather than as discipline-centered departments. His critical account of academic knowledge as "a badly made patchwork quilt" might be seen as supporting the stress on specialisms as a more realistic concept than a discipline. However, it is Clifford Geertz, in *Local Knowledge*, who spells out in detail the profitable breakdown of the defining boundaries between disciplines.

In the first chapter, entitled "Blurred Genres: The Refiguration of Social Thought," Geertz notes that "analogies drawn from the humanities are coming to play the kind of role in sociological understanding that analogies drawn from the crafts and technology have long played in physical understanding" (19). In his introduction to the work, Geertz states that the blurring has become normal in our judgments and has led to important changes in our modes of explaining our existence to ourselves, and in the course of doing so has altered our view of what "counts as science." What I find most striking is the degree of kinship Geertz feels for the interpretative processes applied in humane studies to a literary text. It is in fact the blurring of the distinction between social *explanation* and literary *interpretation* that comes over most forcefully. In a later essay in the book, Geertz describes a presentation in which he compares his findings as an anthropologist with the critical writings of Lionel Trilling: the occasion was a memorial seminar to Trilling at Columbia University. "If Trilling," he says, "was obsessed with anything it was with the relation of culture to the moral imagination; and so am I. He came at it from the side of literature; I come at it from the side of custom" (40).

The change, Geertz suggests, has resulted from the increasing failure of a "law-and-causes" approach to social problems to yield the kind of understanding and predictive power, and the control, at which it aimed. It is, from his point of view, an abrupt shift in direction: "Calls for a 'general theory' of just about anything social sound increasingly hollow, and claims to have one megalomanic. Whether this is because it is too soon to hope for unified science or too late to believe in it is, I suppose, debatable. But it has never seemed further away, harder to imagine, or less certainly desirable than it does right now" (4).

The methods of cultural anthropology suggest Geertz's solution—and the title of his book—*Local Knowledge*. The object of study is seen within the framework of local understandings. What is signaled is to "turn from trying to explain social phenomena by weaving them into grand textures of cause and effect to trying to explain them by placing them in local frames of awareness" (6). I used to inject, as a comment on the partial nature of firsthand experience, the saying that the earwig and the head gardener live in the same garden. But according to Geertz, this metaphor does not go nearly far enough: the knowledge we bring to bear on the life we lead draws on wide areas of knowledge and wisdom of past eras:

> The truth of the doctrine of cultural (or historical—it is the same thing) relativism is that we can never apprehend another people's or another period's imagination neatly, as though it were our own. The falsity of it is that we can therefore never genuinely apprehend it at all. We can apprehend it well enough, at least as well as we apprehend anything else not properly ours; but we do not do so by looking *behind* the interfering glosses that connect us to it but *through* them.   (44)

His example of the process at work concerns the way writers have dealt with rapidly changing responses to the Great War, presenting what he calls "a world view in droplets," and the way these writers' views have created a lasting social framework around the event. And he claims a similar effect from works of fiction: "This is how anything imaginational grows in our minds, is transformed, socially transformed, from something we merely know to exist or have existed, to something which is properly ours, a working force in our common consciousness. . . . The passage is from the immediacies of one form of life to the metaphors of another" (47–48). There can be no doubt in my mind that this account of the breakdown of previously acceptable boundaries and affiliations among the disciplines has broached new understandings and that neither the stability of scientific parameters nor the hesitations of literary ones are unaffected. As far as my own area of interest is concerned, I look for novel developments in theories of the role of literature in the educational program.

Geertz, like Langer, treats common sense as a cultural system, though in his words it is not usually conceived as forming an ordered realm. He suggests that treating it in this way, rather than on its own commonsense terms, as "just what anyone clothed and in his right mind knows" (75), will enable us to distinguish its operational force from the immediate and invariable accompaniment of experience. It will allow us, in particular, to see that there are individuals who do not merely use their ears and eyes to read a situation, but do so actively and discriminatingly; who may judge whether to accept or to amend or to reject altogether what common sense would urge. It is Geertz's concern to note that common sense as a system has certain common characteristics wherever it appears, but also many unique features in different cultures. In attempting to define the common features—a task that he finds there is no obvious vocabulary for—he speaks of the qualities to be associated with what is "natural, practical, thin, immethodical, and accessible" (85). "Thin" is the puzzling item: he explains it elsewhere as a reference to the process of reminding people of what they already know. Naturalness is a fundamental requirement and will color what may appear to us as far from natural: intersexuality, magic, witchcraft. Practicalness will indicate the quality that characterizes local knowledge of one's environment, directly or indirectly involved. "Immethodical" might be viewed as celebrating the surprises and the shocks of experience—perpetuating, perhaps, what William James called the "blooming, buzzing confusion"—and applying clearly to the contradictory nature of many commonsense claims: "Look before you leap" and "He who hesitates is lost."

Geertz closes his account by contrasting common sense with cultural systems of science, art, ideology, and the rest as "what is left over when all these more articulated sorts of symbol systems have exhausted their tasks" (92). One must wonder whether he regards the commonsense system as capable, in favorable circumstances, of growth toward articulation and novel ways of knowing. As for "these more articulated . . . symbol systems," the restricted languages of the disciplines, I believe that what is required of the writing specialist—a role I take it that Lee Odell and Charles Bazerman are concerned with—is to work in close association with the subject specialists on whose tasks students are engaged. And that, surely, points the way to the kind of interdisciplinary study necessary on a substantial scale if we are ever to know the precise terms governing the practice of a discipline in a particular institution. As a linguist, I believe I can contribute something to such a study, but, having in mind Polanyi's conception of tacit components in a practitioner's thinking, I realize that nothing we might know of the nature of language in general could fill its place. Practitioners may be unable to convert their tacit knowledge into explicit terms. But their acceptance or rejection of the interdisciplinary conclusions would still be a necessary step.

Development of a Learning Theory

My career as a teacher began in 1930, when I was appointed to teach physical education to boys in a Middlesex grammar school and English to the coeducational classes. I was singularly fortunate that I had been prepared for this work by an original and gifted teacher—a linguist who was also a specialist in literature—Percival Gurrey, my tutor at what was then the London Day Training College (to become, soon after, the University of London's Institute of Education). I could not have had a better springboard. Within a few years I had committed myself to a view of curriculum by writing a text to cover two years of the secondary school English program, a language and composition course. Unfortunately—no, fortunately—I came after a time to an understanding that I had nailed my colors to the wrong mast. Not that there is any reason why one should not teach a language-study and writing course, but to suppose that that is the necessary combination for all students was an undisturbed relic of a former philosophy. Accumulated evidence from research, experience from teaching itself, and knowledge of schools in which grammatical instruction was not featured and the written work did not suffer convinced anyone who had managed to keep an open mind that, much as we might enjoy studying and teaching grammatical knowledge, it could no longer be considered a royal route to improvement in writing.

It was many years before I found opportunity to make anything like a full statement of my conception of the curriculum for English teaching. *Language and Learning* was the outcome of teaching, at advanced level, a course to practicing teachers and a parallel course for would-be teachers at the London Institute of Education. In the book I state explicitly that I had not written about the subject matter of English teaching but about the role of language in education. I had begun to define for myself the field that I would later call "predisciplinary" learning theory. It is in the preface to *Language and Learning* that I make my confession and launch myself, with the help of my colleagues, into a problem. Having expressed my gratitude to students and colleagues who had played a part in the course, I went on:

> To other colleagues, in the dens of their disciplines, I offer my apologies, for in applying what I have learned from them I have certainly taken risks they will find it difficult to excuse. Expertise is dangerous, used in the open, and the choice is between taking risks with it or leaving it alone—which, as I judge it, is no choice at all. After all, if I must confess, I am not a philosopher, a psychologist, a sociologist, a linguist and a literary critic; for the sake of the confessional I could have said *"or,"* but not for the purposes of my argument. (7)

The first opportunity I had to pursue further the notion of a theory appropriate to the study of education came some years later when, in 1977, James Squire, for NCTE, invited me to contribute to *The Teaching of English*, the seventy-sixth yearbook of the National Society for the Study of Education. My chapter was to open the book by dealing with "language and the nature of learning," setting out the processes by which children acquire initial competence in using oral and written language. I completed my essay with advice and assistance from nominated readers and from the editorial committee, but the latter determined that a subtitle be added to the effect that what my chapter offered was "an individual perspective." Not, I hope, so individual today as it was then reckoned to be.

My thirty-eight-page account deals with most aspects of the curriculum in literacy for the early years; the "individual perspective," the learning theory, covers little more than the first two pages. It is a very tentative statement, but positive in its insistence on the need for research in the relevant disciplines: psychology, linguistics, sociology. It is equally firm on the need for a learning theory that is not the equivalent of any of them. The argument rests in part on the fact that a teacher must work in areas for which there is no agreed disciplinary view—as, for example, on the precise manner in which learning to read is related to learning to write. Thus teachers have to find ways of making up their own minds on the matter from whatever clues they can pick up. In the words of my original:

> If in the face of a range of problems the teacher succeeds in becoming an active and constant theorizer, psychological theories (for example) will be of help to him; but, as teacher, he does not become a psychologist since his theorizing stops at a point nearer to the phenomenon than does the psychologist's—and the phenomenon in our case is the child using language to learn and grow up. The teacher is thus something of a psychologist, something of a philosopher, linguist, sociologist—never one of these because always something of each of them.   (2)

The 1977 essay closed by suggesting that the term "predisciplinary" should describe this learning theory, thus reserving the term "interdisciplinary" to describe cooperations between the exponents of cooperating disciplines—the "academic tribes and territories" of the Becher study.

It is interesting to record that when in the writing research project at the London institute we reported our means of classifying kinds of writing by function and by intended audience, Michael Halliday's comment on our work, at a time when he was actively working on "a social semiotic" (a diagramming of the networks of social communication), was that our categories applied well to the data beneath them but articulated badly with the more general categories above them— the upper levels of the social semiotic. This was, in effect, what we intended these categories to do, since they are "predisciplinary" and stay at a level close to the phenomena classified.

My concern for the nature of education as a discipline was grounded in the work of earlier writers. Joseph Schwab, for example, had suggested in 1969 that a necessary aspect of the study of education must be to account for "the arts by which unsystematic, uneasy, but usable focus on a body of problems is effected among diverse theories, each relevant to the problem in a different way" (1). The thinking of Geertz— his blurring of the genres, his application in anthropology of the interpretations customary to literary critics—will have prepared us for such a view. Certainly one of the problems in the field of education is to define the proper relation between research and practice. There survives a view in our field, derived from the physical sciences, that there is in learning theory hard knowledge that is cumulative and grows steadily in scope and complexity. This view must be faced and corrected. Perhaps what, as teachers, we need from research is that it should guide our thinking rather than our actual practice.

My latest return to the theory of education is contained in an article written jointly with Merron Chorny (of the University of Calgary) in

Handbook of Research on Teaching the English Language Arts. I close this section of my essay by repeating the warning we deliver in that piece. We suggest that our view of the field of education—one that stays close to the phenomena and draws on many disciplines as contributors to its theory—could lead to a damaging eclecticism. Categories that have been divorced from the systems they comprise may come to be seen as rough equivalents and so become distorted to the point where they mean very little. To define a *personal construct* in Kelly's analysis ("Man's Construction"), for example, as the rough equivalent of a *concept* as Piaget would define that term would lead to some confusion. The proper course for our predisciplinary study lies in pursuing parallels, but under the full control of a just and sensitive response to the phenomenon itself.

Education among the Disciplines

Having decided that I wanted to finish with a brief look at how education relates to the customary or established disciplines, I realized that the wording of this section title might suggest I was anxious to put the cat among the pigeons. So be it. There is likely nothing surprising in my claim that most incumbents of the disciplines in prestige subjects and prestige establishments wear their learning with very little thought of how they came by it.

And yet I doubt if that is the whole story. A great many academics are also parents of growing children, and we can imagine that in "teaching" their children, they might be led to reflect on their own learning. Even where their own sources of knowledge and skill remain hidden, there must be some payoff in terms of the value these academics accord to schoolteachers. If this were not so, we would have to rely on the proverbially traditional and outdated educational conceptions of party politicians, without the shaping effects of social concern.

Judith A. Langer in the present volume looks at teaching within the disciplines and finds that teachers have a great deal more to say on the specific content of what should be included in a syllabus than they do on the ways of thinking—and writing—that are appropriate to the various subjects. Further, she finds that where revised ways of thinking have been explored and advocated in the disciplines—as, for example, in the physical sciences, where the sense that knowledge is objective and verifiable has largely been abandoned—these new theories of knowing have produced very few changes in the procedures that occupy the classroom.

Langer's findings suggest to me that improvement in teaching is not likely to arise from new disciplinary theories. A predisciplinary theory of education seems, in contrast to a disciplinary approach, a very different kettle of fish. It has no function as the substance to be taught—whether teaching means that it should be transmitted or paraphrased or somehow induced. It is, rather, a method by which a teacher comes to an understanding of what will result in an understanding on someone else's part. It is clearly, and perhaps totally, a matter of language.

I have been talking about "predisciplinary theory," and I have tried to make clear what I take the term "predisciplinary" to mean. I will conclude by saying as best I can what I mean by the term *theory*. Kelly has put it this way:

> In essence a theory is simply a way of highlighting events so they may be viewed in some kind of perspective. And yet, regardless of how well events are illuminated, it is quite unreasonable to hope they ever can be so completely revealed there will be nothing left to look for. The best one can ever expect of a theory is that it will enable [one] to see what [one] has never seen before, and that it will be succeeded in time by another theory which will disclose some of what still remains hidden.   ("Behaviour" 260)

And taking the other end of the spectrum—but not, I think, in the final analysis contradictory—here is George Miller's "What's in a Theory?" from his book *Spontaneous Apprentices*. Note how close, to Miller, the theory must be to the data:

> Different lexical fields can be organized very differently. For example, the best way to organise colour terms is in a circle; the best way to organise kin terms is at the corners of a three or four dimensional solid; names for times can be mapped onto a line; verbs of motion seem to require some complex lattice of shared concepts that is difficult to visualize spatially. . . .   (22)

Here I leave my topic, poised somewhere within the scope of these two views of a theory: the general claim set out in philosophical terms by Kelly and the intriguing particulars displayed in Miller's analysis of theoretical method. My concern has been a view of what goes on in school classrooms, and that seems to demand a catch-as-catch-can mode of attack, rich in the effects it can bring about, concerning not so much *what is known*—as the disciplines are—as *who knows what*.

From Cultural Criticism to Disciplinary Participation: Living with Powerful Words

Charles Bazerman

The author is professor of literature, communication, and culture at the Georgia Institute of Technology.

When I started teaching writing, twenty years ago, I soon became aware of the ways in which college students needed to write about the materials they were reading in their courses. (See my textbook The Informed Writer.*) In investigating the social organization of disciplinary writing, I became drawn to the sociology of science, which has influenced all my work since then. (See* Shaping Written Knowledge.*) I continue to be interested in questions of how knowledge is constructed, reproduced, and used through the material, social, and textual practices of different disciplines. How literate practices are inextricably bound with the entire matrix of disciplinary and professional activity is the organizing theme of the volume* Textual Dynamics of the Professions, *which I coedited with James Paradis.*

Critical commonplace now has it that disciplines are socially and rhetorically constructed and that academic knowledge is the product of sociolinguistic activities advancing individual and group interests. Literary theorists readily assert that knowledge (at least of the academic kind) is made up out of words and other symbols, that words are made up by people, and that people have their own concerns to look out for—or, even worse, that people are so imprisoned by the words they use that words use people to reproduce themselves. Words almost seem a form of linguistic DNA that ineluctably re-creates itself through the appliance of human beings. In simplest terms, you can't trust words to tell you the truth. Such a conclusion, logically unexceptionable within its assumptions, is a great disappointment to foundational hopes about the enduring verity and universal authority of the results

61

of our academic labors, but it is a great encouragement both to the humanist case against the perceived hegemony of sciences (natural and social) and to the radical case against all forms of institutionalized authority that may be perceived as sources of oppression.

This commonplace is precisely critical: rhetorical perception used as a means to distance ourselves from the everyday practice of the world's business in order to reveal and evaluate the hidden mechanisms of life. Indeed, such criticism can challenge us to remake our world according to our own best lights instead of according to the masked advantage of the few or the imperatives of autonomous symbols beyond the interest of anyone. A much more ancient commonplace dear to the academy suggests that we live meaningfully only when we have examined our lives. The more precisely we learn how the symbols by which we live have come into place, how they function, whose interests they serve, and how we may exert leverage on them to reform the world, the more we may act on our social desires. Exposing the choice making that lies behind the apparently solid and taken-for-granted world forces us to address the ethical question of our responsibility for our world.

Criticism, however, is only the beginning of action. Action is a participation, not a disengagement. Participation is the other side of rhetoric: the art of influencing others through language in the great social undertakings that shape the way we live. In contemporary America, the academy has become one of the chief institutions of society: in creating concepts and practices that pervade culture and political economy, in advising and educating social leaders, and in influencing the education of all. Participation in the academy is a significant means to individual and group influence in the constant reproduction and reshaping of our society. Because the academy is one of the great levers for social change, critical disengagement from its active projects, unless in the realistic hope of forming some other equally influential and better means of realizing social desires, is withdrawal from a great social power. Retreat into critical purity leaves that power in the hands of the very people theorists criticize for parochialism, narrow interest, and lack of social imagination: the epigoni of the disciplines.

Indeed, the cultural rhetorical critique of disciplinary writing tends to bring into prominence the epigonistic formulas that may make the disciplines seem static things. Critiques that expose how outdated beliefs, power, and interests are entrenched in disciplinary discourse draw a conservative picture of disciplines as they have come to be but not as they are now becoming. To highlight the residuum of the past, rhetorical critiques delineate the current synchronic system of base-

line expectations, the seemingly taken-for-granted disciplinary assumptions that have emerged from the prior negotiations of language.
These assumptions necessarily reflect the way things were for those
who had influence and power in that negotiation, not the way things
are now. Discourse is always in dialectical tension between what came
before and what is now: contenders jockeying for position, as they do
in any vital, communal endeavor. The notion that the rhetoric of a
discipline is a uniform, synchronic system hides both the historical
struggle of heterogeneous forces that lies behind the apparent regular-
ity and the contemporary contention and complexity of discourse that
is played out against the school-taught formulas of current convention.
Rhetorical criticism, especially if it is carried out with broad sweeps
of condemnation, may make disciplines seem purveyors of hegemonic
univocality rather than the locales of heteroglossic contention they are.

In bluntest terms, cultural criticism of disciplines may fall far short
of its mark because it believes too readily, and is thus too readily
disappointed in, the textbook accounts of disciplinary work—that the
disciplines are simply what they represent themselves to be to neophyte
students. When we, standing outside a particular discipline, discover
that a discipline is not all it says it is, does not achieve the irresistible
harmony of irrefutable knowledge without serious contention, is not
purely separable from its social consequences, and must depend on
social forces for its support, we then may too readily believe that the
discipline is unredeemably suspect. Yet people who push beyond the
101 textbook in a given field begin to learn its complexities: its history,
its culture, its production and use of knowledge, its relation to other
institutions in society, and its border skirmishes. They also feel, and
must consciously contend with, the constraints and focuses put on
their work through the habits, standards, and practices of the discipline. They come to recognize, too, the strains among contending elements in the field and recognize poachers from neighboring fields. As
they advance in their participation within their discipline, they learn
to locate themselves and their work on an ever-changing, complex
field where communal projects, goals, and knowledge are constantly
negotiated from the individual perspectives and interests of participants within and without the field. These acts of participation are
all necessarily responsive to those powerful but nonetheless fluidly
interpreted and reconstituted social facts of disciplinary institutionalization and control.

The overt teachings of a discipline, beginning with textbooks for
schoolchildren and continuing through all forms of professional communication, may ignore or even suppress knowledge of the contexts

and forces in which the field operates and that shape the knowledge of the discipline (Latour). The overt teachings may pretend that the work of the field is methodologically pure and intellectually isolatable from the messy, rhetorical complexity described above. Instruction in methodological standards may in fact represent only the rhetorical move of one group, which, having gained the upper hand, attempts to reinforce its position. Even when that position of epistemic hegemony is well institutionalized and entrenched, however, methodological issues and apparently closed borders can be renegotiated as difficult cases and new focuses of concern evolve. Nonetheless, institutionally enforced standards may lead practitioners to relegate the impure facts of daily life to such backstage forms as jokes, late-night beer talk, or "political strategy" sessions (Gilbert and Mulkay).

Rhetorical analysis of the actual communications of the disciplines (whether undertaken by those trained in the arts of language who turn their attention to the disciplines or by disciplinary practitioners who develop self-conscious sophistication about language) opens up these suppressed issues of the dynamics and evolving knowledge production of the disciplines. Rhetorical analysis can make visible the complexity of participation by many people to maintain the large projects of the disciplines. It can recognize the linguistic practices developed in consonance with the goals of such projects, the constant struggle between competing formulations, and the innovation that keeps the discourse alive. Rhetorical analysis can also reveal exclusions and enclosures of discourse to see how and why they are deployed and to question their necessity in any particular case. But even more, it can provide the means for more informed and thoughtful participation. Through this activity we can help the disciplines do the best work they were created for, rather than be the self-protecting domains of vested interest and social power we fear. Such analysis allows insiders to move the discipline effectively and enables outsiders to negotiate with the discipline and regain territory that may have been inappropriately enclosed within the expert discourse.

Teaching students the rhetoric of the disciplines, understood in these terms, does not necessarily indoctrinate them unreflectively into forms that will oppress them and others, although such oppressions do happen often enough, as power and system become their own ends, and practice becomes habit and then rule. Such oppression of the self and others is more likely to occur when individuals learn communication patterns implicitly as a matter of getting along. Explicit teaching of discourse holds what is taught up for inspection. It provides the students with means to rethink the ends of the discourse and offers a wide array of means to carry the discourse in new directions.

Rhetorical self-examination in anthropology provides a striking illustration of the way in which critical exploration of discourse can lead to deeper insight into the projects and knowledge of a discipline and to disciplinary vitality—even when such examination shows that previous discourse was implicated in social, political, and economic relations that we now disown. Historical work on the discourse has demonstrated that the early accounts of anthropologists were part of late-nineteenth-century imperialism, as the United States attempted to subordinate and domesticate the Native American populations through the Bureau of Indian Affairs, and as European nations spread their control over the other "primitive" peoples of the world who were being drawn under their political and economic "protection." The genre of ethnography, with its representation of the primitive other through the suppression of the native informant in representing the way of life and the elevation of the anthropologist as the objective authority, became the chief textual means for Western societies to objectify the dominated peoples.

Recent critical work (J. Clifford; Clifford and Marcus; Fabian; Geertz, *Works*; Marcus; Marcus and Cushman; Mascia-Lees, Sharpe, and Ballerino-Cohen; Rosaldo; Tyler) has not only pointed out these intrinsic dynamics but has also indicated how ethnography has changed in response to evolving understandings of the relations between "exotic" cultures and the "scientific" nations of the West, as well as the decreasing distance between self and other. However, these revelations, along with the rejection of the socioeconomic relations of dominance, have not meant an end of the genre of ethnography. People still need, both individually and institutionally, to represent their own and each other's lives to each other and for themselves. Questions of who speaks, who owns the discourse, who receives, how the self becomes changed in the interaction between self and other, and for what ends the discourse is carried on have opened up new experimental varieties of ethnography (for example, Abu-Lughod; Crapanzano; Dumont; Rabinow) and more sensitive use of all varieties (see, for example, van Maanen). Thus, rather than go out of fashion discredited, ethnography has gained vitality and spread across the social sciences and even the humanities.

Detailed attention to disciplinary writing does not enslave users of disciplinary languages to the entrapments of the past. Instead, it provides choices for reevaluation and facilitates exploration of the flexible and manifold resources available within traditional disciplinary genres, reconceived more deeply. I have found this to be true in the response to my study of one of the most restrictive of disciplinary forms, a writing "style," imposed by leaders of one discipline attempting to advance a dominant epistemology, theory, and research program. The format of the experimental article in psychology, as set forth in the *Publication Manual* of the American Psychological Association, is the result of a self-conscious program of discipline building by behaviorist psychologists over the middle of this century. In the manual's prescriptions behaviorists have indeed found an appropriate rhetoric based on their assumptions and goals and growing out of the dynamics of the professional discourse during this period (Bazerman, *Shaping*, ch. 9). In becoming the official style of the most "scientific" of the social sciences, the APA style has been highly influential throughout the social sciences.

By analyzing the processes, dynamics, and assumptions of this institutionalization of style, I have not at all fostered the enclosed dominance of this discourse. Rather, professionals and students have largely responded that understanding the implied baggage of the discourse has freed them to make rhetorical choices with greater clarity: whether to continue in the traditional forms, to modify them, or to abandon them altogether for discourse conducive to other kinds of projects. The only resistance I have met is from those who do not wish to think of their discourse as "discourse" and claim that their words and arguments carry no freight and are only epiphenomena of their "science." According to such individuals, they are writing the only way they could in consonance with "good science." It is not the serious attention to disciplinary discourse that restricts our intellectual options but the refusal to attend that fosters the hegemony of narrow discourses.

When we do attend to the history of disciplinary discourses, we see complex heteroglossia, even in the most restricted genres, such as the experimental report in science. Each newcomer to a field must come to understand, cope with, and place himself or herself within the evolving conversation. In studying the development of Isaac Newton's way of discussing his optical findings, a way that would have profound implications for all scientific discourse to follow, I saw Newton working to make sense of the discourses around him, find appropriate means of addressing his audiences, respond to the conceptions and objections of his readers, and forge a style that would carry overwhelming force on the discourse field that he only gradually came to understand. His final solutions in the compelling "Newtonian style" seemed to suppress all other voices but actually encompassed them in a way that they could not escape to make alternate claims for a century. In examining

Newton's rhetoric, we move behind the massive social appearance of the supranatural genius Newton, "sailing through silent seas of thought alone," and we come to understand an individual locating himself among others and finding powerful means to advance his own vision and claims (*Shaping*, ch. 4). The history of all scientific discourse is built on such individual stories of people learning to use language effectively and thereby advancing the resources of language.

Once a rhetorical field is highly developed, individuals find themselves in the middle of intertextual webs within which they can act only by modifying the intertextuality through new statements. Our goals and activities influence our idiosyncratic placement in and interpretation of that intertextual field. When physicists read professional articles, they do so with an eye toward promoting their own research projects within a competitively structured argument over what claims are to be considered correct and important and how the literature should be synthesized and advanced (*Shaping*, ch. 8). There is constant negotiation among prior statements, new statements, responses, and further work over what constitutes credibility and creditability (Myers; Latour and Woolgar). By reconstructing the literature around their ongoing work and then representing their new work within that reconstructed matrix of the literature, individuals make the field over fresh and construct a new place for the self.

Discourse studies of the disciplines, which aim to understand the dynamics of each field and the state of play into which each new participant enters, can help build the intellectual foundations for courses that enable students to enter into disciplines as empowered speakers rather than as conventional followers of accepted practice, running as hard as they can just to keep up appearances. Even more, discourse studies can provide an enlightened perspective through which students can view the professional and disciplinary fields with which they will have to deal as outsiders. It is as important, for instance, for an ecologist or a community planner to recognize the complexity of the discourse of biologists, geologists, and petrochemical engineers as it is for those professionals to have command of their own discourses.

Taking the discourse of professions and disciplines seriously provides the understanding students and professionals need to develop as active, reactive, and proactive members of their communities. With a sense of individual power, students can press at the bit of the disciplinary practices they are trained into or run up against. Seeing through the appearances of the discourse allows them to keep the fundamental goals of the fields in front of them. They can ask what kind of communication structures, patterns, and rhetorics will enable the fields to achieve those goals, how they can contribute to those ends as individuals, and in what way the goals achieved through a single disciplinary discourse coordinate (if at all) with social goals from other forms of social discourse. By understanding how knowledge is constructed, they can judge what knowledge it is they wish to construct.

This adventure into the power of language in the modern world should not be a far digression for scholars of literary studies, who have long been examining the power of language to shape the imagination in the religious struggles of the Reformation, the political struggles of the eighteenth century, and the industrial struggles of the nineteenth. Studying discourse might mean looking into disciplines and professions that literary specialists rejected as undergraduates on choosing the life of literary studies, but studies of disciplinary discourse wander no further into arcania than studies of Puritan pamphlet wars. Indeed, to the contrary, the disciplines and professions are always near at hand, as they increasingly encompass every aspect of our daily life.

Nor is the study of disciplinary discourse such a far digression for practitioners of disciplines, for they all, as part of their training, are taught to think reflectively about the tools and methods of their fields. Once they become aware that language is one of their most fundamental, and most sensitive, tools of knowledge construction, they cannot escape the conclusion that rhetorical studies are an inevitable part of methodological training, as much as education in statistics, analytical techniques, or laboratory experimentation. All professionals must have some knowledge of field-appropriate methods of knowledge construction and their implications, and some specialize in understanding various techniques. If certain sociologists, economists, and educational researchers specialize in field-appropriate statistics, why should there not be scholars of field-appropriate rhetoric?

No doubt the development of substantial research and education into disciplinary language will require significant reallocation of resources and priorities both within departments of literary and language studies and within the many other disciplines of the academy. Resistances to this change are likely to be many. However, if we are to create a humane society for the next century, it is precisely the disciplinary and professional words we will have to keep from getting away from us. Insofar as we understand the powerful words of our society, we can live with and through them.

Speaking of Knowing: Conceptions of Understanding in Academic Disciplines

Judith A. Langer

The author is professor of education at the State University of New York, Albany, and codirector of the National Research Center on Literature, Teaching, and Learning.

For the past decade I've been studying the structure of literate knowledge: how people become skilled readers and writers, how they use reading and writing to learn academic subjects, and what this means for instruction. I look at disciplinary writing from a sociocognitive perspective, at the knowledge students use when they make "sense" and the ways in which their thinking is affected by activities and interactions in the classroom. Most recently, I've been studying the nature of literary understanding and its contribution to intellectual development.

Are there essential similarities and differences in the ways various disciplines regard "knowing"? We need to answer this question before we can talk intelligently about using writing to learn in the disciplines. Yet in the literature there are no clear answers. I was led to this question by way of my earlier studies of academic coursework, particularly *How Writing Shapes Thinking*, coauthored with Arthur N. Applebee, which indicated that the overwhelming focus of instruction in English, as well as history and science, was on course content, on the object of study—the facts, to the neglect of ways to think about them. But why this separation? Does the focus on content have a root in the history of the various disciplines, or is there a dichotomy between the ways the fields regard knowledge and the ways schools regard knowledge?[1]

Problems of Knowing and Schooling

I have explored the relationship between academic writing and thinking in a series of studies examining students' writing across a variety of academic disciplines and have traced relationships between that writing, the teachers' values, and the types of learning fostered in their classrooms ("Literacy" and *Process*; Langer and Applebee, *Writing and Learning* and *How Writing*). The studies combined observations of individual classrooms with larger-scale surveys and found that students were rarely challenged to explain their interpretations or encouraged to examine the evidence on which they had based their conclusions. More typically, in all areas of the curriculum, they were asked to summarize information and points of view that had been presented to them by the teacher or the textbook.

In the first set of studies, such findings were attributed in large measure to a lack of effective models of alternative approaches to instruction, especially models that stressed writing as a process of thinking about new ideas and experiences (even though the literature on writing instruction placed great value on such approaches). In response to the need for such models, a second series of studies focused on teachers who used writing in interesting and effective ways, in a variety of academic disciplines. Though these studies were planned as a way to develop a series of models of effective instruction, the major outcome was to highlight serious problems in current conceptualizations of the role of writing in academic learning. It became clear that if new activities emphasize one kind of knowledge but teachers have been trained to look for other types of performance as evidence of learning, the new approaches make little difference.

The findings led to my present concern with the *content* of instruction—with what students are asked to learn and with what teachers look for as evidence of such learning. If teachers are to help students develop higher-order reading, thinking, and writing skills, they must be able to articulate the ways of knowing that are central to particular domains. Only then can they begin to conceptualize student learning in terms of the ways in which students think about and discuss the subjects they are learning, rather than in terms of recitation of rote content.

Generic and Discipline-Specific Ways of Knowing

The validity of this focus on discipline-based content and thought depends in part on the level of specificity that one adopts. Previous studies have made it clear that there are broad strategies of argument or uses of language that are common to the various disciplines (Applebee, *Writing*; Applebee, Durst, and Newell; Britton, Burgess, Martin, McLeod, and Rosen; Calfee and Curley; Langer and Applebee, *How*

Writing). Students of literature, of history, and of science write *reports* about specific events, for example, and also write *analyses* based on their observations. These strategies capture consistencies across varied contexts of language use. At the same time, however, the similarity in underlying purpose may mask important differences in the ways in which these purposes are achieved. These differences are likely to involve fundamental disciplinary concepts—notions of causality and proof, of evidence or warrants for claims, of assumptions that can be taken for granted, and of premises that must be made explicit and defended. Such concepts may lie at the heart of successful performance in a new discipline, as well as at the heart of the development of the higher-level intellectual skills that so few students seem to achieve.

Unfortunately, the earlier studies of effective teachers of English, science, and history have shown that these higher-level intellectual skills are not the focus of instruction. Instead, it is the content that drives curriculum and is reflected in the courses and examinations that students take.

There is another way to view academic learning, however, that transforms the role of writing in schooling. This is to view the classroom as a community of scholars (or of scholars and apprentices) that has its own public forums, with associated rules of evidence and procedures for carrying discussion forward. Students must learn, then, not only the basic facts around which discussion is structured but the appropriate and inappropriate ways in which those facts can be presented in the forum defined by that classroom. Such a forum is partly oral, in the presentations and discussions that make up the dialogue of instruction, and partly written, in the materials that students read and the papers they write. The quality of the reading materials is important, since they provide the most extensive models of what counts as effective discourse; the nature of student writing tasks is also important, since the opportunity for individuals to make extended contributions during class discussion is necessarily limited. Writing (and the thinking that accompanies it) then becomes a primary and necessary vehicle for practicing the ways of organizing and presenting ideas that are most appropriate to a particular subject area. In such a view, writing becomes a major vehicle of instruction in all the academic disciplines.

What evidence can we muster for viewing writing as a way to learn the structure of disciplinary thought? A variety of scholars have put forth related arguments, developing them in the context of an examination of the conceptual, intellectual, or social traditions of a given disciplinary community (Bazerman, "Discourse" and "What Written"; Bizzell, "Cognition"; Kuhn; Odell, "Process"; Roland). Anne Herrington complements this theoretical work by studying the nature of such disciplinary communities, or forums, at the college level. Basing her conclusions on lengthy ethnographies of two chemical engineering classes, she found that even within the specialized context of this subject matter, the demands of the forums in the two classes were very different. Students were learning not only the principles of chemical engineering but the specific types of claims and warrants that were construed as effective discourse in particular contexts. Success in these classes, then, depended in part on learning highly specific strategies and routines that were inextricably linked with the social and intellectual expectations or practices within each disciplinary forum. Other recent studies have also examined discourse features of discipline-specific writing and the social environments in which they are communicated and learned (Berkenkotter, Huckin, and Ackerman; McCarthy; North). In a very different tradition, Applebee, Russell Durst, and George Newell analyzed arguments produced by high school students and published writers in science and history. Using a variety of text-analytic procedures, this study found not only that the text produced by the two groups differed in consistent ways but also that the *patterns of differences* varied in the two subject areas.

Yet characteristics such as those described by Herrington and by Applebee, Durst, and Newell are rarely articulated by the teachers involved, though there may be an intuitive recognition that such differences exist. If we are to avoid a trivialization of instruction, we must articulate the features of argument and analysis that characterize academic learning in particular disciplines. (See Odell in this volume for a related discussion.)

A Study of Learning in the Academic Disciplines

The study I draw on in this chapter focused initially on conceptions of subject matter within particular disciplines as they are presented in their theoretical and pedagogical literatures, and later on how subject matter is treated by high school and college teachers. I provide examples from our interviews with forty-eight teachers.

Perceptions of Knowing within the Disciplines

In each of the disciplines we examined (biology, American history, American literature), there has been an increasing focus on the tentative nature of "truth," leading to an emphasis on the need for active *questioning* and *interpreting* rather than on simple accumulation of facts. Each of the subject areas has shifted away from a belief in a verifiable, constant, and stable body of knowledge toward the view that meaning is fluid and depends on individual interpretation, firsthand evidence, or new information. Such changes seem to be part of the objectivity-versus-subjectivity debate that has taken place during the late twentieth century. Further, discussions in all three subjects have emphasized both specific content and ways of thinking as central to becoming an expert within the discipline.

Biology. The role of these two aspects of knowing has been debated in biology (or more generally in the various physical and biological sciences), where there is a long history of searching for "objective" knowledge and a concomitant concern with codifying a "scientific" method that structures that search. More recently, the validity of both of these concepts has been challenged as scholars have questioned the independence of method and observation, arguing instead that the "facts" we discover are shaped and conditioned by our assumptions, that knowledge and the process of understanding are determined by our general theoretical and methodological presuppositions (Feyerabend; Polanyi, "Life's"). Either formulation, however, would lead to a program of science education in which learning to think like a scientist would play an important role.

History. Discussions of history have similarly placed a continuing emphasis on the twin issues of method and content. The word *history* itself derives from a Greek root meaning "to inquire," and much of the debate in the field has concerned the most appropriate methods of inquiry. Past decades have seen shifts from history as (perhaps idiosyncratic) narrative to history as objective scientific inquiry to history as interpretation. This latter shift, like that in science, has been driven by critiques of claims that "objective" or theory-neutral observations can ever exist and by the emergence of subjective influences as a legitimate, even central, part of the historical enterprise. These debates about historical method have been paralleled by debates about the appropriate content of history (see Berr and Febvre; Carr; Conkin; Dray; Eisenstadt; Gardiner; M. Mandelbaum).

Literature. Discussions of literature also reflect a history of debate about proper approaches to literary texts. These schools of criticism or of literary theory represent alternative formulations of what literature is about and of what should count as evidence in the defense of competing interpretations. The past century has witnessed a variety of approaches (e.g., moral, philological, historical, sociological, New Critical) emerge in turn as dominant in literary studies, but the present decade is marked more by diversity than by consensus. Approaches variously labeled as constructionist, reader-response, Marxist, feminist, structuralist, deconstructionist, postdeconstructionist, and psychoanalytic vie among themselves (and with other theories) for preeminence. Though many of the arguments parallel the more general debate about objectivity and subjectivity that has also influenced conceptions of science and of history (Bleich), no one approach to critical theory in literature has emerged to dominate contemporary scholarship.

Discussions of specific content in literature have usually focused on the nature of the canon: what literary works should one have read. This approach has a long history and continues to play a major role in contemporary debates in which, as in history, many have sought a deliberate broadening of the canon to include works representing a wider variety of authors, cultures, and points of view. An alternative approach to content in literature has focused on developing students' "appreciation," a "habit of lifelong reading," or "critical reading skills"—at which point the specific content of literature begins to merge with the "ways of knowing" represented by the favored school of critical theory, permitting instruction to focus on thought as well as on content.

Emphases in Educational Practice

In contrast, while shifts in educational research and theory have often paralleled some of the concerns in the "pure" fields, they have not necessarily become the major concerns of the teaching journals, nor have they made their way into practice. There is consensus in the abstract about the importance of both specific content and ways of thinking, yet in practice all three subject areas seem to have devoted most of their attention to specific content. This is perhaps most evident in biology, where the long tradition of concern with scientific method has manifested itself both in philosophical analyses of what constitutes "scientific method" and in pedagogical proposals for "inquiry-based instruction." Such a tradition would seem to ensure classroom emphasis on the rules of evidence and procedure that guide the work of the practicing scientist, but our review of the related literature on biology instruction suggests otherwise. Instead, we found that memorization of specific content continues to dominate, despite calls by leaders of science teaching since at least the turn of the century (see Hurd, *Biological*; Yager). Textbooks, which are used by 90% of high school science teachers 90–95% of the time, shape the curriculum, and the textbooks themselves have become almost overwhelming in the amount of specific content they seek to convey. In fact, the typical biology course requires students to master several times as many new words as they would learn if they were studying a totally new language.

Although specific content has been attended to in biology courses, no commensurate attention has been given to relations between scientific thinking and pedagogy. The most promising attempts to focus on such thinking have stressed "inquiry" approaches, in which students would learn the process of science through their own investigations. Such approaches, though enthusiastically endorsed by each wave of educational reform, have never been widely adopted. In the end, most courses seem to stress the value of a "scientific method" without providing students with the procedural knowledge and experience to apply such methods successfully themselves.

Similar patterns exist in history and in literature, where the particular content, and not methods of thinking, has tended to be altered in the course of curriculum reform. Recent reforms have changed "faces" in the textbooks and broadened the curriculum to represent more diverse groups and cultures. In history as in biology, there has been a parallel emphasis on inquiry approaches designed to introduce students to the methods and procedures of the historian; but though often advocated, such methods seem to have made few changes in practice (see Dunfee; Shaver, Davis, and Helburn; Lorence). In literature, methods that place the responses of the reader rather than the specific content of the text in a central role have been receiving increasing emphasis in pedagogical journals and other works, but such approaches seem to have had at best a superficial effect on classroom instruction. (For results of a national survey of literature education, see Applebee, *Study* and *Literature*).

If we look across the three subject areas, it is quite clear that although there are differences in both the theoretical and pedagogical emphases among the three disciplines, in each case the literature on practice reflects little of the underlying principles that are guiding the related discipline-based scholarship. In all three cases the scholarly fields have moved from a belief in the accumulation of knowledge toward one based on the tentative nature of truth, and toward a call for questioning, inquiry, and interpretation as continuing processes.

Perceptions of Knowing at School

Pedagogical concerns and teachers' goals are not necessarily the same. The teachers in our survey wanted their students to engage in deeper thinking about course content and to arrive at more comprehensive understandings of the course material. However, in the interviews the teachers were more likely to talk about general understandings when discussing abstract goals, and to talk about specific content when dealing with the day-to-day details of teaching and learning (there was little variation between high school and college teachers in their comments). For example, when asked about the value of studying the discipline, they spoke broadly about imparting a sense of history, a critical attitude, or a sensitivity to the human condition, as well as providing students with a way to function within the field. Some illuminating excerpts from the responses are presented here.

In literature, a teacher talked about the "study of human values, ethics, knowledge of self and the world around us. All literature helps us become introspective, retrospective, circumspective and helps us to consider society and how to live in it in an open-minded, compassionate, and humane fashion." Another teacher remarked, "American history is part of their heritage. Students learn values in their culture and judgments."

History, a teacher in the field observed, "adds coherence to students' sense of themselves and begins to give students the critical analysis they will need in later life for reading newspapers, voting," and other activities. In the words of another teacher, the discipline "is part of the collective cultural heritage of us as a people. Shared knowledge helps maintain a sense of collectiveness. Also there are certain kinds of problems that can be talked about by using historical materials."

Among the biology teachers we interviewed, one said that his subject "gives students an understanding of themselves and their bodies—like biological existence for survival, ecological systems information, practical health concerns, and career possibilities." A colleague noted that students "learn to think critically through the scientific method—hypothesis testing—to figure out why their sink leaks."

As these examples illustrate, when the teachers spoke about their disciplines in general, they almost never mentioned content. Instead, they emphasized the immediate or eventual usefulness of coursework in student's lives. However, these broad goals were not elaborated on. Although changes in student thinking as a result of exposure to the disciplines were implied (e.g., learning tolerance, understanding the body), how such changes come about, or how ways of thinking differ from thinking in other disciplines, was rarely discussed.

When they were asked about the value of a specific course, the teachers stressed major issues and themes. References to ways of thinking were infrequent.

One of the respondents, for example—a literature teacher—expressed this view: "A few key themes are important, such as our relationship to God, the American dream, being part of a group versus individualism. *The Scarlet Letter, Huck Finn, Gatsby,* and *Death of a Salesman* say much about what we are as a people." That approach was enlarged on by a colleague: "Teaching students to read poems and stories and plays and how to think about writing an essay is important no matter what literature you're teaching. For the American lit course, the idea of Manifest Destiny, that America was going to become the renewal of the world, explains a lot about American culture."

The perspective from history departments similarly focused on key concepts, such as the discovery of "how all kinds of people contributed to the development of this nation. Students come away not with a chronology but a sense of what preceded what—a sense of how America developed and why. Causation is critical." A colleague noted that "the foundation is the Constitution and the amending process, the functions of government, and the major conflicts in this century and why we went to war." It is important, this history teacher went on, "to understand the influx of many cultures—why we have become a global nation."

Biology teachers, too, concentrated on major ideas: "how genes are passed from one generation to the next, a basic understanding of the physiology of bodily functions, prenatal development—things that relate to our lives—biochemistry as part of nutrition, reproduction, sexual function." Concepts like these, one teacher said, help students "be more effective patients when they contact medicine." Students, another biology teacher maintained, should "know the basic systems of the human body, know how humans relate to other species, know how humans do things similarly to and differently from other species." They should know enough basics about human systems "to be able to decode media information, such as fad diets—are they for real or hoaxes? The course can open them up to wanting to read more science."

And when respondents were asked about the value of studying a particular unit, content became the predominant focus, with little linkage to the larger themes or perceptions.

According to an English teacher, for instance, reading *Huck Finn* can give students "a sense of Twain's worldview (e.g., how people treat each other). They can see how use of the word *nigger* functions in this book—see beyond the possibility that Twain is a racist—recognizing that dialect could be a problem and recognizing it early on." A colleague said, "In *The Scarlet Letter,* I want them to come away with the words 'be true, be true' sticking in their minds for the rest of their lives and to have pondered what these words signify for Hawthorne and for themselves."

In identifying significant areas of study, one history teacher cited the "sense of the degree to which American society was transformed as a consequence of industrialism, some of the sense of what the idea 'laissez-faire' means, and contradictions and violations in American tariffs." For another teacher in the field, it is important "to entertain the notion that the settlement of America can be best understood in the context of the time—in terms of motives—rather than approach it from later mythologies (e.g., revolutionary America—about everybody coming here for liberty, freedom, etc.). Words like *freedom* are nineteenth-century terms that have no meaning for seventeenth-century people." Also vital is the concept "that change in society didn't come out of a plan but resulted from concrete problems."

"Students," a biology teacher asserted, "should know the definition of a calorie and be able to solve a calorie problem. I'll come back to calories again and again during the year and want them to have a foundation." And a colleague observed: "They need to assess a trait in a person, to practice with frequencies in math [calculating percentages], and to deduce phenotype and genotype—if you have *xxx* phenotype, what is your genotype?"

Thus the teachers' discussions of their fields and their coursework in many ways mirror our findings from the literature review study, in which we saw that when considerations move from the discipline itself to the pedagogy of that discipline, the focus shifts from ways of thinking about knowledge to particular content. Across disciplines, when the teachers talked about their coursework, there was an implicit notion that the buildup of content knowledge would lead to generalized understandings and ways of thinking. In addition, even when teachers spoke broadly about themes and thinking, their language was limited. And in most of the interviews, teachers discussed content more than ways of thinking.

Disciplinary Differences in Talk about Thinking

When they did talk about thinking, teachers in the various disciplines had different perspectives. Asked about the kinds of reasoning and interpreting they expected from their students, and about the kinds of justification or evidence their students should offer when writing, the teachers spoke from the vantage point of their own field. While their comments may provide us with a starting point for considering discipline-specific approaches to argument and evidence, the teachers' language tended to be inconsistent and unelaborated. Let us first look at the disciplinary differences.

The history teachers focused on recognizing contradictions, looking at circumstances, taking sides on controversial issues, providing supporting evidence, and distinguishing true from false positions. One college history teacher, for instance, said, "I want students to recognize contradictions and make an attempt at figuring out relationships between contradictory developments—also to have a critical bent, to be able to criticize what they read and what they hear." When they give evidence or justification, "I warn them about being abstract. 'Society caused it to happen': I want them to say who. The logic of history is straightforward, simply a matter of taking into account when things happened. Look at the circumstances and the context."

A teacher of United States history said that she wants students to be able "to tell me in writing what they've read and to recognize the main points as distinct from the subpoints, to take a side on a controversial issue and find supporting evidence, to distinguish between good thinking and fallacious positions." When asked about the kinds of evidence her students should use, she replied, "I expect them to raise issues and flesh them out with details—to give at least three different types of reasons relevant to the issues and to give details to support those reasons."

The biology teachers used somewhat different language. For example, a high school biology teacher noted that he would like his students "to make connections, to reason logically, to think critically, to take facts and apply them to problem-solving situations, or to develop a research experience in the lab." About justification or evidence, he said, "Students should use facts and data—reliable data they've found. They should shy away from opinion without establishing the validity of the source, be able to hypothesize and present findings." The approach was echoed by a colleague at the college level:

> I expect students to be able to make probable conclusions from certain kinds of questions that are raised. I really mean predict outcomes, which in essence would be hypotheses. Conclusion will prove or disprove the hypotheses. Reasoning is their thinking in terms of taking a problem, thinking about the possible outcomes, using logical reasoning, and then being able to synthesize to prove or disprove the case. I want them to come up with evidence that's reliable and repeatable—tangible evidence. It would come from the experimental setup and go into a chart or graph.

For the biology teachers, major goals for students included reasoning logically, using facts and data, avoiding opinions, establishing validity, hypothesizing, arriving at probable conclusions, and proving or disproving hypotheses.

The language the English teachers invoked differed, in turn, from that of the teachers in the other two disciplines. For example, one college English teacher wanted students "to have a sense of major themes and motifs in literature, so that they're touching with the wholeness of the work. It's primary for them to have an idea of what the author evokes. But of equal importance are their own responses to their reading, to involve themselves in the work and re-create it in their own minds—not just to be critical analysts." For justification and evidence, "they can start out with points from the novel. Some students are clearer than others, used to supporting their ideas, to knowing the incident and seeing how it relates, to going back to the text."

A high school English teacher offered her view:

> I expect students to interpret. What would you think about the choices the characters made? Would you have done the same things? And to analyze. With honor kids I have them analyze the literary style, and with the others, I have them [compare and contrast] the values of literature with their personal values. Justification has been a dilemma for me, training the kids to do this. For practice we deal with "why" questions—but keep coming back to the text.

At both the secondary and the postsecondary level, the English teachers talked about instilling a sense of major themes and motifs and motivating students to involve themselves in the literature, analyze techniques, use the text to support ideas, and ask probing questions.

Thus, while the concern for facts cut across fields (e.g., a history teacher talks of "details," a biology teacher stresses "facts and data," and an English teacher speaks of "points from the novel"), the teachers in each discipline had a somewhat different vocabulary to describe at least some kinds of reasoning they expected their students to do and evidence or justification they wanted their students to learn to use. Although the language they invoked seems to capture real variations in the ways of thinking typically required in the three disciplines, we can also see that their comments were general, falling short of the kinds of explication that would convey disciplinary argumentation and structures to people who didn't already know them. For instance, having a critical bent, or taking a side on a controversial issue and finding supporting evidence, is surely an important feature of certain kinds of historical reasoning, yet how to be critical and how to judge which ideas are appropriately supportive remain unstated.

Teachers' Responses to Student Writing

The pattern of discipline-specific differences in the language used, coupled with the inexplicitness of that vocabulary, can also be noted in the teachers' discussion of their students' A and D papers. In general, when teachers examined thinking as evidenced in writing, their concerns differed across disciplines, and the terms they used to discuss student thinking also varied. Yet even in their comments in response to student writing, the teachers focused largely on content. Because examples of content concerns appear in earlier sections of this essay, I have selected excerpts of comments on ways of thinking for this discussion. Even so, the teachers' predominant concern for content becomes evident in their discussion of student work—just as it is in their remarks about their teaching.

For example, the college history teacher who wanted students to observe contradictions commented about an A paper:

> The student begins to talk about the subject. He discusses the notion of how Paine had problems with the monarchy. He demonstrates knowledge of what Paine said. And he does the same thing with Mrs. Stowe. He talks about her ideas and morality. At the end he ties the two together. He took two documents and sees similarities and used them to answer the questions asked of him.

In response to the D paper, the same teacher noted that "it's stilted. The stumbling syntax reflects no understanding of what the question entails. The student's not clear about what Paine had to say." There are "no comparisons between Paine and Stowe. The work is semiliterate."

When discussing the kinds of reasoning he expected from his students, the teacher had said that he wants his students to figure out relationships; his comments in response to his students' writing reflects this concern. He points out here that his A student made connections between two documents while his D student failed to do so. The teacher also observes the type of information both students included in their papers. For example, his comments about the A paper stress specific content (e.g., "talk about the subject," "how Paine had problems with the monarchy," "knowledge of what Paine said," Stowe's "ideas and morality"), with much briefer attention to ways of thinking about the ideas (e.g., "ties the two together," "sees similarities"). His characterization of the D paper reflects a concern with presentation as much as content (e.g., "stilted," "stumbling syntax," "semiliterate"), but his reaction centers more on the way the student's clumsy style reflects an inability to understand the content (e.g., "not clear about what Paine had to say") and to make connections than on the student's lack of knowledge of mechanics and surface features.

The college English teacher cited in the previous section noted in discussing an A paper: "This student saw the novel differently from the way it was seen in class. She felt it was an allegory of how the mind works. She used good examples from the book. Validity is in the examples. She's got the basic ideas of criticism: you present an idea and give evidence. She wrote well too." In response to a D paper, he observed that the student had given "all generalities and no examples." The paper "fills up space without saying anything." This teacher had said he wanted his students to react to the work they read, to have an idea of what the text evokes, and to support their ideas with reference to the text. His remarks about his students' papers indicate he values such skills. He comments on "seeing," or interpretation, in the A paper and notes the absence of student response to the text in the D paper. Unlike the history teacher, he does not identify particular information in the papers but rather the ways in which students' ideas are presented. Instead of a concern for content and connections, his focus is on students' ability to formulate a response and to defend it.

Finally, the college biology teacher quoted above described an A paper this way: "The student paid attention to instructions. She eased her problems by following instructions, by following the format (lab report write-up). She was able to go back and forth in her notes and pull out the information and put it in a certain category." The writer of the D paper, he said, "didn't follow instructions." The work was a "bunch of rewritten notes, haphazard information with no conclusion, the result of not putting enough time into it—it was not developed or polished."

Apparently this teacher views his writing instructions as a recipe— as a guide for what students are to do with their notes (e.g., "follow the format") rather than for thinking about what the notes mean. Thus his concern for presentation is quite different from that of the other two teachers. Instead of encouraging students to formulate their own understanding and structure their explanations, he sees good writing (in this instance) as the ability to select relevant information from lab notes and place it in the proper category, according to his instructions. The A student has sorted the information into such categories and reached a conclusion, while the D paper has failed on both counts.

Although this teacher had said he wants his students to think critically, to make connections, and to reason logically, he seems to be looking for replication rather than reasoning in his students' writing.

Thus we see that while the teachers focused much more on the content than on student reasoning about the content, when they did speak about students' understanding (in response to the course papers), their concerns differed from discipline to discipline and the language they used to express their concerns also varied. Most often, however, the language was general. For instance, the biology teacher's comments about the D paper make clear his negative evaluation but provide few clues on how the student might proceed. Surely some "stilted" papers with "stumbling syntax" receive grades higher than D; a focus on both form and content needs to be connected to their role in representing and communicating the student's understanding. While comments about relationships between content and form might have been useful, they were not forthcoming. Although the history teacher's remark about the need for a comparison between Paine and Stowe was an attempt to provide guidance, a student who does not know the kind of comparison to make or how to structure it would be at a loss in trying to improve the paper.

Failure of Articulation

The results of this study parallel other research suggesting that the closer teachers' comments get to their actual work in classrooms, the greater the emphasis on specific content at the expense of the rules of argument and evidence that represent the ways of thinking unique to each discipline. These findings go further, however, to suggest that this problem may stem in part from a general failure by both scholars and practitioners to clarify and articulate those rules of argument and evidence in ways that enable teachers to think about what they are teaching and to guide their evaluation of student work. (A separate question, not addressed in this study, is whether specifying such rules for students would help them learn to use them or would—like the rules of grammar—simply add another layer of content to be mastered.)

The failure to articulate the ways of thinking or the rules of argument and evidence specific to each discipline is apparent in the reviews of the related literatures. At first glance, biology, with its concern for the nature of the scientific method, would seem to have a long tradition of scholarly explication of appropriate methodologies. Yet closer examination showed that explications of the scientific method suffered from two shortcomings that have been pointed out by scholars in the field:

(1) the methods codified do not reflect the processes of problem definition and problem resolution characteristic of skilled scientists but instead present an idealized representation of the results of scientific inquiry, and (2) the focus on scientific method has included little concern for practical heuristics, such as considering multiple ways to solve problems that scientists actually confront. A third problem emerged from examining the literature on biology instruction: we found that even when there was an emphasis on inquiry-based or related methods, little or no attention was paid to expressing the results in "scientific prose"—little attention, that is, to teaching students how to muster arguments and evidence in a way appropriate to their discipline.

When we turned from the literature reviews to interviews with high school and college teachers, their responses reflected the emphases within the discipline as a whole. Biology teachers had a larger vocabulary of discipline-specific forms of argument and evidence than did their colleagues in American history or American literature. In the latter disciplines, teachers relied on a more generic vocabulary (structuring their discussions around such terms as *interpretation, causality,* or *analysis*). In all three disciplines, however, the overwhelming characteristic of teachers' discussions of such issues was their inexplicitness.

In fact, among all the teachers we studied, notions of discipline-specific ways of thinking were mostly implicit. They had a more or less well established vocabulary but not a systematic way to think about it, and so their talk about ways of thinking came and went—unnoticed and unmarked. Perhaps because of this, biology teachers, for example, felt no contradiction in relying heavily on objective tests to measure student achievement, though at a more idealized level they stressed "scientific methods" and "ways of thinking" as goals for their courses. Conversely, when they were confronted with student writing to assess, they were more comfortable with issues of content and scope of knowledge than with evaluation and display of evidence as part of scientific discourse.

In the light of such results, previous findings about students' inability to engage in critical thinking in a variety of academic subjects come as no surprise. Students are unlikely to be learning how to gather evidence and develop effective arguments when their teachers (and the field in general) have not articulated such concerns clearly to themselves. Scholarly emphases on the tentativeness of knowledge and the need for inquiry have not generally become part of the teachers' consciousness—or are either so vague or so tacit that teachers cannot talk comfortably about them. And so, for students, instructional experiences on ways to think about what they are learning are likely to be either unfocused or sporadic, with critical approaches inconsistently flagged and codified.

What does all this mean for college teachers? It suggests that we need to look beyond generic terminology about thinking and reasoning in discipline-based writing, to move beyond general recipes for more thoughtful work, toward finding more specific vocabulary to use in discussion with students about how to create a comparison of historical eras, or to prepare a feminist critique in literature, or to write a summary of the critical features of Mendel's experiments. While the forms of comparisons, critiques, or summaries can be discussed in general ways, if *only* the general characteristics are discussed, then the use of those forms in *particular* disciplinary contexts will be lost. This in no way suggests the need for labels to be memorized and treated as content, but instead calls for communicative "signs" that can be used to talk about the shapes of knowledge within a discipline. Such language can permit teachers and students to think through and discuss options and possibilities and can help them become better able to identify (and also value) alternative moves toward successful comprehension and composition. Such language becomes embedded within the social network of learning, providing overt conversational tools to help students think about planning, organizing, and presenting their ideas in discipline-specific ways.

NOTE

[1]This chapter is based on a collaborative effort between myself, Arthur Applebee, Elise Earthman, and Steve Athanases. Earthman was responsible for doing the literature review and writing the chapter on biology, Athanases was similarly responsible for the review and chapter on history, and the two shared responsibilities for English. These chapters appear as parts of the complete project report in *Speaking of Knowing: Conceptions of Learning in Academic Subjects*, Judith Langer and Arthur Applebee, Final Report to the U.S. Department of Education, Office of Educational Research and Improvement, Grant No. G008610967, ERIC ED 297 336.

Context-Specific Ways of Knowing and the Evaluation of Writing

Lee Odell

The author is professor of composition theory and research at Rensselaer Polytechnic Institute.

I work with Rensselaer's Writing Intensive Program and have conducted writing-across-the-curriculum workshops at a number of colleges and universities. Currently I am directing a writing-across-the-curriculum program for teachers in the Fort Worth, Texas, public schools. My primary interests are in identifying the thinking processes writers engage in as they gather and reflect on information and in determining ways those processes vary from one academic context to another.

A colleague at my school recently showed me a paper—the collaborative effort of a team of three undergraduate engineering students—in which the writers were recommending a particular course of action to the management of a hypothetical chemical plant. At one point in the students' text, there appeared an approving comment, "well-written," and at the end of the text, another: "very nicely done—your report is simple, clear, and authoritative." Although these comments were made by a composition specialist who was trying to help these students with their report writing, the engineering professor told me he agreed with the writing teacher's assessment. And he gave the report a grade of C. This professor's overall judgment was that the group "writes well . . . but they write well about nothing."

This comment, of course, reflects the practical stylist, or "formalist" (Fulkerson 344), view that judgments about writing can be divorced from judgments about content. From this perspective, *writing well* means observing conventions of diction, usage, syntax, and organization, conventions that are presumed to apply to all good writing and that can be identified even if one knows little about the subject matter

86

being discussed. Although this view is widely criticized in composition theory and research, it appears to be alive and well in many college and university classrooms. In conducting writing-across-the-curriculum workshops, I routinely find that many participants— English faculty members often chief among them—accept the formalist distinction between *writing* and *content*. These participants are also likely to assume that evaluating writing is the primary responsibility of English instructors and the assessment of content is the exclusive province of faculty members in other disciplines.

Such a distinction creates a couple of problems. For one thing, it relegates English faculty members to the role of proofreader rather than to that of a colleague who might have substantive insights into the work of a discipline other than writing or literary study. Even more important, this distinction seems almost certain to diminish faculty commitment to writing-across-the-curriculum programs. Working with students' writing takes time and energy, especially when one tries to evaluate that writing. Unless the effort pays off in some substantive way, unless both the assigning and the evaluation of writing relate clearly to students' understanding of their subject matter, colleagues cannot be expected to persist in these activities. Eventually, work with writing will simply become too much effort and will be abandoned by all but English teachers and those quixotic souls in other departments who see themselves as defending the last outposts of linguistic civilization.

If we are to solve these problems, we must show colleagues that the evaluation of writing can help both students and teachers better understand the ways of knowing that are important in a particular academic context. In making this recommendation, I am also making several assumptions, some of which are less widely accepted than others. The first, which is taken virtually as a given in current work in composition, is that writing is not only a means of articulating existing ideas (feelings, perceptions, memories) but also a process of formulating those ideas, constructing meaning, discovering what one wishes to say.

A second assumption is that the process of discovery or meaning construction is guided, in part, by ways of knowing—thinking strategies that can be made conscious and can influence a writer's (or reader's) reflection on the subject matter at hand. Although this assumption has a long tradition in the history of rhetoric, it is not universally represented in current work on writing across the curriculum. In some instances, this assumption is specifically repudiated. For example, James Britton and his colleagues argue that conscious awareness of one's discovery processes is rarely possible and usually undesirable, because "such awareness is quite likely to have an inhibiting effect on getting on with the job [of writing]" (Britton, Burgess, Martin, McLeod, and Rosen 40; see also Emig, "Uses"; Elbow, *Writing*). In other instances, scholars (e.g., Summerfield; Belanoff; Thaiss) do not specifically argue against this assumption, but their discussions of writing across the curriculum are premised on Britton's view that the greatest insights arise from the spontaneous, unplanned process of "shaping at the point of utterance" (Britton, "Shaping"). Consequently, these scholars advocate the use of informal, exploratory writing (e.g., journals, learning logs) and typically have little to say about the meaning-making strategies represented in the writing.

Those who believe that the meaning-making process is shaped by deliberate strategies for gathering and reflecting on information (concepts, feelings, memories, numbers, events) do not argue that the process is entirely conscious or linear. Nor do they deny that the act of writing can encourage intuition and lead writers in unexpected directions. But some of these scholars contend that experienced writers have acquired ways of knowing—"patterns of reasoning" (Toulmin, Rieke, and Janik 281), "patterns of thought" (Miller and Selzer 316), or "analytic strategies" (Odell, "Beyond the Text" 261–63)—that help them formulate their ideas. Other scholars, such as Ann E. Berthoff, recommend asking students to formulate their own meaning-making strategies. And still others, such as Verner Jensen or Gary Lindberg, imply an interest in conscious meaning-making strategies when they structure journal writings so as to engage students in specific ways of knowing. Lindberg, for example, invites students to respond to literary texts by noting times when they are "surprised or puzzled" or when they "recognize a pattern—the images start to overlap, gestures or phrases recur, some details seem associated with each other" (120).

Several scholars who are interested in conscious meaning-making strategies are beginning to claim that many of these ways of knowing may be context-specific. During the 1960s and 1970s, a number of scholars believed that people's ways of knowing could be codified and represented in heuristic models that applied in all situations (see Corbett; Young, Becker, and Pike; Kneupper). At an abstract level, it does seem possible to identify widely applicable thinking processes. For example, if one accepts Leon Festinger's claims about the importance of cognitive dissonance in the thinking process, it may be that one basic cognitive process is to recognize when one is "surprised or puzzled" and, as Lindberg suggests, to formulate that surprise or puzzlement as a question or problem.

Certainly, most disciplinary communities require that their members be able to ask meaningful questions. But the nature of those questions may vary so widely that a question that is important in dealing with, say, a particular topic in philosophy may be less important in dealing with topics in chemical engineering or even with other subjects in philosophy. Consequently, some scholars (see, for example, Bazerman, *Shaping*; Herrington; Odell, "Defining") are beginning to argue that different academic disciplines, even different courses within a discipline, may make quite different conceptual demands on writers.

A final assumption on which this essay is based is that some of a writer's ways of knowing are likely to be reflected in a written text. Those who make this assumption (see Bazerman, *Shaping* 18; Miller and Selzer 314–15; Odell, "Written Products" 53) would have to acknowledge that analysis of a written text cannot reveal everything that went on during the process of composing, since it includes reading, formal and informal talk, revisions, and all the complexities that attend the process of "shaping at the point of utterance" (see Odell, "Written Products," for one description of this shaping). Although it is not possible to gain access to this activity simply by looking at a completed text, it is possible to identify points at which the text reflects careful (or careless) reasoning, astute (or superficial) observation. More specifically, it is possible to infer some of the questions a writer is trying to answer and to identify some of the topics or issues the writer has considered in exploring the subject at hand.

All these assumptions, and especially the last one, have clear implications not only for the evaluation of writing but also for the effort to introduce students to the ways of knowing that are important for a given rhetorical and/or academic context. If we judge a text—a journal entry, an early draft, or a final draft—to be well or poorly thought out, we can base our judgment, at least in part, on the extent to which that text reflects the use of patterns of thought that are appropriate for the context at hand. If we devote class time to helping students understand these meaning-making strategies, they should be able to function more effectively as members of a particular intellectual community.

To provide this help, we will need to accept several obligations. For one thing, teachers of composition may need to learn how to do the rhetorical analysis (described by Bazerman in this volume; see also Miller and Selzer) that identifies the thinking strategies that seem most important for a particular type of assignment. Further, composition teachers will need to give up facile generalizations about what constitutes "good" writing and listen carefully to what their colleagues in other disciplines have to say about student work. And finally, as we try to understand the ways of knowing that are important in a given context, we have to maintain a balanced perspective, not only recognizing the benefits of doing this sort of work but also understanding why we and our colleagues may find it extremely difficult.

Analyzing Students' Texts

To understand the ways of knowing that are important for creating meaning in a particular course, we can look closely at contrastive responses to a single assignment—an A paper and a C paper, for example. In this activity, even highly technical subjects become relatively accessible to nonspecialists. What follows, for instance, are excerpts from two papers written for a junior-level course in epidemiology. Students had been asked to summarize a number of journal articles on a topic of their choice and to conclude their work with a comment on those articles. As best I have been able to determine, the instructor did not elaborate on what he meant by the term *comment*; he simply indicated that the comment should make up the final section of students' papers.

Here is an excerpt from the A comment:

> In each of the studies considered above, an effort was made to elucidate some of the specific epidemiological factors involved in the transmission of hydatid disease. In each case, field research was carried out in the affected communities: many people were interviewed and given tests for echinococcosis; dogs and sheep in these areas were often tested as well. In the California Basque study, the senior author actually worked as a shepherd for one Basque rancher. Exhaustive surveys of the available literature were also performed as well. In the end each study linked infected sheep to infected dogs; infective dogs were linked to human infection via permissive husbandry practices. Nevertheless, I feel that a number of important issues were overlooked by these studies; I have expanded upon these below.
>
> It would be particularly useful to learn exactly how prevalent *E. granulosis* eggs are in the grazing areas and ranching communities. Along a similar line of investigation, it might be equally valuable to determine the ways in which eggs come to be ingested by man; i.e., how is infection linked to hygiene? Are *E. granulosis* eggs commonly found in the ranchers' food? Is the local water supply contaminated with eggs? Certainly an investigation of this type would also want to learn more about the climatic conditions

under which *E. granulosis* eggs are viable and available for transmission. These issues were only tangentially addressed, at best, in any of the studies considered. To the extent that they were not considered or seriously acknowledged as important issues, I feel that these studies are, in one sense, deficient.

Reflected in this comment are several ways of knowing. The student begins by noting similarities in research methodology. That is, she points out that each of the studies did the following: tried to "elucidate . . . specific epidemiological factors"; carried out field research; presented "exhaustive surveys" of the literature; and noted linkages between the infections that appeared in dogs, sheep, and humans.

At the end of the first paragraph, the student displays another strategy, that of identifying "important issues [that] were overlooked by these studies." The next paragraph shows several instances of this strategy, by stating or implying questions that have been "only tangentially addressed at best." For example, she indicates that researchers still need to know "how prevalent *E. granulosis* eggs are in the grazing areas."

For purposes of contrast, here is an excerpt from the beginning of the comment section of a paper that received a grade of C:

> In all parasitic diseases which involve a parasite having a complex life cycle, it is interesting to find out how the various stages of the parasite seek out their specific intermediate hosts. Host finding is never a guaranteed process in nature, and it is amazing to realize how many larvae never make it to the adult stage. In adapting to this stress of survival, most parasites expend a large amount of energy in reproduction. In endemic areas this is unfortunate for man and in order to prevent a high incidence of disease, man must learn to control the parasite population.

Three phrases in this passage seem especially significant: "it is interesting," "it is amazing," and "this is unfortunate." The first two are followed by what appear to be factual references to the materials the student has read. The third phrase makes a value judgment about a preceding factual reference. In all three statements, however, the student's principal analytic strategy seems to be to note ways in which factual materials relate to his knowledge or to his values. At no point does the student's writing suggest that he has used either of the strategies the first student used.

This analysis raises questions about both the process of composing and the process of evaluating. When the writer of the first essay was engaged in the composing process, did she consciously try to determine whether there were any common elements in the research methodology reported in these articles, or whether the researchers had overlooked important questions? Or did she just start writing and only in retrospect—if at all—realize that she had intuitively used the ways of knowing identified above? What about the second student? Might he have used some of these ways of knowing and discounted them because they seemed uninteresting or inappropriate for the assignment? And what of the instructor's bases for giving one paper an A and the other a C? Was the instructor aware that the two comments reflected the use of different thinking strategies? If so, did those differences influence his grading?

No text, of course, can ever tell us all we want to know about the composing process, nor can a final grade tell us exactly why the reader thought a piece of writing was successful or unsuccessful. Nonetheless, a text—especially when viewed in relation to comparable texts—can tell us a good deal. Even though we do not know everything that went on while these students were composing their texts, a careful analysis indicates that the first student did, at some point in the process, reflect on her subject matter in ways that differ from what we see in the second student's paper.

On the face of it, the different ways of knowing seem worth our attention. For one thing, they both have heuristic and epistemic significance: each can be a useful strategy for reflecting on one's subject matter. Moreover, we can identify a research tradition that might lead a reader to value one set of activities over another. That is, both in the humanities and in science and technology there is a scholarly tradition that values efforts to identify common themes in research and to identify shortcomings. Consequently, we have a reasonable basis for talking with the instructor who assigned these papers. We can go to this colleague and say: Here's what I see these students doing. Does my analysis make sense? Are there other thinking strategies that should have been reflected in these papers? Did differences in ways of knowing influence your assessments of the student's work? Are there other factors that underlay your decisions about the quality of these two pieces of writing?

Understanding Colleagues' Perspectives

As noted, the student samples cited above are comparatively accessible even to those who are not trained in the field of epidemiology. There was not a great deal of specialized vocabulary, and it was easy to find a scholarly tradition in which these pieces might be located. In other cases, however, we may find ourselves on less familiar ground. Consider the following excerpts from student reports for a mechanical engineering process design course. The assignment was to design a mechanical device that could be used to develop the "technological awareness" of fifth-, sixth-, and seventh-grade students. The engineering students were to work in groups of three or four to prepare the necessary design and do the technical calculations as well as to write an introduction to the group report. Individual students would then write their own versions of one section of the report, the design description.

Students in one group decided to design a "mock wind tunnel" that would allow schoolchildren to test the aerodynamic qualities of model cars and, thereby, get some idea of the engineering work that went into familiar objects such as automobiles. In his design description, one student wrote this initial paragraph:

> The mock wind tunnel is designed to demonstrate, in a crude manner, the behavior of air flow over a child-size model of an automobile that the child assembles himself. By attaching tufts of yarn to their models and then placing their design in the wind tunnel, the students will be able to witness either smooth or turbulent air flow around their models.

Another student from the same group began his design description this way:

> The mock wind tunnel consists of a tube 46″ long, 3¼″ ID [interior diameter], 3½″ OD [outer diameter]. The tube is supported at each end and in the middle. There is a fan and a 1″ deep diffuser mounted at one end, and a ¼″ by 3″ by 9″ platform placed at the opposite end with the end of the tube and the end of the platform flush. The diffuser is a ¼″ × ¼″ grid with 3¼″ D [diameter] and a web thickness of ¹⁄₂₀″.

The writer of the first passage seems to be considering at least two questions: What is the purpose of the wind tunnel? ("the mock wind tunnel is designed to demonstrate") and How does the wind tunnel function? ("By attaching tufts of yarn"). The second student seems to concentrate solely on one question: What are the physical properties of the wind tunnel?

Clearly the two paragraphs are different, and the differences noted thus far are characteristic of each text. Throughout his design description, the first student stresses the big picture, paying special attention to the social significance of the object the group designed. The second student consistently focuses on the properties and functions of this particular object. The question is, what is the significance of these differences? Is one approach preferable to the other?

Answers to these questions become apparent only as we understand the stated goals for the assignment and the ways a reader is likely to interpret the particular section in which these paragraphs appeared. The point of this assignment, indeed of the entire course, was to introduce senior mechanical engineering students to the type of work they were likely to encounter in their first job. According to the professor, beginning mechanical engineers are often given a relatively ill-defined problem (e.g., design a device that will . . .). They will have to design the device, do the technical calculations necessary to ensure that it will work, and then write up the project in a way that will persuade a supervisor that the device is technically feasible. In reading the design description section of the write-up, from which the two paragraphs were taken, the instructor said he asked himself the questions he felt the student's supervisor would surely ask about this section: Do I think the device would work and could I make it?

In this context, the instructor said he much preferred the second student's work. The detailed attention to the physical properties of the wind tunnel (for example, the specific information about the inner and outer diameter of the tube used for the tunnel) let him decide whether the student had, in fact, designed a product that could be built and was likely to work as the student hoped it would.

This is not to say that the ways of knowing reflected in the first essay are unimportant. The instructor was sympathetic to the effort to see the "big picture." Indeed, the instructor thought that the group report reflected a "nice vision," that the students had "looked beyond the narrow confines of what their problem could be" and tried to show how their product would improve the quality of life for the people who might use it. Moreover, he found it useful to have an overview of the project, a basic sense of what the device looked like and how it functioned. However, he said that he usually looked for the "vision" in the introduction to the project and for an overview of the device in the flysheet, a one- to two-page section that contained a drawing of the device and listed its principal features. He said that he did not particularly mind if elements of "vision" or "overview" found their way into the design description. But he was adamant that this section should contain the specific technical information that would let him assess the feasibility of the students' work: "What we're looking for here is . . . if we were to build this design, is there enough information here to convince us that it would work? . . . Then, secondly, is there enough information to build it?"

As we look closely at texts from other disciplines and listen carefully to colleagues, even highly specialized discussions—whether from chemical engineering, philosophy, or social science—begin to make sense. Consider, for example, the following passage from a chemical engineering report:

> The single pass conversion was chosen to be 40% since the volume of the reactor is dependent on the conversion (we had to choose a conversion that would not make the reactor too large).

Granted, this passage is presented out of context. But for someone who is not a chemical engineer, the context is not very enlightening, since it is filled with references to such things as a "single-stage partial reboiler," "catalysis," and something called a "Panevis horizontal belt filter." When English faculty members are confronted with such a passage (or a highly technical passage from any discipline other than their own), the formalist perspective may begin to seem attractive. If catalysis is beyond our ken, syntax is not.

Indeed, some aspects of this passage (the phrase "single pass conversion," for instance) may always remain a mystery to a nonengineer. However, the professor's comments about this passage begin to make it intelligible, even to a colleague who has no background in chemical engineering. In discussing this passage with me, the professor observed:

> What they're saying is they made a decision here. In other words, they had some idea of what "too large" was, or "too small" . . . and I just wanted to know what went into that decision. In other words, what did they look at? They would have put it somewhere. What did they mean by "too large"? Too large doesn't mean anything. It's a general term.

This observation, combined with a number of others from our interview, makes it clear that in designing chemical processes, students would have to make decisions—about the size and type of equipment used, for example, or about the type of calculations to be used in testing their process. In these instances, the professor expected a clear statement as to what the decision was and a "justification," a technical rationale for that decision.

If explaining decisions and providing technical rationale are two of the important ways of knowing for these reports, it is possible to see part of what is good and what is bad about the passage concerning "the single pass conversion." The students explained why they had to make a choice about the single pass conversion: "the volume of the reactor is dependent on the conversion." However, they did not explain their decision about the size of the reactor. Exactly how large did they decide the reactor should be? And what was the technical rationale (i.e., what were the calculations) underlying that decision?

It would be a mistake, of course, to expect students to go into great detail about each decision they mention in their reports. Some decisions, the chemical engineering professor noted, are not justified by detailed calculations: "Some decisions we make, we feel. . . . You can look at [some designs] for a size and you say 'I feel the size . . . doesn't look right.' You just visualize it and it doesn't seem right, intuitively." Furthermore, this professor pointed out that writers would not include routine calculations that served only to demonstrate that the writer understood procedures any competent engineer would be expected to know.

In other words, both students and evaluators must exercise judgment concerning the ways of knowing described above—or, indeed, concerning the use of any meaning-making strategies. They are not algorithms that will inevitably lead students to a single correct answer. Nor are they textual features that evaluators can simply count, giving higher grades to papers that contain more instances of a particular way of knowing. Nonetheless, an awareness of these ways of knowing can give students a better sense of how they might improve their discussion of a given topic. Such an awareness can also give evaluators a better sense of how to explain to students what they are currently doing well and what they should begin doing or do differently on subsequent assignments.

Maintaining Perspective

Efforts to analyze students' ways of knowing and to learn from our colleagues have the potential to make the evaluation of writing more interesting to instructors and more useful to students. But these efforts are not likely to make the evaluation process any simpler. Consequently, we have to maintain our perspective, balancing our interest in this work with a recognition of the difficulties and objections we are likely to encounter when we work with colleagues.

One difficulty is that, as Judith A. Langer has demonstrated in this volume, teachers at all levels may be more comfortable in discussing the content of their disciplines than in identifying the methods of thinking or analytic strategies needed to generate or reflect on that content. Through our experience as students, teachers, and scholars, we have somehow acquired—and continue to acquire or revise—these strategies, perhaps through someone's explaining them to us, perhaps through trial and error, or perhaps through observation of more experienced or more skillful colleagues. But some of these ways of knowing may become so internalized that it is difficult to bring them to conscious awareness in order to help someone else understand them.

Even if instructors can articulate context-specific ways of knowing that might be useful to students, they may still raise objections to doing so. For example, they may feel a conflict between developing students' ways of knowing and explaining "content" that will be reflected in questions on a standardized test or a single examination given to multiple sections of the same course. In such cases, we and our colleagues will have to work together either to change assessment procedures or to identify ways in which at least some of the items on the test invite ways of knowing that we value. Or colleagues may feel that students should come to them better prepared, so that the instructor can concentrate on the subject matter of his or her course. In the latter case, we may have to work, initially at least, with faculty members who are interested in doing something about students' lack of preparation rather than simply asserting that the problem should not exist. We can collaborate with these colleagues to develop instructional practices that will demonstrate the benefits of helping students gain a clearer understanding of the ways of knowing that are important in a given context.

One final obstacle to the sort of work proposed in this essay may arise when some instructors—in particular, colleagues who still accept a formalist perspective—have to rethink their assumptions about what constitutes good writing. But such colleagues may not be the only source of difficulty. Consider, for a moment, the two design descriptions presented in the preceding section. When I discuss these passages with colleagues in English, most of them prefer the initial passage because it is immediately accessible to a nonspecialist and gives a clear sense of the nature and purpose of the design. Yet my colleague in mechanical engineering had strong reasons for valuing the second, highly detailed passage. We ignore such reasons at our peril, even though acknowledging them may require us to put aside our own sense of what the passage should be like.

These difficulties notwithstanding, it seems important to establish evaluation as part of a larger epistemic process. If teachers in any discipline want students to engage in meaning making, the students will surely benefit from evaluations that help them understand that process more fully. If composition specialists are interested in promoting the process of meaning making, we will need to understand how that process manifests itself and how it is valued in contexts that differ from those in which we routinely work.

And finally, if the writing-across-the-curriculum movement is to flourish, we must persuade both colleagues and students that judgments about the quality of writing cannot be separated from judgments about the quality of meaning making reflected in that writing. As long as student writing is evaluated from a formalist perspective, there is no reason to expect students or faculty members in history, say, or mechanical engineering to take seriously our claim that writing is part of the meaning-making process. Nor should we expect students to be particularly patient with readers who are unable to look past the surface features of their language and somehow apprehend the "content" that is thought to exist separately from that language. If we persist in separating ways of writing from ways of knowing, we shouldn't be surprised if students persist in writing well about nothing.

PART III

Teachers' Voices:
Reflections on Practice

Introduction

In this section we hear the voices of teachers who are talking to one another—and to you—about why they use writing in their classes. We hear as well the voice of a teacher who has shaped a faculty development program in writing in the disciplines, one whose assumptions and practices are generally characteristic of the faculty development that accompanies and helps constitute writing in the disciplines.

The talk is enthusiastic and positive, as it tends to be when college and university teachers are asked to talk about their teaching. There are, as Art Young and Toby Fulwiler have demonstrated, "enemies of writing across the curriculum," but the presence of these foes is not felt here.

In the interchange among the four faculty members, we hear differences—different reasons for using writing and different approaches. Beyond these, we see something of the complex mix of factors that explain these differences. As Michael Abbott, one of the interchange faculty, writes, "It's pretty clear ⟨to me⟩ that our responses reflect strongly the nature of our disciplines; probably less strongly the nature of our institutions; certainly very strongly . . . the nature of our clientele; and for damned sure (but how can we quantify this?) our separate personalities." While all four participants in the interchange underscore the influence of personality (and read here, too, personal history and personal systems of value) on the choices we make as teachers, we rarely talk about this influence, at least not in our scholarship. These instructors do talk about the influence of who they are on what they do, as they reflect on why they use writing in their teaching, why they use it in the ways they do, where they find common ground, and where they find difference. As they do so, they may create a space in which we can reflect, too, on the pedagogical choices we make.

In essence, the interchange participants model the kinds of reflection, and the resultant revision of teaching practice, that can occur in a college-wide writing-in-the-disciplines program. Jacqueline Jones Royster demonstrates what can be accomplished in a college-wide program as she traces for us the development of such a program at

Spelman College. From the perspective of a program director, she describes the excitement and challenge of the enterprise, as it follows what David R. Russell in this volume sees to be a characteristic progress: from a program that aims to improve students' writing to one that strives instead to understand the learning and teaching that take place in the institution. "I have found," Royster writes in her essay in this volume, "that somewhere between the points of terror and exaltation in looking microscopically and telescopically at our work, faculty members make sense of the experience of teaching" (125).

The Spelman faculty development program has encouraged deep reflection on the place of language in the teaching and learning that are the college curriculum. This reflection can lead to classroom-based research along the lines of the three studies described in section 4, "Studies in the Classroom." Just as important, it can motivate discussion among individual teachers, and across disciplines, of the kind we have called for in the interchange essay. Here we see not systematic research but clear, individual perspectives on the relations among writing, learning, and teaching. As Royster notes after reading the interchange, "These colleagues have found their own way to see writing, to contextualize it within their disciplines and their lives, and to use it in their teaching. They have also found their own connection to others who are trying to do the same thing. In my estimation, then, we have acted responsibly as professionals in this arena in terms of both theory and practice. I believe that our students benefit tremendously from our efforts."

Interchange: A Conversation among the Disciplines

Michael M. Abbott, Pearl W. Bartelt, Stephen M. Fishman, and Charlotte Honda

Michael M. Abbott is professor of chemical engineering at Rensselaer Polytechnic Institute.

For fifteen years I have worked with Rensselaer seniors in our capstone design course. In this course we do our best to simulate professional reality, including effective communication of technical results. Hence my concern that my students write well. My job is perhaps made easier by a personal reverence for the written word: I am a poetry addict.

Pearl W. Bartelt is professor of sociology at Glassboro State College.

Throughout my career, I have worked with students on writing in my sociology classes, including both formal and informal writing. This interest motivated me, in 1989, to attend a ten-day residential workshop on writing across the disciplines conducted by Northeastern University at Martha's Vineyard. At Glassboro, I have worked with colleagues to develop a program in writing in the disciplines, and in 1990 I cochaired a full-day workshop on the topic. It is exciting that this "thing" I have been trying to do—getting students to use writing as a viable aspect of their sociological training—now has a name and proponents.

Stephen M. Fishman is professor of philosophy at the University of North Carolina, Charlotte.

At a workshop in 1983, I learned two things: that writing could be a tool for discovering as well as reporting and that personal risk and commitment are keys to quality composition. As a result I changed the way I use writing in my classes, pushing for more student ownership, increasing my role as coach rather than judge. To enable students to be active rather than passive, I created a classroom that grants authority to students to construct their own knowledge and honors multiple voices. Borrowing from Bakhtin, I call this environment "heteroglossic." In collaboration with Lucille Parkinson McCarthy, I have been examining the harmonies and dissonances of my multiple-voiced introduction to philosophy classroom.

Charlotte Honda is associate professor and chair of health and physical education at Bronx Community College.

I was inspired to integrate writing into my courses because Bronx Community College enrolls a largely Hispanic population, and it became obvious to me that communication between me and my students needed reinforcement. I have come to believe that a brief, regular journal-writing session reinforces course content for students and provides opportunities for reflecting personal ideas and feelings regarding the course material. The inclusion of WAC keeps altering my traditional perceptions about teaching, as well as biases about ESL students.

Editors' Note:

We began the epistolary exchange that follows by asking the four correspondents, "Why do you use writing in your teaching?" The correspondence continued, following different threads, for three rounds. With the advice and consent of our authors, we have selected and brought together passages from the correspondents' prose. The exchange begins with the four rather different answers to our opening question. Michael Abbott concludes the section, summarizing and landscaping what he has read. The authors then turn to ways in which writing is meaningful to them, as persons and as professionals. Finally, in a chorus, or quartet, the four writers write collaboratively. There is throughout this correspondence evident enthusiasm and commitment; there is, as there is in the writing-to-learn movement generally, no clear party line.

Pearl Bartelt:

I use writing in my classes to foster understanding, whether it be of a statistic or a concept. I have found that when students write about an issue, they grasp the issue at a deeper level. As it fosters understanding, writing lets students see the gaps in their knowledge. Often students don't know what to write about because they don't have the information they need. They assume that they can't write when, in reality, as soon as they have the necessary information, they can write.

Along with the notion of understanding, in one class that I teach, statistics, writing is important as an explanatory device. If students cannot explain what the numbers stand for, those numbers have no use. Writing requires them to be precise about what they have found. As their explanatory capabilities improve, so does their understanding of statistics.

And although I never thought of this before, I guess I use writing as a tool to teach decision making. In oral discussion an assertive student can influence a large number of students in the class. The quieter students hide behind the reigning viewpoint and won't risk an independent opinion. When they are writing by themselves, these same quiet students have to take a position on the issue. Even the most timid students realize that the world doesn't end because they made a decision, that I won't hate them, no matter what they decide, and that the only way not to complete the intent of the exercise is to fail to reach or to justify a decision.

In the advanced courses I teach within the sociology major, I place a heavy emphasis on writing. Students in these courses are generally juniors and seniors and, because they are soon to leave college, I feel writing is part of their presentation of self. Few of these students will go on to graduate school, yet I require them to write in formal academic language, using appropriate footnoting and bibliographic entries. It is not that I am into high torture, but I find that in the academic world as well as the larger marketplace, writing is a part of the presentation of self. Just as people are often initially judged on how they look, students are often judged on how their written work appears. Misspellings and major grammatical blunders can influence a person's perception of the writer. As we read a paper, we respond to the content, but we also respond to sloppiness, incompleteness, and error.

I have found that when I use writing in my classes, my students often gain self-esteem. I realize this initially sounds oxymoronic. *Writing* and *self-esteem?* Students leave the class with a product, generally a product that far exceeds what they thought they could do. I find students become proud of their work and proud of their abilities. They learn that a first draft will not satisfy them, indeed shouldn't satisfy them, and they realize that with work their papers get better.

I have students write so that they can revise. A spoken sentence can be revised only if you remember exactly what was said. It is hard to reflect on an orally expressed thought and revise on the basis of this reflection. When my students write, they can use their first writing as the basis of reflection. They can put this draft aside for a few days and return to it with a fresh perspective. As the revisions accumulate, students have a developmental trail at their fingertips.

As I write this, I realize that I use writing in my courses because I can't take all my students home with me each week. Their writing gives me a way to stay in touch with their progress. It affords me the flexibility to work with them at three in the morning if I choose, whereas I definitely do not choose to have office hours at that time.

I use writing in my classes so that students will not have to suffer with writing the way I did. Why didn't anyone tell me that almost all writers have to rewrite? I thought I was a terrible writer because I had to write multiple drafts. In the first two years of college the rule at the institution I attended was that you failed an exam if you had three misspelled words, one run-on sentence, or one sentence fragment. It is easy to see why I never thought of developing content first and then, at the end of the process, fixing the mechanics. It is no wonder that I didn't feel able to write freely.

Ultimately, I use writing as a way for my students to learn and refine information and opinions. I use writing as a planning device, as a tool for making comparisons, and as a means for students to experiment with issues. Mostly, I hope I use writing in my courses as a way to transcend barriers rather than have the writing be a barrier itself.

Charlotte Honda:
I have always had difficulty with writing, lacked confidence in my ability to write, and have agonized endless hours trying to make sense of what I wanted to say, how to say it, and where to put colons, semicolons, commas, and periods. As I reflect on my formal education in English during the late 1940s, 1950s, and early 1960s, I recollect that those who were talented in writing received attention, while those of us who were less talented fell by the wayside. Also, for various reasons, my home environment failed to give positive reinforcement in the use of correct grammar in speaking or writing. I was, however, encouraged to read and made regular trips to the public library. English was the primary language spoken at home, but it was consistently mixed with Japanese. Also, I was a very active child, prone to daydreaming and much too impatient to concentrate on how to write properly in the confines of a classroom. In retrospect, the preceding personal history may be the point of reference for my writing insecurities—perhaps, in some respects, not too unlike some of my ESL students. Therefore, as I participated in a WAC workshop in January 1989, I empathized with my students, but I also recognized the value of writing as a tool on many levels, not only as a way to help my students but as a way to help myself.

Before the workshop, writing was not, for me as a teacher of movement, a priority in my teaching process. Yes, I gave some essay-type questions on midterm and final examinations, and I even assigned term papers, in part because the college encouraged instructors to do so. But I must admit I questioned these practices because my students, largely first-semester ESL students, wrote fractured and/or incomplete sentences and did not punctuate or spell steadily. I was, of course, focusing on the way they were writing, not what they were saying. Thus, in my explicit questioning of my students' ability to write, I was also implicitly questioning their intelligence, their ability to survive the demands of college work, wondering if they would ever graduate. Such arrogance! Perhaps I was projecting my self-evaluation, past and present, on my students.

In addition, my education and training in how to teach movement was on a physical, physiological, and neurological level. This training included, among other teaching strategies, an emphasis on kinetic awareness and mimetic drills. Therefore, in my thinking, since I was not an English teacher, there was little reason why writing should exist at all in a moving and doing class. Writing was not going to help students learn how to dance or play a sport. This attitude is not uncommon among movement teachers and is, I now feel, most unfortunate. In retrospect, it is apparent to me that the majority of my twenty-seven years of teaching has been spent avoiding the idea of writing, as well as covering up my own insecurities about writing.

I first brought my new perspective on writing into my classes in the spring of 1989. My classes that semester were in hatha yoga, modern dance, and aerobic dance. I went about incorporating writing as an experiment, told my classes so, and then sought the best possible way to integrate writing into classes that met only one day a week for one hour and forty minutes. I also aimed to make writing as nonthreatening as possible, assuring students that the class would be concerned with just the experience and opportunity to write: nothing more, nothing less. There would be no grading of their writing, just a check indicating that I had read what they had written. The process became a five-to-seven-minute journal-writing session, discussing a "question of the day" relating to some aspect of the class experience, course content, or both.

I have been growing and changing with WAC for several semesters, and the shift in my perceptions about ESL students has crystallized as I have suspended judgment on *how* something was written and focused on *what* was being said. In a WAC follow-up workshop, I was struck by the leaders' observation that my students' journals demonstrated their continuity of thought and ideas, despite the fact that their grammar, spelling, and punctuation left much to be desired. I was struck by the fact that cognitive learning was taking place—that abstract reasoning was evident in these journals. The workshop leaders helped me see and hear what my students were writing. They helped me read beyond the obvious.

Through their journal writing, my students have taught me a great deal. The students' journal responses often determine where I need to be clearer, what material needs to be reviewed, and when I should introduce new ideas. The journal writings sensitize me to individual student differences that I overlooked before—particularly since my classes meet only once a week. My understanding about writing as a viable and valuable means of communication and learning tool, regardless of subject matter, continues to be enriched and deepened. It is no longer a matter of "why I use writing in my classes"; it is simply that I must.

Michael Abbott:

I am occasionally asked by an engineering student why I want her or him (an *engineer!*) to write well. If the question occurs in my office, as it often does, I retrieve from my desk a packet of three-by-five-inch cards. I ask the student to choose a card, on which will be found a response to the question. The selected response is always one of the following four (this 52-card deck is rigged!):

1. It can make you a better person.
2. It can make you feel good.
3. It can make you famous.
4. It can make you rich.

Each response is, or could in some sense be, "correct." Whatever the response, it provides a basis for discussion. Here are brief elaborations:

Response 1. Writing is both a skill and (at its higher levels) an *art*, practiced well by few. In the eyes of most, an engineer or scientist who writes well is an *artist*: to the rest of the technical world, a "better person."

Response 2. Doing anything well should make one feel good. Whether it's playing bridge, running miles, making love, or proving theorems, the standards are there: sometimes personal, sometimes set by one's peers. Writing well, after one has developed or accepted standards for comparison and evaluation, is an extraordinarily satisfying experience.

Response 3. This one is fun. Question: Can you name for me six chemical engineering professors from schools other than Rensselaer? Answer (sometimes with a little prodding): Professors U, V, W, X, Y, and Z. Question: Why do you think of these names? Answer: They wrote my textbooks. (Comment: Inevitably, four of the six are textbook authors. The other two are usually "legendary" types, or names that a Rensselaer professor may have dropped in class.) Question: Why do you think we choose these textbooks? Answer: Because the authors know their stuff? Question: *We* know our stuff. Try again? Answer: Because the books are well written? And so it goes. The point is easily made and easily grasped. Global "fame" in this business usually obtains from *authorship*: more often authorship of well-written texts than of scholarly papers.

Response 4. Engineers are and must be result-oriented, but a hard fact of corporate life is this: good results communicated poorly are no better than poor results communicated well and only marginally better than no results at all. One's boss will pass judgment on the technical quality of one's results; the boss's boss—the real keeper of the gate to promotion and riches—wants to be quickly and cleanly informed and (perhaps) entertained, not confused and (possibly) bored. Without special connections, the major route to the boss's boss is the written word. WRITE IT WELL.

Stephen Fishman:
There are many reasons why I use writing in my courses. The most important is to help students see the relevance of philosophy to their own lives and to help them gain control over their own learning. For example, in my introduction to philosophy class I push students to start with personal problems. I urge them to give me as much detail as possible and to use a narrative form. What I want to do is engage students in philosophic reflection rather than merely introduce them to the canonic or influential theories. My own assumption (prejudice) is that philosophy is reflection on cultural conflict, and by conflict I mean those incongruities that develop when different beliefs or values clash, when there are inconsistencies between beliefs and practices. Another assumption of mine has to do with students. More than two decades tell me that students have a difficult time getting excited about articles and topics in typical introductory anthologies. So I avoid such texts and use student narratives (about personal problems) as a way into broader cultural conflicts. Let me illustrate. A student in one class wrote in his first draft about a problem with his former girlfriend. They weren't talking anymore, and he was upset about that.

As a result of a conversation between the student and myself—really, some writing back and forth—the student decided that his core conflict had to do with ways of dealing with disagreement. He discovered that he chose to avoid disagreement rather than to confront it. I asked him to look at everyday examples to enrich the definitions of his key terms and to look at cultural practices to see which practices support confrontation and which support avoidance. Although this task is not a philosophic problem that appears in the canon, I believe this sort of work gets students to philosophic analysis while exploring problems in which they have a keen interest.

Other reasons I use writing are to build community, to help students participate in class discussion, and to give students multiple perspectives on different issues. As students complete required drafts, I respond with letters about how I think philosophers would go about developing the conflict at the core of their papers. I do not grade these drafts and I encourage students to complete as many drafts as they have energy to write. With these drafts and letter-response exchanges I hope to build community between myself and individual students.

The in-class writing I use, what is usually called "focused freewriting," facilitates the class discussions that follow the writing. It helps students learn about philosophic dialogue and about careful listening to the different positions. When I ask people to express their view of an issue, they have something to read to the class; they do not have to respond from an empty deck. In-class writing also helps develop bonding within the class as a whole. It is like breaking bread together. The classroom becomes quiet, as if we have found a safe place to work, a chance to do something we know we should be doing but just don't get around to often enough.

My deepest purposes for writing are concerned with learning about inner dialogue and the joy of writing itself. The old LIU basketball coach Claire Bea, himself an author of over one hundred adventure books, used to say that players should treat the basketball backboard as a friend. I want my students to see *writing* as a friend. I want students to see writing as an interlocutor, a friend with whom they can converse and, in the process, learn that they really have something to say about a particular issue. Often students claim they have nothing to say, but I believe that if they use writing to explore an issue, rather than just to report work already completed, they will develop confidence in self-reflection and inner dialogue. I also want students to discover that learning can be exciting, that learning through writing is an emotional "high," a taste of the creative experience. I hope students experience the joy of beginning with a blank page and filling it, writing so quickly, becoming so one with the meaning of what they are writing, that they lose all sense of time and find sentences coming to them that are startling, that appear as if from the Muse herself.

Michael Abbott:
1. It's pretty clear (to me) that our responses reflect strongly our disciplines; probably less strongly our home institutions; certainly very

strongly (especially in Charlotte's case) our clientele; and for damned sure (but how can we quantify this?) our separate personalities.

2. So let me play a game. I see (feel?) a kind of spectrum here. Let's not worry about what we're trying to correlate, but it feels something like this:

Mike $\longleftrightarrow$ Pearl $\longleftrightarrow$ Steve $\longleftrightarrow$ Charlotte

3. OK, what does the spectrum reflect? Perhaps, most obviously, *discipline*. Pearl and I, more than Steve and Charlotte, work in pretty quantitative areas. (Apologies to Steve if he's a logician.) My comments, and Pearl's also, addressed the importance of writing as a *professional* skill.

4. Steve and Charlotte, more than Pearl and I, stress the importance of writing as a vehicle for personal (vs. professional) development. Charlotte's approach is totally nonjudgmental; Steve's less so. I see here a Bartelt-Fishman link: they both stress the importance of revision.

5. The above items stress differences, and this would be a pretty dull exercise if there were no differences. But what of similarities? I made for myself a little table. . . . The details are uninteresting, but the "reasons for writing" that three or four of us appeared (in writing) to agree on are that it is an important personal skill, is an essential explanatory device, fosters self-esteem, serves as a vehicle for evaluation, and fosters understanding of the subject.

Felt here, but not strongly expressed from all quarters (e.g., mine) is the importance of writing as a means for self-expression.

I hope I haven't overdone the engineer's penchant for classification and analysis by pigeonholing the four of us as I've done here. What's clear to me is that we're all serious teachers and that we're all serious about writing in the classroom. If any items in my list stand out as truly important, they are the first and third: "important personal skill," and "fosters self-esteem."

Stephen Fishman:
Mike, in his 12 June response, says that the way in which each of us talks about writing strongly reflects our discipline. He also says that our approach to writing as a teaching and learning device has much to do with our individual personalities—our histories and biases. Encounters with members of my own department have led me to this same conclusion. My colleagues in philosophy reveal a range of attitudes toward classroom writing. At one extreme, some give numerical grades for each paragraph on essay exams, and, at the other extreme, some use peer-faculty panels to evaluate student portfolios.

Why is Mike's point important? I think it calls into question a notion, common among writing program directors, that writing that occurs across the curriculum is primarily determined by discipline. Mike's point also calls into question the assumption that in classroom research the only personalities worth studying are the students'.

Why are we shy about discussing teacher personalities? Two reasons immediately come to mind, both having to do with authority and both assuming that authority and objectivity go hand in hand. The first reason is that teachers want to believe that their ways of instruction are demanded by their disciplines. We want to believe that our teaching reflects our field's special ways of knowing and writing. We hope our classroom practices are not the result of personal choices but neutral faithfulness to our discipline's tools and findings. The same assumption about authority underlies classroom studies. Despite calls for greater reflexivity, researchers still focus on students rather than their own or the instructor's histories.

The second reason for neglecting the instructor's personality has to do with language. How would instructors tell about their own initiations into their field? The most convenient form would be autobiographical narrative. But academics scorn autobiographical narrative. Storytelling does not distinguish us as professionals. It does not show objective mastery. Far from being neutral, good stories carry with them the smell of a particular writer.

So I believe Mike is on to something. Although we cannot quantify our personalities, we can examine their effects on our classrooms by telling how we became teachers. Teaching stories would be valuable additions to the WAC literature. The power of narrative is detail, its ability to make us feel we are there. And the instructor's story becomes central if we are to learn how much of someone else's teaching practices are applicable to our own. I suggest that future classroom research include profiles of WAC teachers, include answers to questions like What was the teacher's own disciplinary initiation? Is the teacher a disciplinary insider or outsider? Does the teacher believe that learning flows from master to apprentice, or that it takes place when equals exchange their different sorts of information?

Charlotte Honda:
I reread all of our "round two" contributions and was particularly impressed by Steve's discussion regarding what he considered the stages of good writing:

> My own good writing—whether memos or APA style reports—comes from personal writing. Again, I have little data, but I have

in mind the journals of Einstein and Camus and Darwin. For these good learners and writers, personal pieces formed the scaffolding—the discarded scaffolding—for their formal work. Obviously there is a long jump from personal to professional writing, but drafting and redrafting require commitment, require that authors believe that their work is valuable, so much so that it is worth the effort to make it clear and effective. And that is why if forced to choose I would stand with Charlotte's approach. It stresses the first stages of good writing, stages in which students write to find out what they care about. Without sufficient work at this first stage students run the risk of writing "uncommitted" papers, papers they do not care enough about to do the necessary reworking and editing. I also choose Charlotte's approach because of its implied ideology. Students are the silent ones in American education, yet students learn best when they have a personal stake in the classroom. I believe that personal writing is a crucial step in education, no matter the discipline or field.

The philosopher Steve has sounded a note that resonates with my thoughts and feelings.

Steve also raises an interesting point regarding my approach to WAC and my attempt at bridging the gap between the students' native languages and the language of the classroom. Steve suggests the possibility of permitting the journals to be read in class. I am aware that I am responding to his point out of context; however, I feel it is important to state that I would not allow journals to be read aloud in class. Journals are personal excursions in self-expression, and I feel privileged that my students allow me to witness their journey. Such a practice would break the contract between us: that I will be the only person to read their journals during the semester. An important issue here too is that many of our ESL students are often afraid to write. I believe that much of their anxiety is based on the fact that they are struggling to express themselves in their writing and speaking. They are perhaps overly sensitive to critique, positive or negative, that they receive regarding their language deficiencies. They may also find themselves struggling with the perceived value judgments that accompany their status as "ESL students." I need not elaborate on the effect such judgments can have on their academic success.

Lastly, Mike raises the issue of "our separate personalities." I myself think that our own experiences, and our ease or dis-ease regarding modes of communication and self-expression, are important factors in the development of our personalities. Consequently, I con-

sider our histories a factor in the development of our teaching styles
and personalities.

Pearl Bartelt:
I would like to return to something that Steve discussed when he
distinguished between *professional* and *personal* writing. I agree that
Mike and I emphasize professional writing. Mike's assumption that
this emphasis may be discipline-based is probably accurate. There are,
I assume, agreed-on writing styles in engineering. In sociology the
formal presentation style is the most prevalent, although more informal styles are used by those following certain theoretical schools—
mainly symbolic interactionism and ethnomethodology. The reading I
have done in philosophy is also quite formal in presentation. I would
expect that, in a movement class, writing would deal much more with
feelings than in the other disciplines.

Having said this, I must also say that I, like Steve, have found that
my best writing comes out of personal writing. It is personal writing
that gives me most joy. Yet I have had to be able to move from personal
writing to the more professional modes to complete degree requirements. For a number of years, concentrating on the "shoulds" of sociology, I forgot about personal writing. It has been a joy to rediscover this
neglected part of myself. I agree that students learn best when they are
personally engaged. I guess I find the personal engagement of students
such a basic tenet of education that I never mentioned it in my previous
writings to you. I try to help students make decisions and take stands
in their writing. But notice I am still using "I." I am still the teacher
keeping the classroom under control. A point well-taken, Steve.

I do feel, after reading our collective offerings, that we probably all
do combine both the personal and the professional orientations. I have
students use far more personal writing in The Sociology of Women
than I do in the statistics and methods course. Yet this semester I am
having statistics and methods students keep a journal. My hope is that
among the many educational and personal reasons for journal keeping,
the process will help them build a base of personal writing that will
contribute to their formal research paper. I wonder if I presumed that
the personal writing predated the section drafts I see? I'm pretty well
convinced that the students feel that they should be able to write the
final formal treatise without the journal phase. Just because Einstein
had to keep journals . . .

I have tried each semester to bring to my class all of the false starts
and arbitrary pieces of paper that have gone into whatever research I
am currently doing. This gives tangible proof that my own writing is a

personal and messy process and it debunks the myth that students seem to hold with steel-like grip: that all academics write final drafts, beginning with the first sentence and working on to the end. These academic papers, students are convinced, emerge from the printer or typewriter in publishable form.

One last thought. As I was reading all our second-round entries, I wondered how each of us would teach movement. Would we choose a combined professional and personal orientation? Would the more structured among us become more flexible?

Michael Abbott:

Steve in his letter of 19 July suggests (I believe) that we might examine our personal histories, with a view perhaps toward understanding our approaches to WAC. Clever devil, that Steve: He knows how much academics enjoy talking about themselves. I grasp this straw; "A Little History" is my topic for this round.

By the time I finished my degree work, in 1965, I was sure that I'd seen enough of universities for a lifetime. Not that I'd had a bad time of it: my undergraduate experience had been good, and my research professor was a fine man, from whom I'd learned a lot (including— and this was certainly a major early influence—the importance of writing well). But twenty-plus continuous years of schooling is a lot, the job market for PhD chemical engineers was super back then, and so I took a job with Exxon at its engineering center in Florham Park, New Jersey.

The job at Exxon was great. The problems were interesting, I was working with good people, and the salary was OK. And here I learned my first postgraduate lessons in written communication. Details are not important here, but the message certainly is: Exxon took writing very seriously. I made lots of mistakes (probably most often rhetorical), and did more rewriting than I had since high school. We of course had a company style manual, which was good news and bad news: good, because it's important to be able to write within constraints; bad, because the constraints set by company style manuals are often perversely local in nature. It was probably at Exxon that I learned to hate the passive voice.

After about three years away from university life, I began to miss it. And so I returned to the university . . . the same one from which I had received my degrees. This was in 1969.

The first five years after I returned I spent as a postdoc, but in the last two years of the postdoc stint they let me into the classroom. Finally, I had a chance to teach! Wisely, they put me in a graduate course in my area of expertise. I was terrified for a while, and I made the usual collection of mistakes made by all green teachers, but I found quickly that I enjoyed it: I had in fact a talent for explaining, I enjoyed immensely the scholarship that goes with effective teaching, and I appreciated the opportunity to work with talented young people.

I should back up a bit. While still a postdoc, I was invited by my mentor (my former research professor) to collaborate with him on a couple of thermodynamics textbooks. These were my first professional adventures in writing for an audience of nonexperts. These writing exercises helped a lot to prepare me for teaching—good expository writing is teaching, although of a very different sort from the classroom variety. Tenure came in late 1977, and with it the freedom to focus more on what to me is most important: teaching, writing, and the scholarship that goes with both. Since then, I have continued to keep up with and publish in my field but have really concentrated on the classroom. Joseph Campbell would have said that I have found my bliss; most Rensselaer administrators would rather that I had found $250K per year in grant money. But I am happy with what I am doing, and truly believe that teaching is the most honorable profession.

Let me back up again. There are surely other items in my history that influence my attitudes and approaches to writing in the classroom. My nonprofessional passions have always been reading and music. My tastes have of course changed over the years, but I think I can say that I am open-minded, to a fault, about both: I really will give a couple of reads or listens to almost anything. (Some litmus tests: John Milton, Diane Wakoski, Ravel's *Bolero*, Steve Reich. They are all acquired tastes. They all "pass.") I suppose that my tolerance and enthusiasm for almost any serious literary or musical effort has helped me to survive the efforts of my young colleagues to put their thoughts to paper.

So what have we here? With all of these data, we ought to be able to make a few observations. I shall observe as best I can from my vantage point, using a couple of Steve's questions as a platform.

1. My disciplinary initiation was conventional, but labored: undergrad, grad, industrialist, postdoc—culminating in an academic appointment at age thirty-five. (By today's standards, I really took my time.) What does this mean? It means that I had lots of bosses before I had the chance to be, once in a while, my own boss. It means I had the chance to write for lots of different audiences. It means, in short, that I had to switch gears a lot of times. Mine is not a hazing mentality (I did it, so "they" must do it . . .), but I do not believe that it hurts my students to have to do a bit of gear-switching.

2. I am a disciplinary insider—of sorts. I go to an occasional conference, give an occasional paper, review a dozen or so papers and proposals yearly, and know most of the folks in my field. But my reputation is that of a teacher-explainer-synthesizer—not that of an innovator—and that's the way I want it. How does this affect my approach to WAC? I want student writers to tell a good story: that's one of the things good explainers do.

3. My extraprofessional interests (poetry, music, literature) have surely influenced my approach to and attitudes toward WAC. Good writing is good writing: the same standards apply everywhere—without defining *good* in detail, this is what I believe. Some good writers: Paul Halmos (a mathematician), Erwin Schrodinger (a physicist), Clifford Truesdell (a continuum mechanicist). Some good writers: G. Chaucer, W. H. Auden, Thomas Pynchon. Some good writers: J. S. Bach, Duke Ellington, I. Stravinsky. Make up your own lists, hand out your favorite examples, play your favorite records, tapes, CDs. The styles are various, the subjects (even media) are different, but what comes through? *Craftsmanship*! One doesn't even have to understand the message (Halmos? Chaucer? Stravinsky?). This, I think, is good news. Young folks can comprehend this: that these artists wrote or write, carefully and critically according to some set of standards, often set by themselves. Many of them were revisers (Bach and Halmos were not, but Auden and Stravinsky were), and in all cases the finished products involved a lot of thought.

A Chorus, or Quartet:

The philosopher, the engineer, the sociologist, and the movement specialist: We sing different parts; we make better music together than alone. If students are to hear the totality of the music, they must go from course to course, taking each different voice with them as they move. One lone writing course—no matter how well taught—leaves a student without the full sense of the music.

Despite these differences in our voices, we share important assumptions about learning. We assume that students learn best when they can explain the numbers, when they have worked to construct their own position rather than mindlessly repeat someone else's. We share a commitment to demystifying our professional expertise. By sharing our writing experiences with our students, we are trying to let them behind the professional curtain. It is a way of altering the power structure of the classroom, showing students that academic skills are painstaking achievements rather than products of genius. Finally, each of us finds a place in our courses for personal writing, something that dramatically influences the way we initiate our students. Pearl uses personal writing in her sociology of women course and journals in Statistics and Methods; Charlotte employs journals in dance and movement; Mike says he wants student writers to tell a good story; Steve encourages his introduction to philosophy students to explore moral conflicts using personal narrative. This tells us something about our view of academic initiations. Instead of trying to substitute academic discourse for students' native languages, we see our task as relating these languages, as relating the student's own driving concerns to the concerns of our disciplinary communities.

Recognizing the value of personalized writing as a first stage to professional writing, enhancing communication between teacher and student, structuring the process for developing clear, organized thinking on paper, and providing a venue for self-expression: these seem to be major reasons why the four of us incorporate WAC in our classrooms. We have been energized by the variety of ways we all work—the diversity of who we are, coupled with the diversity of our disciplines. In the eight months that we have been sharing our ideas, we have learned a great deal and have come to know one another as kindred spirits who care about our students and the value of using writing in our teaching.

From Practice to Theory: Writing across the Disciplines at Spelman College

Jacqueline Jones Royster

The author is the director of the Comprehensive Writing Program and associate professor of English at Spelman College.

In 1972, I taught my first college-level writing course and discovered the threads of concerns that have held my attention for two decades. We have since named the general arena for these interests literacy studies. *For me, this arena includes also the interdisciplinary perspectives of women's studies and African diaspora studies, and I find myself continually crossing disciplinary boundaries and considering dialectical relations. As the director of a cross-disciplinary writing program since 1978, I have brought my concerns together in ways that have allowed me to feel both productive in my own work and helpful to others.*

Since 1978, Spelman College has had an active, well-supported writing-across-the-curriculum program. We began with the notion, as did many other institutions throughout the nation (see Griffin, "Programs"), that greater success in developing communication skills called for an extension of this responsibility in reasonable and productive ways beyond the English department to other departments across the curriculum. This strategy seemed capable of enhancing our efforts to produce graduates who can perform well in graduate and professional schools and in the world of work.

The program began as a faculty development program: the running of workshops and seminars, the identification of strategies and resources. It was designed to improve students' skills by assisting faculty members in incorporating writing more effectively into their courses. The concentration of effort, typical of WAC programs at that time, was on assignment making, classroom activities, evaluation, feedback, and grading. We assumed that students needed more opportunities to write throughout their academic programs and more opportunities to receive varieties of feedback on their writing. As the coordinator of these activities, I assumed that the practice and the feedback would help the students operate with greater awareness of what they were trying to do as language users in various contexts and that this process would strengthen their abilities to perform.

In 1983 we received funding that allowed us to systematize and improve support mechanisms for both faculty and students, and by 1985 we concluded that the program was operating with some success. Each year we set reasonable objectives in terms of faculty participation and course development across the disciplines, based on our needs, concerns, and resources. Each year we met our objectives. We found that we were helping faculty members incorporate writing activities more effectively into their courses, we were providing support for those activities through the Writing Center, and we were changing the ways in which instructors and students thought about and talked about writing.

By the end of 1985, our cross-disciplinary perspectives on skills development provided us with ways to look at the challenges differently. The Committee on the Improvement of Communication Skills had surveyed faculty members who were teaching general education courses (a level of the curriculum specially targeted for writing-across-the-disciplines activities). These instructors perceived the program to be successful in three ways: in enriching classroom dynamics, in conveying a clearer sense of the importance of skills development regardless of a student's major, and in emphasizing that students should expect to write in courses other than English and would be held accountable for conventional usage.

Beyond mostly attitudinal changes, however, we discovered that these faculty members were not confident that the performance levels of students had changed to any significant degree. As we explored the implications of this perception in informal follow-up discussions, various instructors raised concerns, not about form and structure in writing but about content, the quality of the ideas. Now that students were more careful about honoring conventions, we were able to see more clearly that they were not writing much better because they were not thinking critically enough. We began to pay more attention to the notion that "good writing is good thinking."

This new concern led us to wonder just how our students were actually operating—not just as communicators, but as thinkers, learners, problem finders, and problem solvers. We decided to give specific and conscious attention to developing what the literacy community now calls higher-order literacy skills. In essence we had changed the conceptual frame of the program. In the beginning, our target ultimately was to improve performance levels in writing. After 1985, the goal was to enhance the operational strategies of students as thinkers and learners through a variety of skills development mechanisms, including writing. We looked for existing structures, systems, and strategies to develop critical-thinking skills and experimented with others that might increase the effectiveness of our students' learning. We examined more closely what individual teachers and courses were doing, what departments and divisions were doing for majors and nonmajors, and what roles clubs, organizations, and special programs were playing in our students' learning. The explorations included systems not just at the classroom and departmental levels but also at the institutional level. In the third phase, our current phase, we recognize that writing is a multidimensional strategy that has a vital role to play as we talk about the construction of knowledge from discipline to discipline and across disciplines; as we use writing to operate and interact with people within and across those disciplines, as well as in nonacademic settings; and as we measure knowledge and performance from point of entry at the college to point of departure.

Faculty-development workshops, which not so long ago were devoted to classroom strategies, now focus on explorations of the ways in which students acquire knowledge and understanding, think about subject matter, articulate their thoughts, and meet varying disciplinary expectations. In these workshops we discuss the college and the classroom as learning environments, strategies for teaching and learning, and the ways that we, as teachers, measure success. Our concerns have become pedagogical: how we teach, how students learn, and the nature and quality of the spaces we create that allow for the actualizing and maximizing of potential. The result is that we now see writing—and reading, listening, speaking, thinking, problem finding, and problem solving—as dynamic threads in lively processes that we call teaching and learning. Such is the legacy of more than a decade of writing across the curriculum at Spelman College.

At this point we are well distanced from our beginnings and reasonably positioned to reach beyond the documenting of specific objectives and outcomes as they provide evidence of institutional culture or institutional effectiveness. We can now ask, after years of faculty development and supportive activities, after years of thinking and rethinking, "What have been the consequences of our work?" For me, the most important consequence is that our brand of writing across the curriculum has led me to formulate an inquiry model for teaching and learning. This model has been shaped by the experiences of faculty members from across the disciplines who have used writing and other learning strategies more specifically and more consciously in their courses.

As we consider writing across the disciplines, we are better able to transcend the microscopic view of skills and strategies and see larger pieces of the teaching and learning fabric laid whole. In doing so, we discover that cross-disciplinary practice reaches for theories—not of writing, but of teaching and learning. With a heightened consciousness of what constitutes or should constitute writing and learning, we can create worlds, shape experiences, talk, think, and listen, and we can do so in communion, not in isolation, through cross-disciplinary programs. We can pool our talents, resources, and our thinking in the interest of individual and community concerns. With perseverance, we can bring epistemological and pedagogical theories together with classroom practice in a powerful and provocative dialectic of success and failure, trial and error, truth and illusion, issues, needs, and concerns, all of which have the potential to produce a highly charged academic endeavor that folds and refolds theory and practice into each other until we know that the enterprise is a good one despite the ever-present feelings of chaos, disintegration, and resistance that often accompany ongoing inquiry.

Creating a World

My experiences as a classroom teacher, as the director of a cross-disciplinary writing program, and as a workshop leader on my own campus and at other institutions have led me to concentrate on helping colleagues to establish useful directions for learning and to find productive ways of sustaining momentum. My primary effort has been to raise questions that encourage faculty members to operate consciously and systematically as they define for themselves the tasks of teaching and learning and as they choose points of departure and a range of options to carry out those responsibilities.

Imaging

I begin most dialogues by asking instructors to "image" what it is that they see themselves trying to do in the classroom. I encourage them to take note of the images that emerge as they think about students, their subject matter, and the roles that they themselves typically play in managing courses and classroom activities. I encourage them to think metaphorically, analogically. What usually results is a collection of images that enable the articulators of the images to see themselves and their efforts in the classroom with greater clarity. They identify strengths and sometimes see directions for change.

Three examples come immediately to mind. One person saw himself as a portrait painter and considered one of his tasks as a teacher to be to "paint" for his students the people that they represent themselves to be and thus help them clarify for themselves who they really are, what they understand, and what their possibilities are. Another person saw herself as a bus driver who stops along winding trails to invite students to travel with her, inviting them to take a comfortable seat and to take advantage of the resources along the way. A third person saw herself as a bridge over a deep cavern, a structure that gave students access to new territory.

Imaging offers a vocabulary and a context in which to talk about classroom interactions positively, with a focus on the full-bodied nature of the effort, not just on short-term objectives and outcomes. The images reflect who we are, who we may not be, who we are trying to be, who we might be instead. We bring our selves and our students more proactively into the teaching and learning process, along with the other players that have been privileged toward the spotlight: content, objectives, strategies, and outcomes. We acknowledge not just the work but the human dimensions of the academic enterprise. We embrace our values and visions, and we see pieces of ourselves in the trials and tribulations of others who share our values, problems, and concerns. We find community.

This type of dialogue can be contextualized within the national dialogue on good practice. In 1987 Arthur W. Chickering and Zelda F. Gamson identified seven principles of good practice for undergraduate education. They concluded that good practice encourages student-faculty contact, cooperation among students, and active learning; gives prompt feedback; emphasizes time on task; communicates high expectations; and respects diverse talents and ways of learning. Three years later, the National Council of Teachers of English published a working paper that goes even further in detailing a range of assumptions and in listing pedagogical guidelines for the teaching of English and language arts. This document succinctly pulls together prevailing notions concerning cultural diversity, classroom climate, classrooms as communities, the interactive and interdependent nature of learning, the social construction of knowledge, language as a tool for learning, growth, and change, and notions about relationships between language and power.

The national dialogue provides considerable evidence that we are taking into account complexities of literacy development and learning

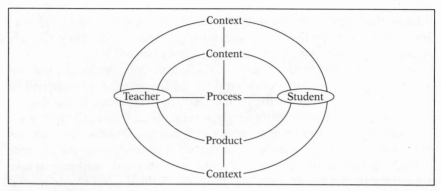

Figure 1. Creating a Learning Space

in new and different ways. Clearly, we are being more inclusive than ever before of the array of factors that can either hinder or support the academic success of our students.

Choosing

The continuing dialectic between theory and practice evokes a sense of teacher as decision maker. Because of the complex of issues, assumptions, and perspectives, setting up a course is very much like creating the world according to us—our own world, our own culture, and we recognize that in this choosing there is privilege and obligation (see Porter; Purves and Purves; Brandt; Strenski; Dean). Within our institutional, disciplinary, and interdisciplinary cultures, we have the authority to choose, and we have the obligation to make these decisions in good faith and good conscience. Operating with integrity demands that we teach consciously, not only in acknowledgment and awareness of values, assumptions, and expectations, but also with sensitivity to the ways in which perceptions of knowledge seem to be changing and to such dynamics as the sociopolitical dimensions of literacy and learning.

Primarily, though, we are the ones who determine what type of arena for learning there will be in our classrooms. We decide what we want, and we set up systems that, we hope, will nurture and sustain those choices. Even so, the goal is still fundamentally to create a space in which learning is possible and then to energize that space so that learning potential can be brought forth and maximized.

The elements in figure 1, Creating a Learning Space, show where the task of weighing and choosing alternatives can begin. The circles and the connecting lines indicate the dynamic relationships in this mix of ingredients. Each factor represents a point of focus, a lens through which to view the classroom; it provides a set of values and concerns that allow instructors to clarify what they're trying to do, how they are trying to do it, and the ends that they are trying to meet. Each lens can be focused by asking questions.

Context: What is the ethos of the classroom? What are the general expectations for knowing, being, doing in this environment? What is appropriate and inappropriate behavior? What constitutes good citizenship, good learning? What level of trust will be engendered? Will students be encouraged to take risks, allowed to make mistakes, and motivated to learn from error rather than be punished for "wrongdoing"? What kind of place are students entering and how should they be acculturated and acclimated?

Teacher and student: How much of yourself and your experiences will you bring to the classroom? What will you allow your students to bring? What systems and structures will enable you and your students to take the greatest advantage of the opportunity to learn? Who will talk? to whom? about what kind of information and experience? What types of information and experience will count? How? What will nurture and sustain teacher and students as they grow and change?

Content: What information, principles, processes do students need to see and understand? What should they value in order to do well? What behaviors, skills (reading, writing, speaking, listening, thinking, problem finding, problem solving) will they need to use, exhibit, and demonstrate?

Process: How will you know where to start? How will you recognize strengths? How will you set and help students to internalize criteria? What strategies, techniques, ways and means of knowing, being, and doing will you use? How will you engender attitudes and behaviors? How will you sustain the direction and momentum for learning? How will you monitor growth and development? How will you judge, rank, and file?

Product: What will you use to measure growth, progress, success? To what ends will these measurements be directed? When is the best time and what are the best circumstances for measuring? What kind of feedback will students need? What is the best time to give what kind of advice and feedback? Who can give advice or feedback? How will students know how they are doing?

I have found that somewhere between the points of terror and exaltation in looking microscopically and telescopically at our work, faculty members make sense of the experience of teaching. The inquiry permits meaningful dialogue to take place, dialogue that is often gloriously ill-structured. At our most successful moments, I have found that the search is not for answers but for options, options that grow from our thinking again about the values, assumptions, and expectations of our disciplines, about what we mean to do when we teach, about how we can help our students to learn.

Shaping a Whole Experience

Traditionally, as faculty members who teach at the college and university levels, we have found it rather easy to decenter ourselves and our students from what happens in classrooms. Until recently, we talked more about knowledge than learning, about our fields of research than our teaching, about facts, figures, and measurements rather than people and processes within immediate contexts. Privileged in this talk were content, received standards of excellence, and notions of objectivity in what constitutes reason, quality, and achievement. However, writing-across-the-curriculum activities have encouraged many of us to reconsider. We have been moved to ask, "What is it that we are really trying to do?" Inevitably, as we face the challenge of determining ways of knowing and seeing, we encounter the challenge of finding productive ways of being and doing.

Demystifying the Task

Simply stated, the fundamental problem is to help students to learn and to perform. Not so simply, the task is to determine how we (with more knowledge, experience, and expertise) can help students (often with very different knowledge, experience, and expertise) to operate effectively and efficiently within our disciplines. Typically, the cardinal effort is to demystify the context and process of learning in ways that allow students to handle content flexibly, to move from novice levels of knowledge and performance to levels of expertise. In addition to the constant challenge of specifying the appropriate "what" of learning, the task is to determine when, where, and how to intervene in our students' learning in order to make a positive difference in their efforts to see, know, be, and do.

As we explore students' pathways to learning and empowerment, we bring into play sensitive questions about classroom authority. We need to lay bare the ways by which we do and do not share the authority and responsibility of learning. Research and practice in collaborative learning, as evidenced by the work of Andrea Lunsford and Lisa Ede, Anne R. Gere, Kenneth A. Bruffee ("Social Construction"), and others, indicate that we are changing our views of classroom participation and authority. This shifting theoretical perspective raises questions about the need for faculty members to share control, to be more inclusive in

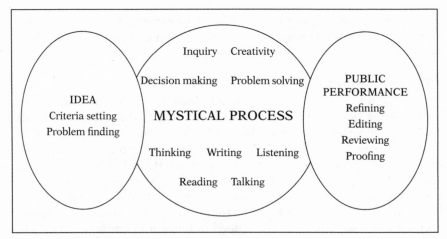

Figure 2. From Idea to Performance

defining the "what" of learning, to enable a diversity of voices and experiences to find respect and appreciation in the classroom, to allow for more social interaction and more varied feedback, and to use multiple measures of success and achievement.

Figure 2, From Idea to Performance, conceptualizes classroom activities as whole learning experiences. The overlapping circles indicate various points of emphasis as we reconsider the wholeness of particular activities. This concept suggests that we find ways to help students negotiate the space between starting an activity and finishing it. Within each circle are mechanisms by which instructors can intervene in learning. We can do more than give an assignment and judge it on the due date. We can think about structuring activities throughout the "mystical" process of completing an assignment. We can help students know that they are on an appropriate path and proceeding in ways that are respected by the particular discipline.

Highlighted in each circle are basic tasks, processes, and strategies that students can use to activate themselves, to engage in conversation thoughtfully, and to measure movement and success. Initial points of focus in designing activities include the need to set criteria, to help students internalize the criteria, and to help them find and articulate appropriate problems. Interim points of focus include structuring activities and using a range of strategies (writing, reading, thinking, listening, talking) that help students engage in inquiry, use their creative energies more effectively, make decisions, and think through and solve problems in keeping with disciplinary expectations. Culminating points of focus include activities that refine, review, and edit performance, again in keeping with disciplinary expectations. These latter activities can remind students of their responsibilities to make their performances ready for public viewing and judgment.

Defining Literacy

As we begin to think of classroom activities as whole experiences, we find that we need to redefine *literacy*. As indicated by Jerrie C. Scott and by a collection of essays edited by Eugene Kintgen, Barry M. Kroll, and Mike Rose, new definitions of literacy take into account varying contexts and purposes and force us to ask what kind of literacy we are seeking to engender. Faculty members must become more reflective about the ways of their disciplines. They must consider specifically how their disciplines work, what they value, what students who are seeking to do well in these areas need to know and know how to do in order to be anointed "literate" and productive. They should consider the similarities and the differences in developing literacy across disciplines, even what the relationships are between academic and nonacademic arenas.

Scott's view of literacy has been most usable in my interactions with instructors. Across disciplines, I find that teachers are seeking to help students learn how to gain access to information, to process the information in various ways, to use the information flexibly and productively, and to find or create meaning based on their abilities as thinkers, learners, language users, and problem finders and solvers. Individual faculty members, then, are left with their departmental colleagues to flesh out for themselves the particularities of literacy from their own disciplinary bases. Seemingly, we can never abandon the struggle to establish what is appropriate within either specific or general territory in terms of content, objectives, operations, procedures, outcomes—to establish what constitutes literacy and learning (see Scott, Davis, and Walker). This challenge seems to be pandisciplinary and perpetual.

Managing Options

Clearly, a broad array of definitions, values, beliefs, attitudes, preferences, and predispositions yields a multiplicity of options that faculty members need to consider in shaping specific directions for the teaching and learning task. Colleagues may feel inundated by details but can reduce this complexity, for the sake of finding a point of departure in managing the task, by recasting the task. Useful questions include How do you help students to become "literate" in your classroom? How do you help them to gain access to information, to process the information in various ways, to use the information in keeping with disciplinary habits and expectations, to find and create meaning? The dialogue that springs from these questions helps us stand back from the complexity of day-to-day teaching so that we can function more easily, not just in decision making but in action. We are able to see exactly how we can make the activities work.

At the specific, microscopic, immediate level of what individual teachers can do, we talk about points of departure. The attempt is to move our thinking from ideas to action in careful consideration of the systematic activities that we each deem necessary to achieve desired outcomes. The task is not just to conceive of classroom activities but to discover how particular procedures can be used to translate those conceptions to action. This nuts-and-bolts approach encourages faculty members to design classroom activities in anticipation of what students need to see and understand (information, principles, process); think and feel (values, beliefs); do and be able to do (behaviors, skills— reading, writing, speaking, listening, thinking, problem finding and solving) in order to be successful.

Again, needs become questions, and questions become conceptual frames informed, in this instance, by my own experiences in classrooms and the experiences of others with whom I have worked over the years. The effort on this lower, more concrete level is, again, to think through the learning experience as a whole experience; to design activities that help students gain authority, experience, comfort, and confidence in knowing what to do and how to do it; to create a range of mechanisms to help both teacher and learner monitor progress and achievement. There are three sets of questions (which reflect questions raised in the explanation of figs. 1 and 2) that I have found to be useful.

1. *How will you start the learning activity?* How do you determine where to start? How do you come to know where students are with the subject matter, what they know and do not know, what they can and cannot do? What do they need to see, understand, think, feel, do, be able to do in order to succeed? How will students know what is important and what they should know and do? What will you be responsible for? What will they be responsible for?

2. *How will you sustain the direction and momentum of learning?* How will students know that they are progressing well? How will you know that students are progressing well? How will you determine when it is most reasonable for you to intervene? What will help guarantee that the learning outcomes that you expect will be the learning outcomes that you get?

3. *How will you end the learning unit?* What activities and strategies will you use to bring closure? With a more liberal view of what consti-

tutes assessment, to what ends will you use assessment mechanisms and at what points during the course? How will you measure success?

In using this model, which I have presented here as an inquiry model, a teaching heuristic, I have never found that finding writing strategies (or reading, thinking, listening, or problem-finding and problem-solving strategies, for that matter) are a problem. Faculty members' experiences are usually rich, and resources from the literacy studies community are plentiful. We simply fill in the blanks. Finding the blanks—that is, finding, or sometimes acknowledging, what is missing in the teaching and learning interaction—is the more difficult task, especially for those not accustomed to taking these types of risks with their work or with their thinking.

Using an inquiry approach helps instructors see for themselves alternative ways of doing things. As illustrated in figure 2, they see writing as a tool to help students move through the "mystical" process from ideas to performance. They see the need to

- encourage students to take responsibility and authority for their own learning;
- find a productive place to start in structuring positive and productive learning experiences;
- help students extend their thinking;
- help them understand operational systems and identify solutions;
- help them refine their thinking in keeping with specific values and expectations;
- encourage them to make their performances ready for public viewing and judgment.

Generally, faculty members come away from this model (creating a world and shaping whole learning experiences) with a clearer sense of themselves as teachers and scholars and with a clearer sense of the academic enterprise—not just what it means to write but what it means to teach and to learn. Faculty members see that thinking consciously and specifically can help not only their students but themselves. If they remain connected with colleagues who are also experimenting, they find it easier to maintain balance, to keep the dialectic going, and to reinvest in the process.

The Spelman story is a story of evolution and change, shepherded by vigilance. One way to describe the process of this evolution is to say that writing has remained at the center of our concern, but the spaces that serve to contextualize this center have been raised to bolder relief. We can also say that our understanding of writing in its dynamic interconnections with other aspects of the academic enterprise is considerably deeper than it was in 1978. Have we moved away from writing? No, we have not. Quite the contrary! What we have done is to become more aware of ways to sustain writing as a vital element in the teaching and learning that we do.

Again, the evolution has been "shepherded by vigilance." Someone has to keep watch, to name, to nag, to warn, to remind, to affirm, to say again—to facilitate the ongoing process of keeping the connections between skills, strategies, and processes clear, strong, and vibrantly attuned to theoretical and pedagogical constructs. In that regard, writing across the disciplines has worked flexibly at Spelman because specific people on the campus are committed to making it so.

At the final balancing, I believe that the real strength of writing across the disciplines, as we have known it, is that colleagues can work together. We can find our own pathways to learning and empowerment within collaborative groups that question, nurture, and support the pulls and tears of growth. In the academic arena, where habit has pushed us to work alone, these opportunities to form community permit us to discover options that might have been overlooked or unacknowledged.

Over the last few years, various scholars have proclaimed strengths and weaknesses of the writing-across-the-curriculum movement (see Tchudi; Fulwiler, "Reflections"; Blair; McLeod, "Writing"). They have taken the lead during this period of reflection, assessment, and projection in helping us look backward and forward, to find value and achievement, to contextualize our mistakes and weaknesses. Even though there is still a need for comprehensive research designs from which we can draw broad conclusions and fashion agenda, there is also room for singular stories and visions like the one presented here. We must hear them, examine them, and use them in the creating of different, more hopeful stories for greater numbers of students whose potential remains significantly untapped.

Part IV

Studies in the Classroom

Introduction

*Neither researcher nor teacher has the power over outcomes
he or she may want. But both have more power than they may
know.*

—Tom Hilgers

In this section, we move from the personal reflections in the interchange to empirical studies of teaching and using writing in specific
classes. Beyond this likeness, the three studies are quite dissimilar in
their empirical approaches and different focal points. Two follow the
methods and genres of traditional studies, reporting and drawing in-
ferences from information: Susan Peck MacDonald and Charles R.
Cooper's quasi-experimental study of two types of journals demonstrates how each promotes a distinct kind of learning; Joy Marsella,
Thomas L. Hilgers, and Clemence McLaren's qualitative field study of
students' writing in seven university classes focuses on factors that
influence the way these students accomplish that writing. In contrast
to these two approaches, Toby Fulwiler uses a composite journal to
report on writing and collaborative learning experiences in one of his
American literature classes, creating his "story" of the course while
trying not to generalize from the particulars he has chosen to report.
As he explains, in correspondence with the editors, "my point was to
present my experience and invite readers to enter in and witness and
participate in making meaning with us."

While two of the essays focus on writing in literature classes—one
in American literature, one in Chinese literature—the three studies
raise several questions that are relevant to teachers in any discipline
and suggest a range of response. In each study, the researcher asks,
"To what degree should a teacher direct and control what happens?"
After reading the other essays in this section, Hilgers speaks of the
balancing of "professorial versus student ownership of the learning
situation," and Fulwiler acknowledges the trade-off between "writer
freedom" and "academic training—a useful trade sometimes." The conflict between student freedom and teacher constraint is most obvious

in the contrast between the open-ended, student-directed personal journals used in Fulwiler's course and the more structured, teacher-directed academic journals used in the MacDonald and Cooper study. Clearly, these scholars' preferences for different types of journals reflect different priorities for learning in their classes. Fulwiler uses journals "to help students build a bridge between their own personal lives and the academic world they have entered," whereas MacDonald and Cooper intend "to help students actually develop the ways of knowing demanded on papers in the course they studied." Reflecting on their study and Fulwiler's, they comment: "We are not opposed to using journals for students to express feelings, puzzlement, annoyance, surprise. We think personal writing in journals can serve useful purposes. We don't, however, think it will by itself lead students toward typical argument and explanation of the kind widely practiced in the academy and on the job." As Judith Langer's research indicates—and we suspect MacDonald and Cooper would agree—we cannot take for granted what those typical ways of knowing are, since they may vary from discipline to discipline, course to course.

A second question has to do with the *nature* of the direction we provide. If we want our students to use writing as means of learning, how do we achieve this goal? Like Lee Odell, MacDonald and Cooper advocate focusing on the ways of knowing valued in a given class. In the Marsella, Hilgers, and McLaren study, some of the teachers seem to focus more on formats for writing assignments and procedures for working through an extended writing (e.g., drafts, peer review). Taking yet another direction, Fulwiler foregrounds the nature of interactions between students and teacher and the nature of writing activities, as they both contribute to ways of learning and experiencing literature.

A third question relates to our knowledge of our students. How much do we need to know about our students' backgrounds, values, and circumstances if we are to challenge them to use writing in new ways to contribute to their learning? Marsella, Hilgers, and McLaren stress the powerful influence that students' prior writing habits and present situations have on how they define the writing tasks they are given— they influence not only the time students invest but also the ways in which they go about the process. Marsella comments that their own research and the Fulwiler essay demonstrate "how powerful the contexts of [students'] lives are in motivating their writing and learning."

Contributions of Academic and Dialogic Journals to Writing about Literature

Susan Peck MacDonald
and Charles R. Cooper

Susan Peck MacDonald is assistant coordinator of the Dimensions of Culture Program at the University of California, San Diego.
My interest in writing in the disciplines grew from two sources. When I began writing for publication in literature, I experienced the novice's difficulties in moving from one discourse community to another or from one level to another. From my freshman writers—particularly the weakest—I discovered how hard it is to write well without a clear context. In coordinating a writing-in-the-disciplines program at the University of California, I observed the variety of textual practices between, and sometimes within, disciplines and became convinced that learning to write requires an understanding of the ways of knowing particular to an academic course.

Charles R. Cooper is coordinator of the Dimensions of Culture Program and a professor in the Department of Literature at the University of California, San Diego.
I'm interested in the contribution of writing to learning and in the possibilities for students to experience and understand, through writing, the ways of thinking and knowing in academic disciplines. In 1984, I organized a sophomore-level writing-in-the-disciplines program to complement the Third College Writing Program, our first-year course at the time. Our program, coordinated by Susan MacDonald, integrated writing into general education courses in the humanities and social sciences. We assigned journals and conducted several pilot studies to examine the relation between frequent writing and students' learning in their courses. Out of this work came the study we present in this essay.

During the 1980s, the rapid spread of writing-across-the-curriculum programs has resulted in courses embodying different assumptions about how "writing" may connect with "learning" (see, in this volume, Martin; Russell; Britton; and Bazerman; see also Anson, "Toward"). Yet these programs and courses have been accompanied by little empirical research that could shed light on how writing promotes learning in the varied contexts of our universities.[1]

Through research such as Judith A. Langer and Arthur N. Applebee's (*How Writing*), we know that different writing tasks have different consequences for learners. Langer and Applebee examined the effects of four kinds of high school writing tasks—taking notes, answering study questions, summarizing, and writing "analytic" essays—and found the tasks to have different effects. Work like theirs, and similar work by George E. Newell and by James D. Marshall, is important in revealing how much more we need to know before we can see the relation of any writing assignment—lab report, dialogic journal, study question, in-class or take-home essay exam, paper, research report—to learning in a particular course in a discipline. But we must go beyond such broadly defined categories as "analytic writing" if we are to understand how different kinds of writing tasks may affect writing and learning in the highly differentiated contexts that exist in higher education.

In evaluating the contribution a type of writing assignment makes toward learning, we must ask not how writing affects learning in general but what kind of learning a particular kind of writing promotes. Because of the complexity of interacting variables in any course (e.g., institutional setting, subject matter, purpose, discipline, and writing tasks), it is difficult to evaluate whether it is writing or some other variables that enhance learning. It is also hard to predict how a writing task may function in another context. We can, however, examine the way different writing tasks operate within the same context; through comparison, we may come closer to discovering what a given task has contributed.

In the research project described here, we constructed two kinds of journal writing assignments—dialogic and academic journals—so that we could explore whether different kinds of tasks have different effects. The two kinds of journals embody some of the competing assumptions to be found in writing-across-the-curriculum programs.

The *dialogic journal* requires students first to select what to comment on from a text and then to write reflectively on the initial comments. This kind of journal is modeled on a type frequently proposed by journal advocates. Ann E. Berthoff, for instance, proposes a double-entry "dialectical notebook" as "a way of making writing a mode of learning and a way of knowing, because its dialectical/dialogic form corresponds to the character of the inner dialogue which is thinking" (15). Berthoff sees the double-entry journal's virtue as arising from the "heuristic power of language itself"; she believes it fosters learning in that writers must "learn to look," identify ambiguities, keep things tentative, and acquire the habit of questioning (13–16).

Students' control over what they write about is a distinctive feature of the dialogic journal approach. Henry Steffens, for example, says of journal writing in history courses: "All too frequently, we insist that [students] write about questions which we set for them generated out of our own interests, in the context of our own understanding. Our questions are not the students' questions" (219).

By contrast, our *academic journal* assumes that the process of reflectivity and freedom to choose one's own topics for commentary may not help students learn to write in a course with unfamiliar subject matter and the need to meet a professor's expectations. The academic journal requires students to respond to questions and problems posed by their instructors and to make claims and offer evidence. The academic journal assignments we devised are much like "epistemic" sequences that develop a single theme, idea, or particular way of thinking and writing through frequent, carefully articulated assignments and "reach-back" assignments, in which students use previous writing to reflect on and consolidate learning (see Gibson; Coles; Dowst; Klaus and Jones). Our academic journal assignments also reflect the inquiry activities advocated by George Hillocks, Jr., who has demonstrated their effectiveness in comparison-group studies.

With these two different kinds of writing tasks—both analytical, both inviting reflection, both allowing informal language, both intended to promote learning—we were able to evaluate the results of writing in a specific disciplinary context. Our study compares three groups—two groups of journal-writing students and one group that did not keep a journal—in a course on Chinese literature in translation. In this particular context, the kind of writing the professor valued was what we term "claim-and-evidence" writing; it involves the making of claims and the support of these claims with evidence drawn from the texts under study. Our design allowed us to answer two questions: (1) Would students making frequent entries in journals in a Chinese literature course concerned with claim-and-evidence writing perform better on an end-of-course, three-hour claim-and-evidence essay than students not writing frequently? and (2) Would one kind of frequent writing produce results different from another on a three-hour essay in the same course?

Research Setting

The Course

One hundred forty-five students who were enrolled in a Chinese literature course met three times a week in a large lecture hall, as well as in
small section meetings averaging fifteen students. The lecturer in this
course, at the University of California, San Diego, was a Chinese
scholar in the Department of Literature, a professor with an international reputation whose work is informed by current literary theory
and particularly influenced by the new historicism. He welcomed our
study, allowed us to construct a three-hour essay exam that posed a
full rhetorical explanation of the task, and guided us about the central
issue of the course for the question to focus on.

During a ten-week quarter in the spring of 1988, students read three
stories from traditional China, seven from the Republican period
(1912–49), five from the People's Republic of China, and two from contemporary Taiwan. The sociohistoric context of these stories provided
the focus of the lectures twice a week, with films on Chinese history
and current events taking up the third lecture hour. In addition, students were assigned a scholarly article on Taiwan's economy and eleven
of the nineteen chapters of a history of modern China (Fairbank).

The lectures concerned the Confucian system, family structure, gender roles, the role of the storyteller in the traditional period, and literary
and political movements of twentieth-century China. The stories were
central to all lectures, with the focus, however, on the cultural background of each text. Closer analysis of the stories was left to teaching
assistants in section meetings. The literature in the course—despite its
spread over more than a thousand-year period—was highly cohesive,
as were the lectures. The role of women was a recurring motif, along
with family and class structure. The overriding theme of the course
was the tension between the individual and the collective throughout
Chinese literature and society. Students in all three comparison groups
wrote two assigned essays of about one thousand words and had opportunities to discuss their drafts with TAs before submitting revisions.
The first essay was on a traditional story and the second on a story from
the Republican period.

Students

At the time of our research, a Third College student entering as a
freshman took two quarters of freshman composition, then began a
"societal analysis" requirement, of which this Chinese literature course

was a part; two of the students' three societal analysis courses were taken in the writing adjunct section for six credits rather than four. The writing adjunct students spent two hours a week in sections, rather than the one hour a week of regular sections. In any particular course, some students were enrolled in regular sections and some in writing adjunct sections.

Six writing adjunct and four regular sections of the course were offered in the spring of 1988. Of the six writing adjunct sections (W sections), we designated three academic journal sections (A sections), and three dialogic journal sections (D sections). In registering for their sections, writing adjunct students knew nothing about our research or which TA would teach which section. One TA taught four W sections, with two A and two D groups, while the second TA taught two W sections, with one A and one D section.

The four regular sections represented the third group in the study. Students in these sections read all the same material, wrote the same two essays and journals on the weekly films, and were given the same final essay examination as those in the writing adjunct sections—though they did not write journals. All students (A, D, and no-journal, or N, students) had the opportunity to discuss drafts of the two assigned essays in a brief conference with their TAs. All four TAs were graduate students in comparative literature.

Table 1 summarizes the basic information about students in the three groups. There are five kinds of difference among the three groups: (1) class level, (2) amount of experience in writing adjunct sections, (3) amount of heterogeneity in verbal Scholastic Aptitude Test (VSAT) scores, (4) percent with VSAT scores below 450, and (5) percent taking the course for a letter grade. The A group had more lower-division students and more of them had already begun taking their writing adjunct courses. In the N sections, there were more upper-division students who had entered as transfers or before the writing adjunct requirement was instituted, in 1985. All groups, however, would have completed a freshman-level writing requirement at UCSD or elsewhere. The amount of previous experience with writing adjunct courses was highest among the A sections and lowest among the N sections, again because it was not a requirement for some students in N sections.

Standardized information in the form of VSAT scores was available only for the ninety-six students who had entered UCSD as freshmen; transfers' VSATs are not reported to UCSD and therefore were not available for forty-nine students. There was no statistically significant difference among the VSAT means of the three groups (respectively 499, 493, and 465). The standard deviation was lowest in the A group,

Table 1. Characteristics of Students in Three Sections of a Chinese Literature Course

	Academic journal groups (3 secs.)	Dialogic journal groups (3 secs.)	No-journal groups (4 secs.)
n	41	44	60
Freshmen (%)	17	23	25
Sophomores (%)	54	32	27
Juniors (%)	22	25	17
Seniors (%)	7	20	32
No writing sec. (%)	0	0	73
1st writing sec. (%)	54	66	17
2nd writing sec. (%)	46	32	8
VSAT	499 n = 30	493 n = 32	465 n = 34
% of VSAT scores below 450	26	37	41
% of students taking course for letter grade	56	64	73

indicating the most homogeneity in the A group, second most in the D group, and least in the N groups. The A group had the fewest students with VSATs below 450, the N group the most. All students had the opportunity to take the course for a grade or for pass/no pass credit. The A sections had the fewest students taking the course for a letter grade, and the N sections the most.

In summary, the A sections were the least experienced academically and most likely to take the course for pass/no pass credit rather than a letter grade—two traits of the A sections that might predict weaker performance—but they were also more likely to have had previous writing adjunct sections. The groups were otherwise roughly equivalent on the basis of VSAT scores and other variables.

The Academic Journals

The academic journal assignments were due twice a week in section meetings for a ten-week quarter. Assignments were developed by the principal investigator after consultation with the professor and the TAs and were devised to work directly or indirectly toward an understanding of the tensions between the individual and the collective, though particular journal questions did not necessarily address that issue explicitly. Journal assignments were constructed also to exercise different kinds of claim-making, thinking, and writing of four types: (1) bottom-up questions, asking students to form inductive generalizations based on concrete events or scenes in the stories; (2) top-down questions, offering a variety of generalizations, one of which students chose to support with evidence from a story; (3) synthetic questions, asking for generalizations tying together elements from more than one story; and (4) reflection on the process of writing claims and using evidence. Assignments required students to pay attention to particulars in a new way and to move up and down from concrete to abstract or vice versa. Here are examples from late in the academic journal sequence:

> Journal assignment 14. Before writing this journal entry on the story "The Execution of Mayor Yin," make sure you have read Fairbank's chapter on the Cultural Revolution. Then, as you did for entry 13, *annotate* "Mayor Yin" as you read it, looking particularly for concrete words, phrases, actions, etc., that describe Hsaio Wu. Next make a *list* of at least 15 such items, drawn from the beginning, middle, and end of the story. Then *inventory* the items you have listed, trying to see what is characteristic about the character's behavior and how his behavior changes (doesn't change?) over time in response to the events in the story (and in the Cultural Revolution). Finally, write a journal entry using the concrete details you have selected in order to construct a claim or claims about the young Red Guard's behavior and motivation during the Cultural Revolution; through a detailed examination of this particular character, Hsaio Wu, you will be able to see something more general about the Cultural Revolution, but tie your discussion very specifically to the story and Hsaio Wu.

Assignments 13, 14, and 15 asked for the same process of close reading (see Axelrod and Cooper for details of this traditional annotate-and-inventory close-reading strategy); question 16 asked for a synthesis built on the more inductive work done in 13, 14, and 15:

> Journal assignment 16. Look back at your last three journal entries (on "Return by Night," "The Execution of Mayor Yin," and "Keng Erh in Peking") as well as at "Chairman Mao Is a Rotten Egg." Write this journal entry on the stresses Communist China placed on the emotional and/or social life of the individual during

this period. (The author of "Return by Night" may approve of such limitations while Chen Jo-hsi is more disapproving, but you should still be able to make some claims that are relevant to individuals in all these stories.)

Thus the academic journal assignments imposed a continuity of discussion on students, encouraging continual reconsideration or modification of their interpretations of the stories in the light of later stories. They also required students to work at different levels of abstraction in different journal entries and to bring concrete evidence to bear on abstraction in a variety of ways.

The Dialogic Journals

The sections given dialogic journal assignments received, at the first section meeting, a three-page description of their journal work for the quarter. We defined *dialogic* for them as follows:

> *Dialogic* refers to discussion or dialogue for the purpose of examining ideas critically, an ancient but still essential activity of serious intellectual life in any academic field or profession.
> Your journal will be dialogic in two ways: (1) you engage in a dialogue with the book or with yourself as you read and, in the process, write in your journal, and (2) the material collected in your journal provides a starting point for dialogue or discussion with your instructor and with other students in your section.

We instructed students to use the facing pages of the notebook for "a dialogue about the events and ideas in the readings," on one side entering notes and comments while reading and, on the other, later writing reflections. We gave students suggestions for a wide range of dialogic writing: comparing a story with previous ones, connecting the story to major themes or ideas in the courses (especially those from the professor's lectures), examining the continuity or change in Chinese society as seen in the stories, relating the story to personal experience or reading. TAs coached students in ways to use the dialogic journal productively within the context of the course. They asked students to read journals aloud in class, urged them to speculate boldly, and probed them to be more explicit about why they found something worthy of comment or why their reflections took a particular direction. Though we intended the dialogic journal entries to be frequent and spontaneous, the TAs generally asked their dialogic sections to write an entry on each story, just as the academic groups were doing, and so the dialogic groups tended to write in their notebooks twice a week, with one entry per story.

In both A and D sections, TAs commented on students' journals and used them in class. TAs approached their A and D classes with similar agendas for discussion because otherwise they would have doubled their class preparation time. When they asked for journals to be read aloud, however, the discussion might take a different course in the A and D section. In the dialogic sections, for instance, a student might have picked out a small detail as interesting or puzzling, and the class discussion would proceed from that point. In the academic sections, discussion would take off from the starting point of the specific question posed in the journal assignment. TAs' written responses to the A and D journals were similar—brief marginal comments, brief assessments of the seriousness and quality of the work, and encouragement to persist.

Methods

Design and Analysis

From our earlier pilot studies in literature courses, we had learned the importance of an outcome measure (our final exam) that allowed extended time for planning and drafting. We also observed students' difficulties in using the full range of levels from concrete to abstract; consequently, we were particularly interested in seeing how writing tasks might affect students' ability to use that range. In designing our study, we drew upon Hillocks's work proposing acceptable design criteria for realistically situated comparison-group studies of writing pedagogy.

Because of a variety of institutional constraints, neither the population of students in the course nor the TAs could be randomly assigned to academic, dialogic, and no-journal groups; this study, therefore, claims only a quasi-experimental design. Policy for rotating TAs' assignments to writing adjunct sections prevented us from assigning TAs to both journal and no-journal sections. Two TAs did, however, teach both A and D sections.

Thomas D. Cook and Donald T. Campbell classify a study like ours as a nonequivalent control group design with a proxy pretest, our proxy being students' VSAT scores. We could not use an essay pretest to establish whether the three groups were comparable in writing abilities because, with our focus on a specific learning context, no pretest could establish students' abilities to write about Chinese literature before taking a course in that subject.

We collected three types of data: scores on a three-hour, end-of-course essay exam, observational notes on course and section meetings, and students' journals and other assigned writings. Essay-exam scores provide group comparisons. Observational notes—which we do not have space to discuss in this chapter—confirm whether our procedures were followed in all sections throughout the quarter and provide rich descriptions and interpretations of section meetings. Every writing adjunct section meeting throughout the quarter was observed by advanced graduate students with special interests in composition studies. Collections of students' writing provide material for case studies of individual students' development during the course, parts of which we present later in this report.

The Outcome Measure

Students in all groups wrote the scheduled three-hour final essay. In consultation with the professor, we devised the final-examination topic before the quarter began. The exam attempts to pose a full rhetorical situation and allows students to choose one story to focus on from each of the four sets of stories they read: from traditional China, the Republican period, Communist China, and modern Taiwan. Here is a central portion of the exam question:

> Your topic is the relation (or tension) between individualism and collectivism in the Chinese literature you have read for this course. You will be expected to make some claims about the relation between individualism and collectivism in each of the four groups of literature. . . . Your claims should reflect both a careful reading of individual works and an understanding of the changes over time—the ways in which the balance between individualism and collectivism may or may not change over the course of time in the four historical settings you have studied. You may find different or similar emphases in the different settings; a number of different claims will be valid so long as they take account of the complexity of the stories and their settings. In other words, you do not need to choose between individualism and collectivism, and you should avoid simplistic answers; you may find a blend of the two emphases in at least some of the settings, if not all.

The question suggests how the student might conceive of the reader—as someone who had read the stories and could be convinced that the student's claim was worth taking seriously if it was "convincingly documented with much specific evidence from the stories."

Measurements

We scored the essays separately for the following characteristics that we take to be important in claim-and-evidence literary essays like our end-of-course exam:

- *Quality of argument* we defined as making intelligent use of course material and devising a convincing, readable argument. This was the most holistic of our measures.
- *Sophistication of claim* we defined as the accuracy, assertiveness, complexity, clarity, and historical contextualization of the essay's initial claims.
- *Amount and quality of relevant evidence* from a story we defined as the extent of evidence that is concrete, accurate, and supportive of the claims asserted.

Since these were first-draft essays, and since we were analyzing students' learning, thinking, and composing, we ignored deviations from Standard (edited) English. We created two further scores from the three scores—an average score and a weighted score, in which the quality-of-argument score was weighted more than the other two. The average score was exploratory, to see what might result if we weighted our three scores equally to create an outcome measure less influenced by overall quality of argument and more influenced by the critical thinking and writing strategies we designed the academic journal assignments to teach: strong claims and telling evidence. The weighted score—emphasizing quality of argument—reflected what we assumed most instructors would value in an outcome measure for courses concerned with interpretive claims and textual evidence.

We arranged to have the three scoring sessions carried out separately on different days; we did so to diminish, if not preclude, the "halo effect" in holistic scorings guided by multifeature rubrics, in which a scorer's decision on one feature influences his or her responses on other features. After a training period with sample essays, each scorer rated every essay on a 1–6 scale. With two scores for each essay, an essay might have a total score of from 2 to 12. Scorer agreement, within 1 point on the 6-point scale, was 91% for quality of argument, 85% for sophistication of claim, and 82% for quality of relevant evidence. Scores more than 1 point apart were resolved through independent

Table 2. Mean Scores on Final-Exam Essay in a Chinese Literature Course

	Academic journal	Dialogic journal	No-journal
n	41	45	60
Quality of argument	7.244**	6.636	6.407
Sophistication of claim	6.951***	5.943	6.627
Quality of relevant evidence	6.890	6.444	6.500
Three-score average	7.025****	6.361	6.509
Three-score weighted average	7.083**	6.415	6.485

Note: All significance levels are based on the Wilcoxon Rank Sum Test. There are no significant differences between means of dialogic and no-journal groups.

    * < .10, academic vs. dialogic
    ** < .10, academic vs. no journal
    *** < .05, academic vs. dialogic
    **** < .01, academic vs. dialogic

scorings by the two investigators. Essays were not identified by writer's name or section.

Results

Our main findings are presented in table 2. Results were analyzed for statistical significance with the Mann-Whitney Test (sometimes called the Wilcoxon Rank Sum Test), a nonparametric statistical measure that does not assume that scores are normally distributed (Rice). Given our scoring criteria and procedures, the academic journal sections outperformed the dialogic journal and no-journal sections on all essay scores, with most score differences being statistically significant—that is, highly unlikely to have occurred by chance.

Beginning with score differences with the highest significance levels, we note that the A group performed better than the D group on the average score ($p < .01$) and on the sophistication-of-claim score ($p < .05$). The A group also outperformed the D group on the weighted score (p < .10) and on the quality-of-argument score (p < .10). While levels of p < .05 or .01 have traditionally been used to establish statistical significance, some composition researchers have argued that because of the complexity of assessing writing and the relative recency of work in the field, probability levels of p < .10 or even higher might be reported and considered suggestive, if not conclusive (see Daly and Hexamer; Lauer and Asher 96–98, 162). The A group scored higher than the N group on all measurements, with the difference on two scores—quality of argument and average score—significant at the p < .10 level. There were no statistically significant differences between the D and N groups, even though, on all but the quality-of-argument measurement, the N group actually scored higher than the D group.

We carried out several secondary analyses, including a number of correlations with VSAT scores. We report select secondary results here only briefly.[2]

1. Differences in final-exam essay scores earned by men and by women and by lower- and by upper-division students were not statistically significant.

2. Neither of the TAs who taught both A and D sections contributed disproportionately to their students' achievement: the higher scores in the A group cannot be explained by the outstanding teaching of one TA.

3. VSAT score differences among the A, D, and N groups were not statistically significant, yet, predictably, VSAT scores were highly correlated with final-exam essay scores. VSAT and essay scores were not as highly correlated in the A group, however, as in the D and N groups. For example, VSAT correlations with weighted scores were (1) .142 in the A group, (2) .437 in the D group, and (3) .394 in the N group.

4. Differences in essay scores of students taking the course for a grade or pass/no pass were statistically significant, with mean scores being lower for students taking it pass/no pass (for example, on quality of argument, 7.20 for a letter grade and 5.69 for pass/no pass). Since the A group had the highest percentage of students taking the course pass/no pass (see table 1), we might have expected these students as a group to be less motivated to do well.

The superior scores of the A groups, in sum, are not attributable to TA, class, or gender variables; scores of the A groups were much less easy to predict from students' VSAT scores, with students with low VSAT scores performing better than expected; and while the grade versus pass/no pass option is a statistically significant result, the A groups did proportionately better than the D and N groups in both credit and pass/no pass groups. All these secondary results point to the fact that the academic journal assignments made a specific contribution to achievement, as defined by this particular pedagogical context.

Discussion

The results suggest that the A group's directed and cumulative journal writing on subaspects of the issue of the individual versus the collective resulted in better overall arguments as well as more sophisticated claims. The dialogic group's inferior performance on those criteria seems to suggest that left to their own devices, students may not articulate the same issues as their professors, may express them in slightly different terms, or may remain at a lower level of abstraction than if they receive help in formulating and working with abstractions.

There appear to be four ways in which students in the A groups benefited from their academic journal assignments: they were (1) less likely to rely on plot summary, (2) less likely to remain at lower levels of abstraction, (3) more likely to discuss central issues identified by the professor in their journals, and (4) less likely to rely on simple dichotomies and more likely to discuss complexities and ironies. For instance, a point that emerges clearly from the professor's lectures is that the Confucian system required the individual's subordination to the collective but that the nature of the collective in China has changed over time. That is, in the Confucian system the family unit is the collective that may oppress the individual. It may also, of course, aid in self-aggrandizement for the family as a unit, with benefits flowing to some or all individual family members. In the Communist period, the state becomes the collective to which either individual or family should be subordinate.

In a discussion of "Return by Night" (1954), one student's dialogic journal entry consists of a half page of factual statements and the following comment: "All I get is that this story is kind of a brain wash telling you you'll be liked and go far if you work hard and are above reproach. Sounds like something in the novel *1984*." This student's three scores on the essay exam were below average (7, 4, and 6). On the essay exam, his comments on "Return by Night" rely on simple dichotomies: he describes the Chinese in this period as considering "any form of individualism . . . extremely forbidden. . . . Everything was for the good of the party and the good of different kinds of groups. In 'Return by Night' there is a kind of feverish desire to contribute to the party, and the conflicts within the characters arise from letting down the group." The student has assumed that individualism and collectivism are opposed in simple ways, that the explicit avowal of the one means that the other cannot be present.

We see other instances of oversimplification in a dialogic student's comments on Confucianism in the traditional narrative "Tu Shih-niang Sinks the Jewel Box in Anger." He relies on broad statements: "During the imperial rule an individualistic attitude swept the countryside" and "Toward the turn of the twentieth century this individualism has changed and shifted to a collective state of mind. No longer were people worried of their own stature and social graces, but everybody's well-being and prosperity." Not only has he equated Confucianism with individualism, but he has assumed that such ideologies sweep in and out of power, without internal contradictions or inconsistencies and without remnants from previous historical periods. He ignores the complexities in the story: that the young man first asserts himself against the family ideals and then sacrifices the woman he loves when he belatedly accepts his father's authority. The student often uses generalizations ("the individualism brought about by Confucianism is very apparent") and takes no account of contradiction or irony ("Also, women during this time were treated more like objects than people").

By contrast, a student in the A group with VSAT scores comparable to those of the D group student shows greater facility with complex generalizations about individualism and collectivism. In response to a journal assignment to support one of three competing generalizations about the story "Hsaio-hsiao," he explores the social and economic dynamics of the Confucian system rather than rely on flat, either/or assertions:

> First of all, the most important consideration for the rural peasants was economics. They needed labor, hence the "child bride." Logically speaking, the child bride makes sense in that more labor is obtained for the family-in-law. This concept may be hard on the bride, but it is better for all, considering the work that peasant families must do. Also during the scandal of Hsaio-hsiao's pregnancy, the family thought she should be drowned or sold. But when she birthed a son, "Hsaio-hsiao didn't have to be married off after all" (235). This was because the family needed the labor of another male. Economic necessities sometimes overruled the orthodox social customs that persecuted certain individuals, as in Hsaio-hsiao's case.

The sustained reasoning the student shows here is part of what we believe most teachers expect of intellectual work in the academy. It is worth noting that the student also shows here a "voice," a willingness to take a strong stand in writing. For its combination of historical complexity (and accuracy) and assertiveness without oversimplification, the entry is a good example of sophistication of claim in our scoring.

And on the final essay, this student received a score of 10 on sophistication of claim, along with scores of 11 on quality of argument and 6 on amount and quality of relevant evidence. His essay exam again shows an inclination to discuss complexity that is missing from the D examples we cite above. In discussing Lu Hsun's "New Year's Sacrifice," for instance, he shows how individualism and collectivism may coexist and complicate each other. The forlorn widow of the story "makes an individualistic gesture in running away from her mother-in-law," but she at the same time internalizes the superstitions of her society, and, "believing the things said about her, she becomes miserable."

In the work of another pair of comparable students, we see how academic journal writing may lead to refinement of abstractions. Both students might be described as below average for UCSD students, with VSATs in the mid-400s and GPAs of C or C +. On the final essay exam, the student in the academic journal group received above-average rankings of 10 and 7 on the quality-of-argument and amount-and-quality-of-relevant-evidence scores, along with a score of 5 on sophistication of claim. During the quarter, this student wrote approximately thirty-five handwritten pages of journal entries that carefully responded to the nineteen journal assignments. In entry 13, she sees the feminist, socialist heroine of "Return by Night" as demanding "respect not only as a woman but as an equal partner or comrade." When the following stories complicated the picture in demonstrating disillusionment about the Cultural Revolution, her journals begin to comment on some of the complexity. By entry 17—a retrospective journal question—she comments more on the ironies involved:

> Perhaps Lu Hsun would be very satisfied with the progress taking place by men and women and their ability to break away from traditional roles, but at the same time the role of the woman in "Return by Night" is questionable. She still belongs to a mass movement following one belief. Lu Hsun would've been greatly upset over this, since he wrote in order to fight against this type of thing. . . . We witness a situation where even the nuclear family is put under tremendous pressure because of a collective belief.

Journal entries 13–17, which approached an issue recurring in different stories, led the student to a more complex sense of ways the stories can be analyzed and the social issues reflected in the literature of the period. Though she does not at first explore the abstract issues or use the abstract terms the professor used, she comes to do so through repeated opportunities to address the issue.

The second student was in a dialogic section. He appeared to take his journal writing seriously, annotating the stories copiously and writing approximately fifty-eight pages of notes and commentary. His dialogic journal entry on "Return by Night" demonstrates that he understood some important historical issues in the story, but he misconstrues the story in writing that it "criticizes the socialist/Communist division of labor and labor unions." And his comments tend to be particularistic: "[The male protagonist] works in the city, with machines, technology and in an enclosed modern facility. She [the heroine], on the other hand, works in the country, with her hands, with animals, out in the open air, and without the modern-day conveniences." From this observation, the student moves to a low-level generalization about the characters' motivation but does not proceed, like the academic journal student, to construct larger generalizations about the role of the individual in Communist China: "Yes, they were comrades and brothers, but their job difference caused a bit of resentment on the part of the girl. . . . Her dream wasn't to work in a factory, her dream was to modernize the farm labor systems. She wanted tractors instead of plows, instead of horses, and instead of carts."

These representative journal entries demonstrate an important difference between academic and dialogic groups. The dialogic student tends to bring up more issues, without pursuing or refining them, and so does not progress from particulars and low-level generalizations to the overarching issue of the relation between the individual and the collective. The academic student brings concrete particulars from the text to bear on abstractions and has a stronger sense of which particulars support which kinds of abstract claims.

Our study suggests possibilities for future research and raises questions about several frequently held views in the field of composition. The first is that empirical research may be an unsuitable vehicle for studying writing in complex social contexts. We think our research demonstrates that empirical methods can be helpful in focusing on context variables and exploring how different writing tasks may match different academic expectations. The apparent differences in our journal groups' facility in moving up and down the ladder of abstraction as they write, for instance, deserves further research.

Second, our research suggests that we cannot assume students will learn to write in ways that they do not practice. If the dialogic journal students had heard about concepts in lectures, written without constraint about their insights in journals, and then performed in the same way as the academic journal students on the end-of-term essay, we could argue that students will master the range of abstraction in the claim-and-evidence essay no matter what sort of writing tasks they are given. Since the dialogic journal students did not perform in the same way as the academic journal students, however, we have to assume that students were more likely to be successful if they frequently wrote about the particular concepts of the course and employed the full range of concrete and abstract terms used in claim-and-evidence essays.

In our study, undirected journal writing was less likely to ensure that students would identify and grapple with the tension between the individual and the collective. If we grant that students have some stake in being able to see things as their professors see them, our research suggests that, left to their own devices, students may fail to perceive the issues, perceive them in ways different from their professors, or remain at too low a level of abstraction. Since the effective claim-and-evidence essay depends on the use of a full range of both abstract and concrete, frequent practice with that range also appears necessary. The only measure in our study on which the dialogic sections performed as well as the academic sections was the amount and quality of relevant evidence—apparently because the dialogic journal helped students use concrete examples more than it helped them construct and manipulate concepts.

The issue of practice should not be confused with that of engagement. Engagement is crucial for learning, and merely sitting in a lecture room is not an effective form of learning; but we do not assume that engagement consists only in being able to choose what to write on. It can come, as well, from writing in response to an intellectually challenging question posed by a teacher.

The possibility that students will not practice refining abstractions without explicit prompting has important consequences for teachers' assumptions about their students' abilities. It is often assumed that students who do not write well lack ability or have arrived at the university insufficiently prepared; such assumptions can lead instructors to expect less of some students or to water down courses for those students. But such assumptions place too much importance on what students bring with them to the university and not enough on what they are required to practice doing there. With regular practice at claim-and-essay writing, students with low VSAT scores in our academic journal group performed better on the end-of-course essay than did students with comparable scores in the other treatment group. This finding suggests that students—all students—will profit from careful, regular writing practice appropriate to the learning objectives of a particular course.

If it is important for student writers to alternate between complex abstractions and concrete evidence, as in the course we studied, then teachers should not simply require frequent writing and assume that students will grasp the range of levels of appropriate evidence and abstractions on their own. Our study suggests, moreover, that it is not enough just to assign claim-and-evidence essays. All three groups in our study wrote two essays in the course, and neither the dialogic journal writers nor the no-journal students performed as well on the outcome essay as the academic journal writers. To teach students both to construct sophisticated claims and to give concrete textual evidence in support of those claims, writing tasks like those in our academic journals should focus students' attention on the act of claim construction, the conceptual complexities of particular claims, the ambiguity of concrete details, and the importance of the concrete.

NOTES

[1] We would like to thank a number of people: William Tay for his advice and his willingness to let his final exam be shaped by our research; Sudhir Venkatesh for his help as statistical consultant; Robert Cancel for allowing us to carry out an earlier pilot study in a literature course; the graduate students who allowed us to visit their classrooms; and those who observed classes and scored essays. We also thank the University of California, San Diego, for an undergraduate instructional improvement grant, without which this research might have been impossible.

[2] Readers may write either investigator for further details.

Writing and Learning American Literature

Toby Fulwiler

The author is professor of English and director of the writing program at the University of Vermont.

In addition to directing the writing program, I teach courses in writing and American literature as well as conduct writing workshops for faculty members in all disciplines. My books include College Writing, Teaching with Writing, *and* The Journal Book. *I am presently working on two collaborative book projects, seeking with professional colleagues the same sense of community I seek with students in writing classes.*

In the spring of 1988, I taught a survey course in American literature to a class of thirty-two general education students at the University of Vermont. I taught this literature class as I teach my writing classes, workshop style, with frequent writing assignments, both formal and informal, and daily peer discussion groups. The case study that follows tells the story of this class through student papers, evaluations, and journal entries; my own journal entries (edited for clarity); remembered fragments of classroom dialogue; and more recent reflections on the whole experience.

December 19, 1987

The problem: to create in next semester's literature class the same sense of community that I find in writing classes. It's the writing that makes the difference, writing taught workshop style, with people sharing ideas and drafts and actually writing *to* each other—as well as for me. But English 24 is introductory American lit, second semester, for people *not* majoring in English. So even if English 24 is aimed at first- and second-year students, it will include juniors and seniors taking late electives. Which also means that motivation may be a problem. No matter why they're enrolled in my section, however, I want to make reading and writing more fun for them. That's really my objective here, not training young literary critics, but making the study of literature both serious and exciting at the same time.

December 20

This morning I woke up thinking about a framework for the writing in English 24. Britton's function categories would serve us well: *expressive* writing daily, to encourage the students to explore personally and react to the readings; *transactional* writing, to shape some of their explorations and reactions into careful and critical published (for me and the class) pieces; and *poetic* writing, to place them in the role of the authors they study in order to diminish their distance from those authors as well as exercise their own creative juices (Britton, Burgess, Martin, McLeod, and Rosen). At the same time, I want to make collaborative learning (Bruffee, "Collaborative") a regular part of what we do, so that people get used to sharing with each other as well as with me. Informal talk, after all, is a powerful mediator between old experience and new. Tomorrow I write my syllabus.

December 21

American Literature since 1865: A Syllabus

Assigned readings
- *The Adventures of Huckleberry Finn*, by Mark Twain
- *In Our Time*, by Ernest Hemingway
- *Black Boy*, by Richard Wright
- *Go Down Moses*, by William Faulkner
- *Slouching Towards Bethlehem*, by Joan Didion
- *The Color Purple*, by Alice Walker
- *The Voice That Is Great Within Us*, by Hayden Carruth

Assigned writings
   Dialogue journal: You will be asked to keep a looseleaf notebook to respond to course readings, reflect on class discussions, and develop personal and analytic insights about the authors, works, and problems in the course. These dialogue journals will be written in part for yourself and in part as open letters to me and your classmates. You will, however, share only those parts of this notebook that you choose to share; I will ask you to hand in selected (by you) entries three times during the course for me to peruse and respond to. [20% of grade]
   Essays: You will be asked to write three two-page essays during this term [40% of grade]:

1. A critical essay focusing sharply and objectively on one specific problem in one literary work.
2. An essay reflecting your personal experience with one or more readings in the course.
3. An imaginative essay in a fictive, poetic, or dramatic mode, focusing on a particular author, work, or problem in the course.

Literature discussion group

Each essay will be shared first with members of your literature discussion group—four to five classmates with whom you will meet periodically throughout the term (both in class and out) to discuss literary problems. At each meeting you will be responsible for distributing copies of your essay to the other group members. [20% of grade]

Final examination

Your literature discussion group will meet outside of class and collaboratively write a take-home examination in response to a significant question posed by your group. Divide your labors equitably and be sure to include references from your dialogue journals and your two-page papers in this final essay (limit: ten pages total). [20% of grade]

January 26, 1988 (First Day of Class)

11:00 a.m. I like to start fast, so I've passed out three-hole-punch journal paper (7″ × 10″) to all thirty-two students and asked them to freewrite for five minutes on the question "What do you know about reading and writing?" I'd better write along with them.
Diane and Joan read theirs aloud to the rest of us:

> I have learned that there are a lot of things to look for when reading. For example—Who is narrating? Does the narrator change? the author's style? Point of view from which story is told, literary techniques (metaphors, exaggeration . . .). When I read, however, I don't always like to look for these things. I just like to read for the sake of reading. I don't like to read into stories as much as some of my former professors have.

> Writing, Writing, Writing! Umm, I *love* it but I'm told that I'm not allowed to use the verb "to be." I've been told *never* to use *never* and never use *always!* Write with *description.* *Action* verbs are best.

> I love reading books—I have read such works as *Huck Finn*, *Moby Dick*, basically all the classics and more. One of my

favorite books was *All the King's Men* by Robert Penn Warren. I get a kick out of analyzing literature, but I have a difficult time putting my thoughts on paper, such as an essay.

Reading a "good" book will bring me *feeling* and vivid descriptions and also helps obtain a philosophy of life (like Mark Twain's). I always (I should never use that word) say if I could have 2 hrs. to chat with any two people it would be Twain and Robert Penn Warren.

January 28

11:00 a.m. "We'll form permanent groups of five or six each today, so sit where and with whom you'd like. Next class, when you arrive, circle your chairs in that same small group and we'll operate out of that formation, six small groups, most of the time."

11:05 a.m. I think my students are curious about sitting in small clusters as the normal classroom structure. I'm trying it, at least in part, as a guarantee against my own talking too much; if I want to lecture, I'll actually have to ask half the class to turn their chairs around. Right now students are sharing last night's journal reactions about reading *Huck Finn.*

> Wow! This book is really great. It is not too hard to read and it is really fun to read. Huck has seen his father and has been dragged across the river to a cabin and been locked up. He was incredibly ingenious when it came to getting away and killing the wild hog so as to make it look like someone killed him. Too bad it was Jim that everyone thought was the killer. Huck and Jim are now on the island and are hiding out. Goodnight.

February 2

Students so far seem to like starting each period with five minutes of writing. At least everyone seems to be doing it—most quite vigorously, in fact. They are supposed to have read the first few chapters of *Huck Finn* for today's class, so I've asked them to write on the question "What do you look for when you read a novel?" My own answer focuses on credibility, surprise, and insight—but so, I bet, will theirs. I ask for oral responses based on their journal entries and write these on a transparency, omitting none. Then, as a class, we identify places in *Huck Finn* where we find pictures in our minds, and so forth. Students talk readily, pleased to be framing our discussion in their own terms.

What do you look for when *you* read a novel?

Pictures in my mind ....The river, raft, people
Keeps my interest
Reputation of the book.............."A classic," Mark Twain
Action
Creating language, dialogue ....Huck's speech
Story
Good characters, believable ....Both Huck and Jim (not Tom)
Suspense
Situation I can identify with
Character I identify with ....Huck's perceptions—honest
Easy reading
A larger message
Makes me think
Makes me feel
Makes me laugh

Jason volunteered to read his whole entry out loud:

When I read a novel I look for . . .
I guess I look for a sequence of events or a plot. I try as best I can to follow what is happening in the novel. I don't look for description.
I get bored when an author spends paragraphs or sometimes pages describing something. I like action. I like to be left hanging at the end of each chapter. I like to wonder what's going to happen next. If a book/novel is really boring, I look to see how many pages are left. If a book/novel is *really* boring, I look to see if there are any pictures. If a professor tells me to look for something specific, i.e., point of view, narrator, *then* I'll look for it. I'm not too good at picking up those things on my own.

It's funny that Jason wrote about not being "too good at picking up those things on my own," since, when I read his journal a few weeks later, I found this entry in which he picks out good things:

Huck is, obviously, the narrator of *Huckleberry Finn*. I noticed for the first time tonight that he makes a comment to the readers as if he was actually talking to us (I don't know what one calls this). At one point he tells the reader to *read*

on in order to see what further bad luck the rattlesnake
brings Huck & Jim.

February 15

11:05 a.m. This morning I've asked everyone to define poetry to themselves in their journals. After sharing entries in small groups, I ask each
group to give me one idea they talked about; we go around several
times, as each group had quite different definitions. I write their responses on a transparency, and we circle those definitions we think
most useful to our upcoming discussion of Robert Frost. Again, what's
important here is acknowledging the validity of their own perceptions—then pushing them a little further.

How would *you* define poetry?

Deep meaning
Tells a story
Lots of description
Word pictures
Condensed use of language
Feelings on paper
Words in pattern
Rhythm, certain repeated sounds
Means different things to different people
Ambiguous meaning
Freedom with words
Can be read in one sitting
Lines are fixed
Patterns on a page
Verbal art

---

*When I read Chris's entry about Frost's "Mowing," which I did not
actually see until a few weeks after he wrote it, I knew that he knew what
Frost was up to.*

"Mowing"

When I first read the poems by Robert Frost, I thought I
was in for a very boring unit of poetry because nothing made
sense and it was a bunch of words. I remembered that you
said it was important to read it over again, and when I did
that, I was able to see more color and hear more sound. This
was the case, reading "Mowing." By reading all the poems

about three times at different times, I was really able to
understand. If you have ever used a scythe before, you would
be able to get a better understanding and a true feel for this
poem. I think the key word here is the word *whispering.*

*I especially enjoyed watching him move from his own experience (Chris
must have used a scythe himself sometime) into the concrete language
of the poem* (whispering*). Chris is interesting—a business major who
refuses to take poetry lightly.*

February 23

A lot of questions in class yesterday about the first paper, which they
read to each other in groups. I sat outside of the groups the whole
time, at my desk, reading, writing—and listening as best I could. I'm
concerned about how fast and (I'm afraid) superficially some groups
talked about their classmates' papers. From the outset I've been anxious
about the critical paper, which maybe should have been assigned second. Students left class with critiques of their first drafts; their final
drafts—revised—are due to me next Tuesday.

March 1

A week later, the night before the second-draft (final) papers are due
to me, Brian writes:

> February 27 12:55 A.M.
>
> Finally, the paper is all done, final word processing and all.
> Wow, what a project—two rough drafts and a *major hassle*
> with the printer.
> I really didn't realize how deep "Mending Wall" was until I
> started to write on it. I kept questioning every sentence I
> wrote as a possible misinterpretation. Then I kept rereading
> and reanalyzing—totally screwing myself up. Yet I think I did
> a good job on it. Should be A— material.

March 3

8:15 A.M. I was right. The papers are really pretty bad—in terms of
both analysis and care in presentation. Paper after paper showed only
the most minor changes, with students apparently praising each other's
work and not offering the kind of critical help I'd hoped for.

11:00 A.M. "Before I hand your papers back, let me show you some
of the first paragraphs I read. I want to show you what I probably

would have said had I been in your groups last week. And it actually boils down to some very basic things: making careful assertions and providing evidence to support them. It's the kind of reasoning and writing that really goes on in every discipline in this university; this one happens to be English, but it, too, demands, at least in critical papers, careful assertion and convincing evidence."

On the overhead projector, I show eight first paragraphs from eight different papers. I do so anonymously, to diffuse the obvious ill feelings that result when one's work is criticized in public. I point out in sentence after sentence where I (or, as I also say, other educated lay readers) would ask questions and want more information or evidence to be convinced. I also point out how one provides evidence in literary studies, by quoting carefully and selectively from the texts under study. I do not want to turn these students into little literary critics (I say to myself, over and over again), but I do want them to learn how to read with a critical consciousness.

I clearly made a mistake here. I should have used a portfolio system and commented on but not graded these drafts. Now they want to rewrite (which I encourage) because they are afraid of low grades, which for these students is anything below a B +. I'd rather they wanted to rewrite because they really want to learn more or write better.

March 3

Chris, commenting in his journal, in class, after receiving my comment on his analytical paper:

> Wow! You killed me. Well, actually I know I killed myself. I did work hard on the paper and I *do* think it deserves a better grade than what I received. When we met to discuss our papers, everyone thought the paper was good and there were no comments to help the editorial content of the paper. I would be more than willing to do the paper over again if it could improve my grade. I need a better grade.

March 4

Chris, commenting further, the next day, about my comment on his analytical paper:

> I have thought a great deal about my paper and the grade that I received and I do think it was fair. It was just hard to take at first because I normally do not receive grades that low on a final paper. I am happy you are giving us the

opportunity to redo the paper because I know now what I can
change and make better. As you said, I did present some
points and ideas in my paper but I did not back them up with
facts. I know now that it is important to concentrate on one
author but I feel that the work of Frost and Hemingway is
similar in the way that they both are against change. When I
sat down to write my first draft of my paper, everything
seemed so clear. Oh, well, I realize that I have an ability and I
know now it is the time to challenge myself.

March 8

11:00 a.m. "So what are we going to do to make the groups more
critical in a helpful, not destructive, way?"

I write this question on the board to start a discussion I should have
had last class but did not have time for. If the groups were *not* helpful
the first time, what guidelines could we create to make them better the
next time? First, journal writing; then small-group talk; then groups
report out.

*The resultant list is first-rate. Many students remembered what went
wrong in their own groups as well as advice from group work in the past.
I copy their suggestions on a transparency, take them home to type, edit,
and add examples. Of the ten guidelines on the final list, two (2 and 7)
were suggested by me, eight by the groups in class. Even though it cost
forty minutes of class time, I am pleased. It's a good list and it's their list.*

Guidelines for Responding to Writers in Writing Groups

1. Listen critically and courteously to each reader and speaker.
2. Ask for the kind of response you want on this particular piece
   of writing.
3. Try to give the author the kind of response that he or she asks
   for.
4. Tell the writer what he or she is doing right. Be positive.
5. Be honest about problems you see.
6. Can you raise questions rather than give commands?
7. Respect and listen for the author's intention.
8. Comment on a few important things rather than everything.
9. Comment on the larger issues (purpose, theme, content, argument) first, the smaller stuff (punctuation, spelling, grammar, documentation) later.
10. Budget time carefully so each writer gets a fair share.

March 10

Chris, writing in his journal three times during the course of an evening's reading of William Carlos Williams and Cummings:

March 7   9:00 P.M.

   I hate William Carlos Williams and E. E. Cummings. I mean, what the hell are they talking about? Frost was not that bad because one was able to at least grasp some kind of an idea of what was going on. It took two or three readings of Frost to understand what was happening, but with my inability to comprehend what is going on, I may be here all night trying to understand what the poems mean. Maybe they are not supposed to mean anything at all. I also do not feel like writing right now because I have so much work to do this week and I also have two exams I have to do very well on, or else.

March 7   9:30 P.M.

   This guy is on drugs. I was thinking earlier about how I would love to understand the poems of Cummings. Now after reading them over once again, I am kind of happy I do not understand them because now I still feel that I am somewhat normal. I seriously think this guy had gone crazy when he was in a prison in France. His images are so spontaneous and off the wall. It seems that he thinks in a different mode. I think to understand Cummings, in my opinion, one has to think in the same mode as him, and I am happy that I do not, because I know I am not that deranged. I know I am the worst speller in the world but I really do not understand or like how Cummings uses words like: "onetwothreefourfive" in the poem "Buffalo Bill's" or "mYve RylitTle", in the poem "I will Be." Even though Cummings gets me mad, I still, in a way, wish I could understand his work. I think if Curt Voughyut (sp) wrote poetry, he would be a great deal like Cummings.

March 7   10 P.M.

   I think there is light at the end of the tunnel for me in terms of my comprehension of poetry. After reading the first two poems, I thought I was in real trouble. The third poem by Williams that I read, "Between Walls," was hard to

understand. Then I read it differently. I did not pause after
the lines. I read it straight through and I understood it very
clearly. I understood the image but I am still not sure of the
meaning. I think that both Cummings and Williams had
something that they had to release within their soul. They
both had something that burned inside and they needed to
vent this frustration.

*Of course, I didn't see these personal entries until a few weeks later,
but their spirit permeated class discussions of Williams and Cummings.
At first, as you might guess, twentieth-century poetry jarred them profoundly. Later, when they caught on—which they did both in their group
discussions and with some prodding, kidding, philosophizing by me—
most of them felt let in on a secret code and liked what they found. In
retrospect, Chris's particular journey from befuddlement to insight proved
more typical than not. I'd call this writing-to-learn in the best sense.*

March 15

11:00 a.m. "Would you please write an evaluation of the class so far,
commenting on the readings, the groups, the papers, whatever. Do
these frankly and anonymously, as I would like to collect these. Thank
you. Five minutes."

In spite of the poor critical papers and the arguments about poetry,
all my instincts tell me these students are thriving.

Here are some selected midterm responses to class:

How is class going for you? I love being in groups. It seems
like so much more gets done, and I always leave class with
different ideas and ways of looking at different literary works,
and I get these thoughts and ideas from being in the group
and hearing what other people think.

The classroom discussions are good because everyone can
voice his or her own opinion or argument on a subject. Then
you can see some of the things that other people pick up that
you miss.

I've learned to think. I haven't had to think in the longest
time. Since 11th grade actually. We did journal writing there
too. It's a good way to get the thoughts and wondering down
on paper so it's not lost. I hate a class where you sponge and

parrot, sponge and parrot. What's the point, it makes me feel like a bulimic.

I think I've learned more questions to ask to get myself thinking and I've also learned to relax when I'm writing in my journal. I think I've learned to read for enjoyment and analyze later—there's no need to dig for things that aren't there. Just read it and think about it later—that seems to be your attitude anyway—I like it!

March 29

11:00 a.m. "What has Faulkner taught you?"
Here is Bob's response:

Well, more than anything, Faulkner has taught me that I do not understand literature—that I am still very much a beginner reader. To this point he has taught me that life is too short to read books that are unenjoyable. He's taught me how much I dislike detail. He's taught me that I like to read for enjoyment & not to be tortured.

He's showed me a very intertwined life style—the effects of black and white, etc.

I can't think of anything, to be honest with you—Oh—he's taught me to watch out for flashbacks.

He's taught me not to read in bed because I will fall asleep immediately.

He's taught me that this is not a book one reads when 50 other assignments are due.

He shows true sides of people and little incidents that happen w/in small towns and areas that otherwise may not happen (in other novels, that is).

I really get burned on Faulkner. I was sure that I could repeat my success with modern poets with Faulkner's modern prose. But *Go Down Moses* didn't sell. I even gave it the better part of three weeks, the longest of any work in the semester, but I never could shake—in the majority of the class—the resistance to his difficult language surface. At one point, early last week, I even bet (metaphorically) that he'd become their favorite writer, but I won with only three or four students.

April 5

We're reading Black Boy *now. I find one of my seniors, who signed up for the class as a late required elective, writing this:*

> In my Poli Sci 289 class today we were discussing welfare—
> whether it is to provide or to change those on welfare, their
> attitudes. It became a pretty hot discussion. There were a few
> in the class who couldn't understand that there were those
> socialized into welfare—that the belief that someone can get a
> job if he wants it is always true. They believe that a person
> can get as far as they want in society if they are motivated. I
> believe that a motivated person can get as far as society *lets*
> them. I feel society can lock one into a life of welfare. I
> wanted to ask if anyone in the class had read *Black Boy*,
> because the story shows Richard's lack of options from his
> perspective. The blacks of the Jim Crow South were locked
> into their suppressed society—with the exception of a rare
> few—Richard Wright for one. Maybe if they had read the book,
> they wouldn't blame the victim but society.

April 7

We had just finished discussing Black Boy *when many of UVM's minority students staged a two-week sit-in in the chancellor's office, located one floor beneath where our class met and which most of us passed to get to class.*

11:05 a.m. "What are your reactions to the sit-in at the chancellor's office downstairs?" Here is one student's response to my question:

> I come from the whitest state in the union. You want me to
> tell you about racism? Well, quite frankly—I've only really
> read of racism. We have only 40 or so blacks here at UVM, my
> high school had fewer, and, as I said, I live in the whitest
> state. You might think that I hate blacks. You may think that
> I'm hiding or running from them. Actually, that's quite
> contrary. At this time in the presidential election—I'd vote
> for a black man. I knew every black kid in my high school. I
> love to listen to black music and I love to watch blacks play
> basketball. Many great athletes are black. I play soccer with
> blacks. I would love to be more educated, cultured, and

surrounded by more blacks in our society. Pour 'em in, I'd love
it. Racism isn't a problem in my life. If it's in our university, I
don't see it because I don't believe in it. I truly believe that
everyone was created equal. MLK says, "Free at last, free at
last, thank God almighty I'm free at last." I hope that
happens in the feelings of these blacks.

11:15 a.m.
Excerpts from class discussion:
"I think it's stupid. They're just trying to call attention to themselves."
"But isn't that actually their intention? To argue with this administra-
tion that minorities should make up more than a mere 2% of UVM's
student body of 11,000?"
"Yeah, I guess, but I've been here two years, lived in two dorms and
a frat house, and I'm telling you this is not a racist campus. I've never
heard anybody make an issue about race here."
"The only minority faculty members are foreign-born. The only mi-
nority group in the state is French Canadian."
"Why would they want to move to Vermont in the first place?"
"Maybe those who are here have something to teach the rest of us
about cultural diversity."
"Even so, in this day and age, people aren't like they were in Richard
Wright's South fifty years ago. I mean, people in Vermont—and especially in the university—aren't racist."
*After several people denied the existence of racism on our campus, I
said, "Let me read you something." I had handed back the personal-
response-to-literature essays that day, essays that the authors had presented to their reading groups earlier. But I still had in my hand the
papers of a few students who were absent. One was written by Fran, a
Chinese American, the only member of the class who obviously belonged
to a so-called minority group. In one passage, Fran wrote:*

"Look at the Chink across the street! Hey, Chink, whatcha
doing?" was the first time I ever heard the use of that word. It
had to have been some time in sixth grade and I was clueless
to the meaning of it. The tone used insinuated that it had to
do with my being Chinese. I just wanted to run and hide from
the high school kids directing the comment to me. I knew
that I was different—the fact that my characteristics of
slanted eyes and the yellowness of my skin stood out among
my Irish and Italian friends. . . .

By the end of the first paragraph the class was silent. In an informal transactional paper, with strong expressive features, Fran went on to detail her experience growing up Chinese in America and concluded this way:

> Till this day, I can honestly say that I wish I wasn't
> Chinese. It's gotten to a point that I've got a complex about it.
> My girlfriends would sit there and try to talk reason and the
> advantages of being Oriental, but so far all it's produced for
> me is heartache and embarrassment.

I felt awkward reading this out loud when Fran wasn't there. I had not asked her permission—which I always try to with works I intend to make public—but I knew her story would add a missing and powerful voice to our discussion.

April 12

Hollis, writing in his journal in response to the class discussion about the sit-in:

> Racism?
> Having never felt what it is like to be discriminated against,
> I really don't feel that I can judge whether or not the
> behavior of these students is wrong. I know and have seen
> how they are treated and have myself treated some of these
> people unfairly also. Looking back now and after yesterday's
> class, I think I have really seen what the problem is and what
> needs to be done.
> After hearing a story on one student's problems with
> racism, I really can see how much it bothered her and how
> unfairly she was treated. How can we let this happen? I feel
> so sorry for her and I know now that I won't ever let myself
> treat a person like that.
> In order to help, we must all realize the problem and make
> some effort to stop it from continuing. So many of us just
> don't know what the problem is, and we won't find out unless
> we listen and learn.

April 28

"Let's read these first drafts of the poetic papers out loud to the whole group and see what experiments people are trying."

Susan, writing in the style of Alice Walker in *The Color Purple*, to

Max, a hippy character in Joan Didion's nonfiction *Slouching towards Bethlehem*:

> Dear Max,
>
> I don't write to God no more, I write to you.
> My sister Nettie laugh when I tell her I'm writing to you instead of God and she want to know what happen.
> I say, Max understand better and I try to understand him. What God do for you, Max? Make you all confuse in your mind. You and the rest on that street in Californya.
> Nettie in shock when I tell bout you using the grass as a cigarette. She just don't understand.
> I ast her, Ever hear of acid? but she say that acid burn holes in our clothes. Does it? You says you go on trips with it and I think I'd like to try some-time.
> Why do you drop it though?
> I tells Nettie, but she say, Hush, God might hear you.
> I say, Let 'im. He should listen to colored women. The world might be good place then. Might.
> I ast Nettie las night if she hear of the Dead.
> You is a sinner, say Nettie, because she ain't understanding it's music not blasphemy. But I blaspheme all I want.

Sandy, writing in the poetic form of E. E. Cummings with numerous references to different essays in Didion's *Slouching towards Bethlehem*:

> California's
>
> California's
> defunct
> and Sacramento too
>   the center for the study of democratic institutions
>   went too far and PloP
>   it brought Cali with it as it fell
>   to the Pacific
>   an EaRtHqUaKe, so a journal tells,
>   (not the bee union or chronicle)
>   the boom mentality
>   *sunken*
>   death valley dead
>   central valley dead
>   sunday's great-aunts dead

Sharon and Max on trip with no return
Lucille dead (deserved it)
Mr. Laski's communist party underthrown
m street gone
n street gone
o street gone
z street gone too
But c street—
just down u.s. 99
past the Delano Tularo Fresno Madera Merced
Modesto Stockton frigates
where to now Ms. Didion ...
there's always New York in just onetwothreefourfive hours

Jesus
it was a bizarre place
                    and what i want to know is
how do you like your golden state
Mister Pacific

For many students, the imaginative assignment was the most difficult. Few had written any poetry or fiction since elementary school. But by the second (and third or fourth) draft, most were catching on, having a good time, and coming to know better the author(s) they wrote about. We all agreed that successful papers would be those whose experiments most closely approximated a given author's theme, form, or style. This time, I asked the students to grade themselves.

May 5

At the end of the last day of class, I wrote notes to the following effect:
The writing (and the talking) made this literature class work as a community of learners in virtually every way I wanted. The journal writing was daily, in response to various prompts by me, and nightly, in self-initiated responses to the readings. I saw selected journal samples ("ten good pages, your choice") three times, and each time learned not only what they'd learned but how they felt about what they learned—and from each I, in turn, learned to adjust class in one direction or another.

The six-group classroom structure also worked, especially when combined with the journal writing that started each class meeting. Writing privately to themselves for five or ten minutes, then speaking to four or five classmates before venturing an opinion to the larger class, provided just the safety net most students needed to begin to trust their own perceptions and find their own voices. From my perspective, when students wrote, and again when they talked among themselves, they were out of my control and so created their own locus of authority—without which classroom community could not happen.

The analytical papers taught another kind of thinking, harder for them, more critical, but necessary. Their third drafts were remarkably better than their second drafts—however, my critique was essential to this process; I wish it wasn't. They would probably get a more thorough workout in analytical thinking in a more conventional literature class—though not if they never revised. Their group's response and my response taught useful lessons about the value of revision for both conceptual clarity and individual authority.

The personal-response paper was the first time many students had been asked for personal reactions to literature: they enjoyed the freedom and power they found in this mode, with papers such as Fran's affecting many others in the class. Here, too, it was essential they revise their first responses, as many played it quite safe and were less than honest the first time.

The final, imaginative paper allowed us to end class on a wonderfully creative note. The gutsy first drafts of Susan and Sandy provoked gutsy second and third drafts from many whose own first drafts had been stodgy and safe. I think some of the students experienced the joys of literary creation in this assignment, which included strong applause from classmates every time someone's poem or dialogue was especially convincing. I wanted the students to share in some of the same creative impulses that motivated Faulkner, Walker, and Didion—and their writing convinced me they did.

I've already thought about some specific things I'll change next time: (1) lead with the personal-response paper and encourage three drafts; (2) follow with *two* short analytical papers and let the students select the best to count toward their course grade; (3) change groups at midterm—several lost the freshness going into the last part of the course; (4) put grades even further in the background by adopting a portfolio system, in which I would give approximation grades at midterm and final holistic grades only at course's end, as I do in writing classes; and (5) maybe teach *As I Lay Dying* instead of *Go Down Moses*.

How Students Handle Writing Assignments: A Study of Eighteen Responses in Six Disciplines

Joy Marsella, Thomas L. Hilgers, and Clemence McLaren

Paul Brown, Teresa Hood, Su-yueh Huang, Healani Huch, Jane Kiel, Donna Lance, Frankie Lucas, Linda Middleton, Nairn Plourde, Melissa Santos, Barbara Schaper, Karen Simpson, Christie Starr, Anthony Wallace, Ke Wang, Morris Young, and Yanyin Zhang

Joy Marsella is associate professor of English at the University of Hawaii and director of the Hawaii Writing Project.

My interest in how students handle writing assignments began in the early 1980s when teachers in summer institutes of the Hawaii Writing Project asked, "How can we design effective writing assignments that teach?" We found that it took five weeks of concentrated thinking, writing, talking, and listening to lead to some answers. In 1987, when I started directing the new university-wide writing program, the question emerged again from the professors who teach the 350 or so writing-intensive classes offered each semester. To answer the question, we developed a research agenda to explore issues related to writing and learning in the various disciplines. Our first study is reported here.

Thomas L. Hilgers is director of the University of Hawaii's Manoa Writing Program and associate professor of English.

In the late 1970s, with an MA in literature, I began graduate study in psychology. On my first seminar paper, my professor wrote, "Highly literary, but not a review of the literature." Later, after I had the PhD in psychology, my English department tenure committee noted that "his articles read well, though perhaps with overreliance on social-science jargon." Now, when I work with colleagues in more than sixty disciplines on teaching with writing, I remember my own baptism into different discourse communities—and suffer again through baptism into the community of administrative memo writers!

Clemence McLaren is a program researcher and doctoral student at the University of Hawaii.

A summer session of the Bay Area Writing Project in 1979 made me a WAC convert. Since then, I've combined my career as educator with my lifelong addiction to writing. I'm especially interested in how writing in a content area helps students move beyond the facts to probe issues, to dare to question and to react to course material.

The seventeen collaborators are University of Hawaii graduate students interested in writing, teaching, and learning in the disciplines.

In an effort to wean students away from the one-shot midnight-oil method of term paper manufacture, Dr. A assigns his upper-level education students a "developmental" term paper. He begins by handing out a calendar outlining due dates for thesis statement, introductory paragraph, first, second, and final drafts. The handout also suggests a five-part organizing plan and describes requirements for handling bibliography and quotations. By mandating frequent opportunities for revision, he hopes to force students to work through multiple drafts toward more powerful, effective prose. So that their drafts can benefit from collaboration, Dr. A sets aside five classes for peer-response group meetings and provides guidelines from Peter Elbow's Writing without Teachers *for responding to texts. He tells his students, "If you don't all get an A or a B, we've all failed."*

At the fifth and final peer-group meeting, Arnold, a former engineering student preparing to teach high school science, is supposed to bring a second draft of the completed paper to share with his classmates. He joins the circle of students with two crumpled pages: a bare-bones outline attached to an introductory paragraph Dr. A looked at weeks earlier. The professor had asked Arnold to clarify his thesis and had critiqued his language, telling him to rethink and replace phrases such as "sufficiency of the schools in providing students with an awareness of the implications of Christian ideas, and their effect on world history."

Arnold has done no rethinking and no rewriting. The University of Hawaii researcher assigned to track him throughout his writing assignment is having trouble understanding Arnold's paralysis. In an earlier interview, Arnold told her that these comments were "the harshest" he'd ever received. He admitted, however, that past teachers had gotten after him for vague language and that he is leery of English teachers (he knows that Dr. A is a former English teacher) because they are "better at spotting bs." In the weeks since receiving this "harshest" of critiques, Arnold has done nothing to make his language more precise, nor has he moved toward clarifying his thesis. One source of his inability to follow the required writing schedule seems to be that he cannot adopt the objective, inquiring, "academic" stance required of him. Arnold is an ardent Christian; he has chosen to write about the ways in which the Judeo-Christian religions are covered in contemporary high school history texts. In Arnold's language we feel both the strength of his faith and the strength of the demand that he be objective: "I will analyze the teaching of religions tied to the life of Christ in Hawaii's schools."

Another source of Arnold's present inertia is his history as a writer. He sees himself "a procrastinator" and seems therefore bewildered with this assignment because it is so "stretched out over time." In this case, his instrument for procrastination is a recent NEA textbook survey on history and religion that he has sent for. "When it comes in the mail," he tells the researcher, "I'll be able to work down my paper." Afraid of being accused of bias, he seems to need this official source before he can go forward with either research or rewriting. Baffled as to how to amend his language to suit the professor, Arnold also remains content-bereft, still waiting for his truth source, the NEA survey, to arrive in the mail. Now, after five writing-group meetings, near the end of the semester, Arnold has not yet begun to write.

What went wrong? The University of Hawaii Manoa Writing Program promises students who enroll in writing-intensive courses that they will receive frequent feedback on their writing, and Dr. A has bent over backward to conform to these expectations. Dr. A's writing assignment is designed to capitalize on the power of peer conferences: an "Elbow with a Purpose" handout tells students, "The members of your group will tell you what is getting across to them." But Arnold has received almost no feedback from his group.

Dr. A anticipated this breakdown of the group process after the first two idea-sharing sessions. "Here's where students are unwilling to give heavy critiquing to one another," he told the researcher. What he did not anticipate was that so many students would have no texts to share, or nothing beyond their original introductory paragraphs. Given this lack of material, the writing groups could not function effectively. During the final group session preceding submission of second drafts, for example, the "critiquing" was minimal. In a forty-minute session, Arnold skimmed a young woman's first page and noted a spelling error, for which the writer thanked him. Arnold and his classmates then engaged in a lively discussion on another subject. Later in the session a student skimmed Arnold's first paragraph and suggested he might want to identify his pro-Christian bias at the outset.

The breakdown of the group process is especially puzzling because peer groups were seen as operating productively in other aspects of Dr. A's class. Students planned and critiqued lessons and worked on similar projects in small groups. Half the course grades were group grades. Yet in the three meetings observed by our graduate-student researchers, only one promise regarding group work on writing was realized for most students: "Your group will provide you with a valuable source of ideas."

Arnold's negotiation of the writing task presents us with a number of *why's*. Why hadn't he approached his professor for help? Why hadn't his peers challenged him or helped him reword his vague "operational definitions" and refocus his thesis? Why, near the end of this semester-long developmental process, was Arnold described by Dr. A as still "really at sea" and as still having "miles to go before he starts writing"?

The University of Hawaii Study: What We Did

In looking for answers to such questions, we hoped to learn how college students and their instructors approach writing tasks in different academic disciplines. We also hoped to offer teachers of writing-intensive classes insights on the complex issues involved in handling writing assignments.

To learn more about student responses to writing assignments, we first polled a sample of twenty instructors of writing-intensive classes and found that most were willing to become involved with observations of themselves and their students. Then the seven teams of graduate-student researchers each selected one of the available classes for observation. Students within each selected class were polled to determine who was willing to make their texts available to team members and to participate in interviews at the beginning, middle, and end of their work on a writing assignment.

Student researchers observed all classes in which a particular writing assignment was addressed. They interviewed not only the eighteen student "subjects" but also the seven instructors. Actual observations occurred over three- to nine-week periods and involved seven classes in six disciplines: zoology (advanced), mathematics (advanced), written composition (introductory), sociology (introductory), psychology (advanced), and education—curriculum and instruction (two advanced courses). While there was nothing either representative or random about the six disciplines, their range allowed examination of a variety of professional expectations and writing assignments.

What We Found: Influences on Students' Handling of Writing Tasks

Our investigation suggests that the gap between professors' representations of students' approaches to writing assignments and what the students actually do is significant. In the course of responding to an assignment, students certainly consider what they know about their professor's expectations in such areas as format, structure, and appropriate sources of information. But many, perhaps most, of their decisions are driven less by their reading of the teacher's expectations than by their own prior experience as writers and by the present contexts of their lives. For many students, their history and their life situation provide sufficient justification for handling a new writing assignment in old ways. How they write is the result of their negotiation among at least three forces: (1) the specification of the writing assignment provided by the professor; (2) the strategies for handling academic writing that students have successfully used in the past; and (3) competing priorities—demands posed by other academic coursework, part- or full-time jobs, personal and family responsibilities, illness, and strongly held values or beliefs.

Arnold's case illustrates the complex interaction of these forces. First, the professor's carefully specified sequencing of the students' writing process created confusion for Arnold, who was, in his own words, "a procrastinator." Second, we see Arnold's reliance on what seemed to us to be his learned writing behavior: dependence on outside sources and the postponement of writing until the last moment. Finally, there is a conflict between Arnold's values and the values embedded in the writing task, as the student seemed unable to negotiate a path between his own deeply held belief in the value of the Christian faith and the professor's requirement that he maintain an objective stance in his research and writing. These forces conspired to present Arnold as a writer who seemed to our student researcher a "hopeless case." But Arnold was not hopeless in the eyes of his professor. Dr. A was apparently accustomed to students who exhibited Arnold's pattern of writing behavior. As a result, Dr. A maintained his optimism, even as the semester drew to a close. "As soon as the student comes in and talks to me, this paper will take off," he told the researcher. We'll return to the story of Arnold's task negotiation in the conclusion. But first, we offer case studies illustrating each of the three forces that shape the way in which a student writer approaches an academic writing task.

1. Professors' Explanations and Specifications

Dr. B requires students in his two-credit, 400-level zoology (Animal Ecology) lab to complete eight reports based on laboratory experiments, "with a quality as close to professional as you can possibly manage." Although students collaborate on experiments, they submit individual, biweekly, six- to ten-page reports based on the five-part scientific format—introduction, methods and materials, results, discussion, and summary. Before students prepare their initial reports, Dr. B devotes an entire class to explaining the qualities inherent in scientific texts, recommends The Elements of Style *(Strunk and White) and* How to Write and Publish a Scientific Paper *(Day), and discusses several models from* Ecology *magazine. He cautions "little—or, better, no—interpretation" and helps students learn to present information as "clearly and in as unbiased a fashion as you can." Words such as* exactly, precisely, *and* facts *appear repeatedly throughout his instructions. Moreover, each section requires specific information—no more, no less—and a certain fact included in an inappropriate section would, perhaps, be better left unstated. Dr. B has a teaching assistant, Jan, who helps evaluate the lab reports.*

Pam, a twenty-year-old student government president and volunteer worker at the Waikiki Aquarium, hopes to become a biology professor. A good writer, she is unsure how to execute her instructor's writing guidelines. In particular, she struggles to write in an unbiased, factual manner. Bewildered by the format's rigidity, she feels that her original write-ups are more important than the mode of presentation. In her first three reports, one remark per write-up reminds her that this is "formal writing," approximately two to three comments per write-up help her adopt zoology's concise language, and many comments address which information should or should not be included in each section. The need to master the five-part format dominates Pam's attention. Initially, she sees her effort to "get the sections right" as complying with the professor's instructions rather than attending to reader's needs. Furthermore, she considers her audience to be her peers, for she does not feel confident addressing the larger professional community. Not used to altering her style and voice, she occasionally slips and includes first-person references and colloquialisms. Making generalizations from complicated mathematical calculations proves challenging.

Models of writing as process describe writers as making choices among information sources, text formats and features, organizational plans, goals, and strategies. Yet Pam and the other subjects had their choices limited by the professor's specifications of their discipline's genre and format demands. Indeed, as Pam wrote, these constraints were often in the foreground. Her response seems the paradoxical outcome of well-intentioned teaching practice. The teachers gave students clear-cut directions for construing and completing the writing assignment. None of their assignments resembled what Linda S. Flower ("Role") has called the typically ambiguous, underspecified "Rorschach blot" college writing assignment. Five of our seven professors supplied models of finished texts—models that students indicated helped them to understand how the required writing was similar to or different from other kinds of writing they had done before. For example, the math professor used examples of good and bad proofs, for which one students reported gratitude because the examples showed "what I could be doing wrong and if I needed more words."

Like the zoology students, the sociology students had to follow an organizing plan and clarify content, but their primary goal was to engage in relevant discovery and thus enhance their learning. In Introduction to the Sociology of Family, the students were, again, given clear and full instructions. They were to formulate a theory of what causes a family conflict, formulate a method of observing the conflict, and observe the conflict to test the theory. They were to compile their results in sections on theory, methodology, observation, and analysis. To lead them through the process, students were given a step-by-step guide, and the professor devoted class periods to small-group activities and large-group discussions in which students could read, respond to, and discuss drafts of their preliminary results. These students, given no models, all said they wished they had had one. (Although researchers saw an early handout as an excellent model for the theory generation, observation, and testing that students were asked to carry out, the professor did not label it a model, and the students apparently did not recognize it as such.)

But while some students wanted even more structure than they had been given, others wanted less. In the introductory written composition class, for example, the teacher's provision of a five-paragraph formula for constructing an argument created frustration for students, because the teacher had also told them to write "only what you believe in or strongly feel." Initially students found the format helpful in focusing and developing ideas, but in the end they found it inhibiting. In structuring their arguments, they all wanted to exceed formulaic limits, but their teacher would allow no deviation. Clearly, whatever their instructor's intentions, these students were discovering thoughts and feelings through composing. And their discovery experiences proved incompatible with the prescribed essay structure. So the students left the writing experience with considerable frustration.

How much prescribed structure do undergraduate writers need? The answer is probably related to the purpose for a particular writing assignment. When writing is intended to encourage or allow discovery, the format specifications need to be flexible, to permit a range of individual variation. When students are learning to write within a particular genre or to follow conventional discourse forms within a discipline, a high degree of specificity seems both desirable and useful. But it is not enough for the instructor to be aware of the purpose for structural specifications. Students too must understand the purpose of prescriptions if they are to move beyond frustration to mastery.

2. Student Strategies

Let us return to Dr. A's education class and the "developmental" term paper and examine another student's response.

Robert, an English major and athlete, works as a wrestling coach while obtaining his certification to teach high school English. He chooses to write on the implementation of the 2.0 GPA rule for athletes in private schools. He will rely heavily on newspaper sources and interviews with administrators and athletic directors. He has written for a school newspaper and is comfortable reporting interview results. He will also draw on experience with interviews he conducted for a sociology paper. He submits a statement of purpose and brief outline on the required due date, although he omits a bibliography. Dr. A comments fully on his statement, notes the omission of the bibliography, and praises more than criticizes. Robert conducts interviews at three schools. At one of these schools, the coach gives him an already assembled folder of newspaper articles. Robert has no text prepared for the classes devoted to reviewing early efforts and thus he receives no peer responses. He writes a three-page first draft the morning it is due, being careful to respond to Dr. A's directive that he provide a definition of the 2.0 rule and concluding his draft with several questions that will guide his additional research. Dr. A commends Robert's use of the series of questions to "help sharpen your purpose." Robert intends to retain these as the first three pages or so of his final draft. He has no additional text for the peer workshop on second drafts. His busy schedule keeps him from putting more time into the paper. On the eve of the due date, he writes the remaining pages in a five-hour midnight marathon. He receives an A.

While professors in our study tried to use writing to foster their students' learning, their students were asking themselves, What's the most efficient way to complete this assignment and get the highest grade I can, given everything that's going on in my life? To find the most efficient way, they most frequently turned to past experience.

In spite of instructors' style sheets, outlined formats, model papers, and scheduled group meetings, many of our students resorted to old bags of tricks. Robert's confidence in past strategies kept him from starting actual writing earlier, even if he might have learned more and thereby improved his paper. Robert understood the task specifications (which included no criteria for evaluating the process) and knew his grade would not be lowered for short-circuiting the group process. And, as he valued the feedback of his instructor over his peers, he took no advantage of assigned group meetings and did very little revising.

Past experience led students in our study to see instructor-writer interactions as more authoritative than peer-writer interactions. Indeed, in three classes where peer-response groups were functioning, students told researchers that groups were a waste of time—even though some received comments on their text that they planned to incorporate in their next revision. We highlight this term paper example intentionally, for the longer the required text and the longer the period of time for completing the assignment, the more likely students were to rely on the past strategies. Past experience also led students to think of any long assignment as a term paper and to bring to that assignment the last-minute writing they associated with the genre. Even though two of our professors consistently referred to their assignments as "emerging models of teaching and learning" or "I-Search" investigations, the students saw their work as the writing of a "term paper" and behaved accordingly.

If, like Robert, our other students had had past success with a writing behavior, they persisted in using it, even if it was not the behavior specified by the instructor. No matter how clear the instructor's scheduling and sequencing of writing activities, students decided to write at the last minute. For example, in spite of the required "incubation" step in writing zoology lab reports, Bill continued to write his reports the night before they were due and got B's or A's. He also continued to make the same grammatical and mechanical errors that the teaching assistant had corrected on three earlier lab reports—as if his prior experience were also telling him, You can still get a good grade without cleaning up your copy.

But the zoology data also show the power of instructor-student relationships to change students' strategies. In the first of three lab reports, all three students in this course included graphs and tables they hadn't referenced and sometimes referenced nonexistent graphs and tables. Dr. B and Jan, the teaching assistant, acting in turn as interpreter and coach, pushed students to see differences between the relevant and the irrelevant and to highlight the relevant. A typical comment illustrates the instructor's prompting: "You've given a lot of background information, but you haven't included any that is pertinent to this study—for example, what types of seeds are produced, timing of reproduction, are plants self- or cross-fertilized, are they monoecious or dioecious?" A similar prompting process happened in the mathematics class as subjects submitted proofs on a biweekly basis.

When instructor specifications and students' learned writing behavior are in synchrony, writing and learning proceed smoothly and well. For example, a student responding to the I-Search assignment described below saw himself as a multiple-draft writer who consciously used initial drafts to explore decisions regarding goals, persona, meaning, and text, and to reveal gaps in his understanding of the assignment itself. By the time he had finished a number of freewritings and four drafts of his paper in conjunction with the other reading and collaborative activities called for in the professor's task specifications, he had solved problems of definition, clarity, and tone that confronted him earlier in the process.

3. Competing Priorities

Professor C has several goals in asking students in her advanced-level education class to write an I-Search paper—a report of their investigations on a topic of interest that addresses reading or writing in some way. (The assignment is an adaptation of that described by Ken Macrorie in Searching Writing.*) Students follow an eight-step collaborative process that begins with personal writing (weekly learning logs to the professor and in-class freewritings to explore the topic) and ends with a publishable text. In a process similar to Dr. A's, students choose a topic, complete a search, prepare a draft, share that draft in writing-response groups to get feedback on ideas, revise the draft, return to the response group once again for editing, prepare the final paper, and share the published result. The professor hopes they will adapt the writing-as-a-tool-for-learning process in their own high school classes.*

Howard, who wants to teach physical education classes and special education students, is taking the class—along with five others—to fulfill a requirement for his professional teaching diploma. He works during the day as a substitute teacher, coaches football on weekends, and is raising a family. (His demanding schedule is similar to that of other subjects of our study.) After some struggle, he eventually focuses his search: he hopes to show that physical education has more to do with cognitive demands than people usually think.

Because Howard is so pressed for time and wants "to get the paper out of the way," he comes to his first writing-response group with a final draft. His text, a "written speech," kills two birds with one stone: he will use it as the I-Search paper and the final speech requirement for the same course. He listens to the group's response and tells the researcher he heard some good suggestions, but he incorporates none of these suggestions in his final draft. Since he is confident of a good grade, the investment of time and energy to draft, share, redraft, and share again—in other words, to perfect his search—is not worth the benefit.

Our case studies show us that academic writing is context-bound. We have seen how part of the context is the writer's prior writing experience. But Howard's case, like the others, shows us that a significant part of the context is shaped by each student's personal circumstances.

We have always recognized our UH students' ethnic diversity. But our data suggest that ethnic differences may be far less powerful in their effect on students' writing behavior than are the differences between traditional (younger, parent-subsidized) and nontraditional (often independent but needy, and responsible for others) students. Our subjects ranged in age from seventeen to forty. At least five held full-time jobs, three were raising families, and most of the rest held part-time jobs. We now understand more clearly than we had before how economic factors influence decisions students make in handling their writing. The responsibilities involved in students' roles as spouses, parents, and jobholders compete with the obligation to satisfy the instructor's expectations. The case of Paul reveals how personal circumstances compete with academic work. While working toward a teaching certificate at the university, Paul was employed to teach at-risk students in a "special motivation" class in one of the more strife-torn local high schools. Although he had enrolled in the class in part because he needed help with his writing, he brought no drafts to peer-group meetings because, as he told the researcher, he was too involved with problems in his high school. He was also uncomfortable because his wife was several thousand miles away, finishing her degree at another campus. Although he seemed enthusiastic about the assignment, in the end he produced no paper at all.

Another student, Chris, a forty-year-old single parent and Hawaiian rights activist, plunged into her I-Search investigation with a clear image of her eventual written product. She would save time and demonstrate her considerable knowledge by continuing work that she had already begun: the investigation of Hawaiian Creole English. However, in the series of required peer-review workshops, she did no revising.

She had such strong feelings about her subject that she was seen by the student researcher as "rudely rejecting suggestions from her peer group." Apparently her firm attachment to her beliefs and her confidence in her prior knowledge about her topic kept her from considering the suggestions of her classmates.

Further, Chris did not adopt the investigative strategy called for by the I-Search approach. Instead, she followed her usual approach: starting with a fixed conclusion and adding data to provide necessary support—an approach that made the collaborative aspect of the I-Search approach of little use to her. It is no surprise that, in the eyes of the researcher, Chris's final product was closer to a "standard school theme" than to an I-Search investigation. Yet Chris told the researcher that she understood the purpose and the framework of the assignment and that her own students would most likely benefit from collaborative experiences.

Helping Students Make Good Use of Writing Choices

Professors, in response to writing-across-the-curriculum ideals, have adopted expectations about the ways in which writing can relate to student learning. These expectations are reflected in the design of their writing prompts. But our data suggest that students do not share their teachers' views about writing as a means of learning. Professors clearly need to do more to convince students to take full advantage of the approaches to learning and choices available to them. Although our data do not supply explicit answers about how best to frame assignments, the factors that influence student writing suggest issues that writing assignments raise. Understanding these issues may enable professors to help students make the best use of the writing choices they have.

Perhaps the most challenging question is posed by students' reliance on old strategies. How can we get students to move beyond "getting the assignment done"? Put another way, how can we get students to move from what Carl Bereiter and Marlene Scardamalia call "knowledge-telling," a useful but limited form of exposition, to "knowledge transforming"? Such transformation is possible only when students are willing to take risks, only when their instructional contexts allow, even encourage, risk-taking. Success with some of the best writing-intensive assignments—developing a personal theory of learning or designing and testing a theory of family conflict—is possible only when the writer's goal is to learn through writing and not to get the "paper" done in the most economical manner. Yet we have no pedagogy that encourages risk-taking, and professors and students alike measure "success" by grades on written products. It is no wonder that students resort to past strategies. The rewards of unlearning in order to learn anew are hard to come by on most college campuses.

Before we look at ways in which teachers can foster relationships that will create better learning, let's finish the story of Arnold, who was having such a difficult time getting started on his term paper. We left him handing in an outline and unrevised introductory paragraph instead of a completed second draft. But deadlines work wonders, and Arnold did manage to produce a draft. He also narrowed his focus, as per Dr. A's original comments, limiting himself to coverage of the Protestant Reformation in one commonly used history text. But he didn't go back and change his original thesis and introduction to reflect this new focus. Although the course had officially ended, negotiations continued. Dr. A handed the paper back for still another revision— Arnold's first. Arnold brought it in on the last day of exam week, hours before the professor needed to submit his final grade. A triumphant Dr. A said, "The paper had improved 1,000 percent—he came through!"

Arnold had continued "working down" his paper until the last moment. Interaction and revision had taken place, and through that process, Arnold found a focus and an appropriate academic voice. Even after dealing with Arnold-style resistance, this professor maintains his belief in the process. Dr. A admits his assignment still needs fine-tuning but feels it's an improvement over the old days, when a single draft was returned to students, covered with teacher comments delivered too late to do anything about.

We must acknowledge that even though students may not comply fully with the assignment demands, they are still using writing to help them learn. For example, even though Howard did not go through the I-Search process as Professor C defined it, he did meet several of the professor's goals: he found expressive writing helpful in defining his topic, and he therefore intends to use journals and thinking and writing logs in his other classes; he confirmed his notion of the important connections between physical education and cognition; and he completed the search.

Still, the experiences of our students lead us to ask how we can foster relationships in class that promote better learning. We clearly need to work at convincing students that the benefit in learning will be worth the cost in time and energy to carry out the assignment as prescribed. In particular, the data suggest that students need help understanding the power of collaboration. It seems clear that collaboration will become part of a writer's available strategies only after he or she has experienced the improved texts that can result from working with other writers.

Then, too, we need to acknowledge, and adjust for, the growing numbers of nontraditional students who are enrolling in college classes. For many, being a student is second to being a single mother, a high school counselor, an abandoned spouse, or an overextended substitute teacher and weekend football coach. A growing number of students, those who are less concerned with choosing a major than with feeding their children, paying their rent, and securing financial aid to cover tuition, may think that writing to learn is a luxury they cannot afford.

We also need to build into our pedagogies an understanding of students' values and increasingly diverse cultural situations. Some may hold to values and beliefs that do not readily translate into the styles of learning, thinking, and writing that are normative in the academy. We've sketched Arnold's struggle to find a way to write about religion. Chris's feelings about the Hawaiian language were so embedded in the rhetorical context of Hawaiian activism that she rejected suggestions for improving her text as if these suggestions threatened her own values.

Our data also suggest that it would be wise for professors of writing-intensive classes to begin the semester by getting to know their students as writers and by helping them link past writing experiences with the new ones at hand. After finding out what previous writing students have done, they might explain how that writing is similar to and different from the writing to be done that semester. Perhaps then the instructor's expectations will seem understandable, even appealing, enough for students to go beyond getting the assignment done.

We need to acknowledge our students' long-rewarded habits of handing in unrevised final drafts if we want to change these habits. Our case studies also suggest that teachers need to do more than spend time in class defining group work and modeling. They must give students practice, and more than once, in how to behave in collaborative groups. They may have to shape and motivate group participation and drafting by evaluating and grading these activities.

Writing-to-learn classes are slowly changing the topography of American college education. In the early 1980s, students in several of the classes we observed may well have done little if any writing. We are moving in what seems to us to be a useful direction. Further, much of the research that has accompanied the writing-to-learn movement has focused, as does our project, on the student and the student's learning. When we adopt this focus on the learning that takes place in our colleges and universities, it becomes clear that we should consider our students as well as our faculty, our learners as well as our teachers, if writing in the disciplines, and indeed postsecondary education generally, is to live up to its promise.

PART V

Disciplinary Values, Discourse Practices, and Teaching

Introduction

This section moves our attention from the classroom to the larger disciplinary and professional contexts that contribute to shaping what happens in classrooms. More specifically, the authors examine the values embedded in the language of disciplinary discourse and relate these values to the writing, teaching, and learning that occur in classes informed by these values. Bonnie B. Spanier, a molecular biologist, offers a critique of disciplinary ideology and practice—in particular, the gender bias in scientific practice and the passive learning that is encouraged by an ideology that represents scientific knowledge as "real," "hard," and beyond interpretation. In contrast to Charles Bazerman, who takes issue with a reliance on textbooks for such critiques, Spanier bases a good part of her argument on an analysis of introductory molecular biology textbooks. She explains her choice as follows: "I would not argue that textbooks embody the complexities and actual practices of a field. In this respect, I agree with Bazerman. Still, textbooks in molecular biology—and each field or discipline has a particular relationship to the role of textbooks in representing the content and practices of the field—embody a major means of acculturation of students. They are one major site of the reproduction of values and ideology in molecular biology." In the second essay in the section, Louise Dunlap examines the discourse practices accepted in the professional field of planning and its related academic program. She describes what she sees as the privileging in some classrooms and some workplaces of a "neutral" style of writing over a "critical" style.

Both Spanier and Dunlap are calling for change within the academic and professional communities they discuss: molecular biology and urban planning. We read their essays as challenging us to examine the same issues within our own communities. After reading Spanier's essay, Dunlap made a comment about the discipline of planning that seems applicable to many fields:

> Planning is a field that thinks it is about reexamining received assumptions about the nature of institutions. Yet it is sluggish

about reexamining some of its own most basic ones—including assumptions about gender bias, hierarchy, and domination. Re-reading Spanier challenges me to think more about planners' ideology as expressed at the level of linguistic choices. My own thinking focuses more on what I consider the shaping forces of that ideology—the material conditions of study, application, and work. For a transformative understanding of the planning discipline and a transformative teaching practice, I need a well-tuned awareness of both levels.

Spanier and Dunlap raise epistemological and ideological questions that many of us have been slow to address in our own fields—perhaps because the questions challenge long-held and firmly entrenched assumptions, perhaps because they force us to address the connections between, on the one hand, our own practices of knowledge construction and disciplinary acculturation and, on the other hand, issues of gender, class, and race. As the two writers have demonstrated, these are questions that relate directly to how hospitable our classrooms are to our students, who are individuals with distinct histories, genders, and socioeconomic and cultural backgrounds. What values are we asking them to hold? What kinds of people are we asking them to become? Textbooks, curricula, and the practices of a given discipline and profession have answers to these questions—answers that we may find not to our liking.

Encountering the Biological Sciences: Ideology, Language, and Learning

Bonnie B. Spanier

The author is assistant professor and chair of the Women's Studies Department at the State University of New York, Albany.

After receiving my doctorate in microbiology and molecular genetics from Harvard University and teaching biology at Wheaton College, I explored the history, philosophy, and social study of science at Harvard and the Bunting Institute of Radcliffe College. Feminist critiques of the sciences raised my awareness of the values embedded in representations of science and nature. My involvement at Wheaton with one of the first major curriculum transformation projects on women and gender crystallized my concern for change that would motivate students of all backgrounds to be active agents in their lifelong education. I see writing across the disciplines as a contributor to these goals.

As a scientist and feminist, I see writing across the curriculum as providing a fruitful partnership of the humanities and the sciences, one that encourages science educators to confront neglected humanistic aspects of their disciplines: values, dominant beliefs, and societal influences that shape the content of science and science education. More precisely, writing-across-the-curriculum projects *that address ideology in the discourse and practice of science* are potentially transformative and may help to alleviate the exclusion of women and people of color from the scientific professions, the crisis in scientific literacy in the United States, and the vast gulf between scientific experts and the public in issues of science and society.

To be potentially transformative, such projects must expose and question several major assumptions operating in the natural sciences (about scientific objectivity, student passivity, and dichotomous divisions such as subject from object and science from society), powerful conventions that work against both student-centered writing and the involvement of certain groups of students in science. In the first section of this essay, I describe these assumptions—a constellation that constitutes an ideology. In the second and third sections, I apply a feminist analysis to the discourse of biology and molecular biology to illustrate insights gained from delving into values and ideologies embedded in the sciences. And in the last two sections, I focus on the impetus for change in science education and the valuable resources in the effort to promote the development of aware and "resisting" students who can take their rightful places in science and, with their scientific literacy, in society. I hope that, as scientists and science teachers address issues of societal values and beliefs expressed in and through the sciences— with writing across the curriculum as a vehicle in this interchange of the humanities and the sciences—the content of the sciences will change. And such transformed sciences and science education will be more welcoming of all participants.

Ideologies That Constrain the Natural Sciences

Among the traditional disciplines in the academy, the natural sciences tend to be slow in recognizing and attempting to correct cultural distortions of our systems of knowledge (such as the belief that women's behavior is inherently inferior to and different from men's).[1] Scientists as a group are less apt to embrace the view that scientific knowledge, like all knowledge, is socially constructed by, for the most part, a small portion of the population and that it reflects the experiences, beliefs, and biases that serve that tiny but powerful population; scientists, that is, tend to embrace a positivist notion of "truth" rather than an understanding of scientific knowledge as highly political.[2] Since many scientists believe in a particular conception of scientific objectivity and in the natural sciences as a model of value-free ways of knowing, it is difficult to persuade scientists that feminist critiques have a significant bearing on science as both a system and a body of knowledge. At the same time, the general belief in science as a privileged model of objective knowledge—a model that has been applied in the social sciences and in the humanities as well—makes feminist critiques of the natural sciences significant in the effort to transform not only the epistemological basis for science but the whole of society.

A key unexamined assumption in science is the concept of *objectivity*. In the objective paradigm, the subject (knower) is separated from the object (that which is known). Feminist and other radical critiques propose that the inequitable power relations into which our society is organized are supported by an epistemology of an unequal, dominant-subordinate link between subject and object (Harding and Hintikka).

An ideology of subject-object separation, the separation of scientific knowledge from other forms of knowledge, and the representation of scientists as the most objective authorities on scientific knowledge, all reinforce a certain passivity in scientific writing and education and exacerbate a "necessary" dependence on the authority of scientists. Whether it is the use of the passive voice in scientific writing ("the test tubes were filled") or the banking model of learning in science courses,[3] many aspects of science and science education encourage a passive learning process and a passive relationship of students to scientific information and its consequences.[4] The assumption that the learner is passive obliterates the knower (and hence any of that knower's particular characteristics such as her or his cultural values and background) and foregrounds knowledge, conceived of as aperspectival scientific facts, universally arrived at and universally applicable. Indeed, there is no equivalent in science education of the reader-response movement in the teaching of literature.[5]

The Resisting Reader and Feminist Perspectives in Science

"Literature is political," declares Judith Fetterley in the opening sentence of *The Resisting Reader* (xi). That "science is political" science educators may acknowledge, but only in a limited sense. The major textbooks in molecular biology provide support for this generalization: they include no discussion of debates about the safety and ethics of recombinant DNA experiments and applications (Spanier, *Gender* and "Gender"). While many scientists may admit that funding for research is somewhat "political" because a few powerful individuals determine the current topics for research, most scientists disallow the view of the new social studies of science (including feminist critiques) that all aspects of science, like any other human endeavor, embody and reflect power relations—the usual inequitable ones.[6]

Fetterley's "resisting reader" is a woman coming to consciousness about the predominance of a particular white, Western male value system (termed *masculinism*) based on those males' experiences—or, more often, their fantasies—in the American literary canon.[7] Conscious resistance to the dominant value system[8] is essential to prevent what happens to women and other subordinated groups in a society:

we internalize those demeaning values about ourselves, so that low self-esteem and even self-hatred undermine us. Consequent socialization to masculinist values brings women into line, makes us complicitous with the status quo of unequal power relations. Thus studies of science students suggest that, even if the structural barriers that block many women and minority students from pursuing science were removed, the lower self-esteem and confidence of women just as qualified as men would keep them from claiming an equitable place in science and other male-dominated professions (Zappert and Stanbury).

The Resisting Reader exposes the ideology embodied and maintained in the canon of American literature.[9] For similar purposes, science education can (and, I believe, must) encourage "resistance" in science students and their teachers. Actually, this constructive, critical stance corresponds well to the theoretical objectives of science: to eliminate biases in our understanding of nature. A healthy scientific skepticism should involve questioning assumptions about factors affecting research design, paradigms, and conclusions.[10] Scott Gilbert and colleagues have made just such a proposal, using the language of experimental control in the scientific method, to persuade scientists to take feminist critical perspectives into account:

> Whenever one performs an experiment, one sets up all the controls one can think of in order to make as certain as possible that the result obtained does not come from any other source. One asks oneself what assumptions one is making. Have I assumed the temperature to be constant? Have I assumed that the pH doesn't change over the time of the reaction? Feminist critique asks if there may be some assumptions that we haven't checked concerning gender bias. In this way feminist critique should be part of normative science. Like any control, it seeks to provide critical rigor, and to ignore this critique is to ignore a possible source of error.   (Biology and Gender Study Group 61–62)

What are the consequences for science and science education if we control for assumptions about gender and, more broadly, about the political nature of science?

Feminist and other radical science critiques have investigated aspects of the political nature of science in its organization, personnel, and content. At the core of feminist critiques of the sciences, like their sister critiques of other realms of knowledge, is the argument that gender—the gender dichotomy of maleness and femaleness—is a socially constructed concept (albeit derived from physical, particularly genital, differences among humans) with pervasive and deeply held meanings (Beauvoir). It is important to recognize that the understanding of "gender" as a social construct refutes several entrenched beliefs in our society: (1) biological determinist arguments and assumptions—that biology determines, for example, male and female behavior; (2) reductionism in an explanatory (rather than methodological) form that views gender as the result of male and female hormones or male and female genes—rather than as socially created "male" and "female" beings, with the precise meaning of "male" and "female" constructed differently in different cultures and different historical moments; and (3) reification of a complex of socially defined, variable behaviors into a single measurable trait, such as "intelligence," "human nature," or "female" (Gould; Hubbard, Henifin, and Fried; Lewontin, Rose, and Kamin). This antiessentialist perspective on gender rejects biological determinist claims of inherent differences between men and women, pointing to the range and plasticity of cultural meanings of male and female in different societies and times and highlighting the evidence that males and females experience overt and subtle treatment that is different depending on their perceived or ascribed sex—for instance, babies are handled and spoken to differently from birth on the basis of their "sex" (Tavris and Wade 221–22).

Thus a feminist position on the social construction of gender is quite different from Edward O. Wilson's sociobiological claims that what accounts for the low participation and status of women in, for example, science—or business or politics—is an evolutionary and hence genetic difference in "aggressivity" in men and women (138)—or that more boys than girls have "extraordinary math talent" because of inherent differences in hormones and brain structure (Benbow and Stanley 1262). Feminist and other radical analyses of such "scientific" claims have exposed serious flaws in the assumptions, evidence, and reasoning used in sociobiology (Hubbard and Lowe)—which nonetheless remains a field in biology at this time, with broad influence in anthropology and other social sciences. Instead of looking to biology as the source of fixed "causes" of the differential status of women and men in society, feminist explanations draw on the experiences, collective and individual, of marginalized groups within the socioeconomics and politics of a given historical context.

Radical critiques have found that sexist, classist, racist, and heterosexist[11] beliefs are often superimposed onto animal behavior and then used as models for what is "natural" for human society. These beliefs, embedded in the assumptions and paradigms of science, are manifest in and maintained by language. Three common types of ideological distortions are found in biology. All are relevant to sociobiology and animal behavior work, but I include some examples from other areas in biology as well.

1. *Superimposing stereotypical gender attributes and language onto animals and even plants.* A group of female animals that associate with a single male is called a "harem," female behavior is termed "coy," and male mallard ducks are said to "rape" a female duck. In the last case, the language has direct consequences, since some sociobiologists then argue that rape is a natural element of human male-female relations because it is an evolutionary "strategy" for the male to pass on his genes as often as possible. A key assumption underlying gender stereotypes is a number of mutually exclusive dichotomies such as female versus male, nature versus nurture, homosexual versus heterosexual. An example that reinforces male-female dualisms is the inaccurate labeling of "male" and "female" hormones, even though they are found in both males and females.

2. *Creating hierarchies of organization with assumptions of centralized control, casting power relationships of "domination" and "subordination" as natural products of evolution.* It should not surprise us that Wilson's assertions of the male's evolutionary superiority in aggression (questionable on many levels: the term is ambiguous and imprecise; how, then, does one measure it?) justify a rightful place for males (usually white) at the head of industry, the government, and the science lab, as well as the National Institutes of Health and the National Science Foundation.

"Control"—in which domination and subordination describe a fundamental and asymmetrical power relationship—is a major focus of feminist critiques of society, since women have been defined as naturally subordinate to men, just as slaves were once defined as having natural masters in white men. Thus feminists argue that dominant-subordinate relationships carry overtones of gender, race, and class associations by virtue of societal beliefs (see note 1). Centralized control in a hierarchical system is a ubiquitous model in Western science and medicine, with the brain as the control tower. Emily Martin's work on the language of medical texts provides a model case study for the subtle influence of gender ideology and related cultural beliefs on the representation of human physiology. She has found that the relation among the parts of the body (the hypothalamus, pituitary, ovaries, etc.) is assumed to be one of hierarchical control, and she suggests the importance of alternative models:

I have presented the underlying metaphors contained in medical descriptions of menopause and menstruation to show that these ways of describing events are but one method of fitting an interpretation to the facts. . . . Would it be . . . possible to change the nature of the relationships assumed . . . ? Why not, instead of an organization with a controller, a team playing a game? . . . Eliminating the hierarchical organization and the idea of a single purpose to the menstrual cycle also greatly enlarges the ways we could think of menopause. (52–53)

As I discuss below, the preeminent model of hierarchical and centralized control has been extended to the nucleus and genes of the cell over the cytoplasm and the proteins.

3. *Claiming that biology determines behavior—for example, a "masculine brain" confers better analytic and mathematical ability.* This particular distortion of our understanding of biology is directly (and tragically) related to sexism, racism, and classism through a long history of biological determinism as a weapon against groups such as women, African Americans, Jews, immigrants, the poor, homosexuals, and so on (Gould; Lewontin, Rose, and Kamin). Cross-cultural studies and changes in gender-appropriate behavior over time challenge deeply held beliefs that being female (having certain genes and hormones) dictates certain female behavior. An underlying assumption in biological determinist thinking is that our biology is rigid and unchanging. In contrast, we have massive evidence that our biology is highly elastic, a product of cumulative, nonadditive interactions of our physical beings not only with food, air, and environment but also with experience and thought. Simply asking students to consider how being in college affects their biology focuses on the complexities of our "biology" and the inadequacies of rigid and dualistic notions of nature versus nurture. Writing exercises in which students analyze the discourse and content of their science texts as well as representations of science in the media can raise their awareness about these and other societally generated distortions in the sciences.

The Discourse of Molecular Biology

How could such culturally generated distortions occur in molecular biology, where the subject matter is not gendered animals but supposedly nongendered cells, genes, and macromolecules (large molecules such as DNA and proteins)? Molecular biology is of particular interest because it illustrates the impact of our prevailing ideology of "difference" on nongendered subject matter. Further, this field demands our attention because it has taken a dominant position in the life sciences since the 1960s.

Distortions similar to the types of biases listed above emerge from my feminist analysis of language, concepts, and organizing principles in molecular biology.[12] Here are three examples of inaccurate representations of the microscopic and submicroscopic worlds, misrepresentations that have broad ramifications.

In the first example, bacteria are misrepresented as "male" or "female," a case of superimposing the stereotypical gender dichotomy onto nongendered beings.[13] Bacteria are called "male" or "female" based on the presence (male) or absence (female) of a "fertility" (or F) plasmid, a tiny piece of DNA like a separate chromosome, and a bridge (pilus) that links the two "mating" cells and allows the transfer of some genetic material from the male to the female. In this process, the receiving bacterial cell (the "female") gains a copy of the F plasmid and, hence, becomes "male." The scientific definition of "sex"—exchange of genetic material between organisms—has thus become confused with the cultural sense of "sex." The male-female designation is incorrect, since bacteria do not make eggs or sperm (the scientific basis for sex designation). It is also sexist in its gender association of presence and absence, active and passive—and heterosexist in its assumption that "sexual" interchange occurs only between a male and a female.

It is easy to understand why such gender attributions might be considered harmless, cute, and even useful for stirring interest in an otherwise dry subject, but we must recognize the way that such language reinforces sexism. Feminist analyses suggest that it is no accident that a gender ideology of essential male and female difference, with the male signified by the *presence* of the F plasmid and the pilus—and as the natural initiator of action—gets embedded in the study of bacteria, so deeply held or unquestioned is our culture's belief that male-female difference is fundamental to nature. The propensity for and tenacity of genderizing nongendered beings, reflected here in the natural sciences, suggests both the power and the function of gender ideology. Unintentional as it may be, such labeling nonetheless promotes a biological determinist view of "gender."

In the second example, the relations among elements are misrepresented as being hierarchical, under the control of one central "master," when they could just as easily, and more accurately, be presented as interactive and nonhierarchical. The textbook language describing the fundamental principles of the field of molecular biology is one of control of the genes over everything else in the cell:

The modern era of molecular cell biology has been mainly concerned with *how genes govern* cell activity. . . . [By 1952] a small group of informed scientists knew that DNA *was the controlling molecule of life*. (Darnell, Lodish, and Baltimore 11; emphasis added)

In contrast, the following quote from the same textbook illustrates the language used to describe the essential function of proteins:

proteins . . . work together to make a living cell. (viii)

Thus DNA controls, while proteins work. Proteins sound suspiciously like laborers who keep things going, while DNA contains the important information, the "blueprints," for controlling the cell from the nucleus, where DNA is contained in the chromosomes. Indeed, the most common term used for proteins is "gene products," defining proteins in terms of their subordinate relation to genes.

The feminist argument that unequal power relations carry gender associations through the history of Western civilization, usually traced back to Aristotle's expressions of misogyny, should be sufficient to appreciate the masculinist ideology built into singling out one component of the cell as controller of the life of the cell. In addition, recent historical studies provide evidence that scientists indeed have gendered the relationship of the nucleus and genes to the cytoplasm and proteins.[14]

Masculinist privileging of DNA as the "master molecule" (Keller, chs. 8 and 9) that controls the components of the cell in hierarchical fashion has not changed from the heyday of the 1960s, even though molecular biology has developed a language that acknowledges complexity in genetics and reciprocity of regulation. Alternatives to this hierarchical model of centralized control are not hard to find. It is just as accurate to say that proteins, in their ability to function as enzymes, in their contributions to enzyme action in structural, positional ways, also "control" genes. Furthermore, a tiny ion of magnesium "controls" the gene by being essential for replication and other activities of genes. Indeed, using the key concept of "regulation," we may characterize the activities of "life" as so intertwined that almost everything regulates almost everything else. To choose one component over all others as "primary" may be a useful heuristic device, but the language and basic principles of early and later molecular biology clearly use the primacy of DNA as a central tenet to organize not just the components of the cell but all biological knowledge. Thus we find a hidden epistemological stance: that DNA determines what constitutes knowledge—knowledge in the study of "life" and "knowledge" in the cell.[15]

In the third example, which encompasses the intertwined problems of biological determinism and inaccurate dualisms such as nature versus nurture, cancer is misrepresented as a disease that has solely physiological, genetic origins, rather than as the result of economic, political, and social forces. One of the consequences of the distortion in molecular biology is evident in common textbook descriptions of cancer, in which the basic question guiding the approach to understanding cancer is: How do genes control everything in the cell? and the guiding methodology is recombinant DNA technology, which sequences DNA and proteins. Cancer is considered primarily through the lens of molecular genetics because of the "extraordinary power" of those tools (Darnell, Lodish, and Baltimore, ch. 24; Watson et al., pt. 10). While that methodology has provided much information about a genetic analysis of cancer, it is incorrect then to assume that a genetic analysis is the *most* important one for understanding what causes cancer and how to prevent or cure it. Consider the difference between thinking that cancer is primarily the result of an individual's unfortunate genetic makeup and thinking that it is a problem influenced significantly by cancer-promoting chemicals and irradiation in our air, water, food, and workplaces—pollutants produced in good measure by industrial processes—and societal conditions and habits (and even the scientific experiments in this field that use radioactive and carcinogenic chemicals). Readers (undergraduate science majors, medical students, and graduate students) of these texts are not encouraged to consider the importance of factors that we know contribute to cancer in various populations. Not only does our scientific understanding of this disease suffer as a consequence of research programs based on this view, but the genetic-nongenetic form of the nature-nurture fallacy privileges the promise of a gene therapy approach to curing cancer while underplaying the data that most human cancers are caused or promoted by environmental carcinogens. The future researcher is encouraged by example to ignore major economic, political, and social forces that contribute significantly to this disease—rather than think of cancer as a disease not only of whole living-dying beings but of society.

I could provide additional examples of misrepresentation in the written discourse of science, but what I have presented should make my point: that a belief in centralized control and unequal power relations remains the overriding paradigm in molecular biology textbooks and scientific literature. The predominant meaning of "difference," even in progressive texts, carries strong overtones of "better than" and "power over," along with "fixed and hereditary," biologically determined by "genetics." With a natural hierarchy of power reinforced at yet another level of our worldview, all ideologies of "difference" are further cemented into a superior-inferior relation. Feminist analyses of this discourse demonstrate how pervasive are such beliefs about natural differences. To introduce into the biology curriculum such analyses of textbooks would, I suggest, give voice to many views in the classroom, but it would require a shift in emphasis, content, and ideology in the curriculum.

Impetus and Resources for Change in Science Education

For transformative writing projects in science classes and transformative science education to take place, explicit and implicit values and ideologies in the sciences must be assessed. But before we can evaluate hidden beliefs, we must acknowledge them. The impetus for such change may be found in concerns about projected shortfalls in the number of scientists and engineers and the lag in scientific literacy in the United States, as well as in the newer disciplines of the social studies of science and women's studies.

While some teachers have been working on a reorganization of the science curriculum to reflect social and political concerns and the major social challenges of our time, such as pollution, health care, the environment, and energy issues,[16] wholesale questioning has not reached the "canon" of college-level science education.[17] However, fueled by the pressures of economic competition, especially from Japan, and a concomitant increase in nationalistic chauvinism over United States preeminence in science, politicians, educators, and scientists alike have declared a crisis in scientific literacy. The organization that represents the largest number of scientists in the United States—AAAS, or the American Association for the Advancement of Science—has responded with a major project to transform the science curriculum in public schools. If successfully implemented, this curriculum would serve as an impetus to change in science education at the college level as well.

What is striking about Project 2061[18] of the AAAS is that it includes just those elements of science education that have been, for the most part, left out by most educators as "not science"—but that have been emphasized in the new social studies of science and women's studies: the dynamic interdependence of science and the society that creates it.

Thus, among the basic recommendations for scientific literacy are not only "understanding key concepts and principles of science," as expected, but also "knowing that science, mathematics, and technology are human enterprises and knowing what that implies about their strengths and limitations" and "using scientific knowledge and ways of thinking for individual and social purposes" (*AAAS*).[19]

This is a welcome effort for educators like myself and those engaged in potentially transformative writing projects. My experience teaching both biology (molecular biology, microbiology, and biochemistry) and women's studies courses (in particular on women, gender, and science) highlights the clash of the prevailing values in science and the ideals of the humanities. Students trained in the sciences find it difficult at first to overcome a passive, nonexpert stance and place their views into assignments about science in a social context. A telling illustration of this initial difficulty surfaced when many of the science majors who took my course Women Scientists in America: The Difference They Make[20] had to ask me several times if I *really* wanted them to use "I" in the papers they were writing for the course. I had told them to begin their papers by telling us why they had chosen their topic, and I had asked them as well to include their responses to the issues embedded in the topic. With encouragement and reassurance those students wrote excellent papers, in which each one's voice was clear and distinctive, each "I" placed well in the context of the analysis. But to do so, the students had to overcome their training in science—and related disciplines.

In contrast to these students trained in the sciences, seasoned women's studies students, educated to take themselves seriously and to place their knowledge and values at the center of their education, learn a balanced intersubjectivity. Feminist students try to integrate their diverse educational and personal encounters in their education. As a corollary to these observations, it should not be surprising that feminist students who bring their integrated approach to knowledge into the traditional science classroom are often discouraged by their science teachers and ultimately find it difficult to reconcile their feminist values with their interest in science.

Thus faculty members leading writing-across-the-curriculum projects in science courses may find discomfort or resistance among science educators and science students in assignments that require students to find a voice and have an opinion or perspective on the subject matter. The lack of awareness that the students or researchers have a perspective, and one that derives from their cultural experience and background, from their socioeconomic and religious upbringing, from their gender and their racial and ethnic identities, is not an accident. It is part of a basic tenet of "science" and "scientific objectivity" that *who* the scientist or student is has no bearing on the way she or he perceives the world, defines what is a problem, poses answers— hence, creates scientific knowledge.[21]

Yet we know that most scientists—and most college and university teachers of science—are a rather homogeneous bunch. Most of them are white, and most of them are male.[22] And the evidence mounts, from feminist and other radical critiques of science (Bleier; Gould; Haraway; Hubbard, Henifin, and Fried; Keller; Manning), that it matters, that our sciences and even our mathematics are distorted and partial views of nature because the group of people allowed to be scientists, allowed to define what science is and what problems are the important ones to give societal resources to, constitute a narrow slice of the population and claim to—but simply do not—represent society's interests in general. Antiscience stances that blame scientists alone for this problem and the ills science and technology have brought to society are inadequate for the kind of change most critics envision (Spanier, "Transforming"). Scientists do not act nor are they socialized independently of other sources of power in society; therefore, the gender, race, and class of our legislators and judiciary are significant, as well, in shaping what science is and who can practice it. Again, an integrated analysis of the distribution of power in society reveals the mutual reinforcement of dominant ideologies—and similarly reveals mutually reinforcing efforts to eliminate injustice.

A basic tenet of women's studies is that women deserve to be taken seriously as students (Rich). We can extend this principle to all students while we maintain an awareness of the differential societal treatment of women and people of color. Giving students permission and, more, encouragement and training to place themselves into the discourse of science is one way of breaking through the constraints of traditional science education. But what could students have informed opinions about in a biology or other science course? Among the many possibilities, the problems of overtly biased ideology identified and challenged by feminists can be useful. For example, a chemistry professor devoted one of the weekly three-hour laboratory periods in an introductory course to a discussion of scientific and media articles on gender differences and mathematical performance.[23] The teacher reported:

> Class discussion, a notoriously difficult goal for a college freshman course in chemistry, was explosive during this session where

every student participated eagerly for the entire three-hour period. Most importantly, the distinction between statistical facts and their theoretical interpretations, and the necessity for exploring the logical assumptions hidden behind each theory, became abundantly clear to students who were not always eager to think logically about drier issues in chemical theories.   (Pastra-Landis 207–08)

It is noteworthy that, in their short reaction papers, students placed themselves into the critical analysis, with comments such as, "I grew to realize the necessity of analyzing data for oneself, and the importance of questioning opinions that are not backed up by facts" and "It seemed obvious to me that a conclusion could not be made from these data alone." These students are taking an active analytical stance, not that of passive recipients of knowledge.

Who Will Do Science?

At the risk of overgeneralizing about the state of science education and the practice and communication of science among professional scientists (researchers and educators), I would suggest that the ideologies and practices that make it difficult to incorporate student-centered writing into the curriculum may also tend to alienate certain groups of students (that is, white women, women and men of color, and, perhaps to a lesser extent, counterculture white males) from science education and the scientific professions.[24]

The identification of a national science personnel emergency has increased awareness of the waste of human resources and generated projects to encourage the participation and retention in science of underrepresented groups. The impact of gender, race, and class as major categories of organization in society becomes quite clear when we look at who does science: women constitute only about 20–25% of molecular biologists; underrepresented racial-ethnic groups constitute perhaps 2–4%. While institutional barriers are probably the major reason for the disproportionately low participation of women and people of color—along with the general belief in science as a masculine and elitist endeavor *and* the (perhaps unconscious) prejudices by scientists against women and people of color as colleagues—I suggest that the impact of certain ideologies on the *content* of biology and molecular biology may also contribute to the exclusion of individuals and groups from these fields.

While it is difficult to prove, we must consider the possibility that these ideological problems may affect women and other marginalized groups in science.[25] Molecular biology (and biology in general) may unknowingly promote the exclusion of politically aware women, people of color, and certain majority men as well in the following ways: reinforcing a sexist (and, by analogy, racist) ideology of difference by adding another dimension at the cellular and molecular organization of living beings, widening the gap between science and society, and selecting against individuals with egalitarian, antisexist, and antiracist values (these tend to be women and members of other underrepresented groups). My interviews and discussions with women, particularly feminist scientists and science and engineering students, point to the interweaving of issues of participation in science and of issues of the content of science. In their experience, feminist, Afrocentric, and other radical political and ethical concerns frequently clash with the practices and values of science. Thus acknowledging and reevaluating dominant ideologies in the content of the sciences may serve to empower a more diverse cross-section of science students, a necessary effort if we are to open science to all segments of the population and eliminate our scientific literacy problem.

While many scientist-educators may be uncomfortable with the discussion of explicit values and ideologies in the classroom, there are encouraging movements afoot from several quarters to support potentially transformative science education. The introduction of a nontraditional perspective from outside the discipline—from writing-across-the-curriculum projects—holds the promise of increasing scientists' awareness of the norms of their profession, a necessary change if we are to attain equity within the profession and eliminate distortions in our understanding of nature. A constructive view of conflicts between conventional biology (and by analogy the other natural sciences) and transformative writing projects is that the points of tension are both deterrents to successful writing projects in the sciences (to be addressed in such projects) *and* opportunities for writing across the disciplines to effect changes in the norms of the college science curriculum. Thus writing projects in the natural sciences curriculum have the potential to foster important changes in scientists' perspectives on the relation of science to society—and to empower all students to gain access to scientific knowledge that is informed by critical political perspectives.

NOTES

This work has been generously supported over several years by grants from the State University of New York Faculty Research Award Program, the Nuala Drescher Award of NYS/United University Professors, and Irving and Roselyn Solomon Spanier. I would also like to acknowledge the Lilly Endowments Grant on Women in American Society, Bunting Institute of Radcliffe College, 1978–80, which allowed me to start my work on science and feminism.

[1] Many great thinkers of Western culture, such as Aristotle, Thomas Aquinas, and Saint Paul, believed that it is in the nature of being female to be subordinate; it was similarly asserted that it is in the nature of slaves to serve their masters. See Agonito; Osborne.

[2] For example, the editor of *Science* magazine wrote, "[T]he goal [of *Science*] should be to present as close to the unvarnished truth as it is possible to achieve" (Koshland).

[3] Students are seen as passively taking in a set of "objective facts" before they have the background to understand how to think about the creation of scientific knowledge; thus, too many students have not been taught how to critique scientific information or how to think creatively in science.

[4] It is a commonplace that, after several biology courses, a biology major does not understand her own body. In contrast, feminist courses such as Biology and Women's Issues (taught by Ruth Hubbard at Harvard University) and Women and Their Bodies in Health and Disease (taught by Marianne Whatley at the University of Wisconsin, Madison) break down the false duality of subject and object.

[5] My statements are generalizations about the dominant modes of science education and are not blanket criticisms of science educators. There are certainly many individual science instructors who teach from a different set of beliefs and concerns, but few departments or institutions. An important exception, fueled by concerns about the discouragement from science of women and minority students, is the science curriculum at Hampshire College. It includes the first-year seminars The Biology of Women, Human Movement in Physiology, and Ethical Issues in Biomedical Research, a seminar for majors about women in science, and a pedagogy that encourages collaboration and collective learning about scientific topics of particular relevance to societal problems (Strauss).

[6] This view asserts that inequities may derive from the particular situation, but all are informed by structural, institutionalized power relations such as male over female, white over nonwhite, dominant culture over subordinate "subcultures" (even the language reflects the reluctance to admit the possibility of "co-cultures").

[7] This is not an essentialist stance about inherent abilities. While Fetterley's original work justifiably focused on women as resisting readers, I am not assuming that a "resisting reader" (or a liberatory science teacher) has to be female. A feminist perspective is an achieved consciousness, more often

achieved by women (than men) through experiences as women in our society. "Experiences as women" means being identified as and treated as females (recall the movie *Tootsie*), experiences that vary widely with race, class, sexual preference, age, ableness, and so on.

[8] The dominant value system, deconstructed from a feminist perspective, includes hatred and envy of women, especially women who try to act independently from men. Women's resistance, then, is often fueled by anger at perceiving societal woman-hating at the foundation of our literary education.

[9] The "resisting reader" does not stop reading the canon. She (and, we hope, he, too) does, however, read it with an expanded gender consciousness that recognizes and questions the hidden ideologies of sexism, heterosexism, racism, and classism. Then the "resisting reader," at least in my experience, hungers for her own voice and the voices and experiences of the excluded. Eventually, as a result of many resisting readers, the canon is transformed in ways that go light years beyond "add-women-and-stir."

[10] See Harding (*Science Question* and *Whose Science?*) for the complexities of feminist empiricist, feminist standpoint, and feminist postmodern epistemologies.

[11] *Heterosexism* refers to the institution and belief in the naturalness and superiority of heterosexuality as compared to homosexuality. Since sexism includes the belief in the natural sexual complementarity of male and female, heterosexism is actually embedded within sexism. But homophobia (the fear of homosexuality) often prevents us from understanding that aspect of sexism.

[12] My study analyzes the discourse of scientists in formal communications with one another—that is, in scientific journals and annual reviews—and with their students, who may be the next generation of molecular biologists—that is, in major textbooks directed at serious students of biology (Spanier, *Gender* and "Gender"). Textbooks in this field play a critical role in conveying, to the next generation of scientists, the values and beliefs of the leaders in molecular biology research. Thus the examples in this essay are taken from an excellent and widely used introductory textbook, written by three outstanding researchers in the field.

[13] This example can be found in all textbooks in molecular biology. Two of the excellent books that repeat this error are Darnell, Lodish, and Baltimore and Watson et al.

[14] Specifically, Scott Gilbert's studies in the history of cell biology document the association of the nucleus with the male and the cytoplasm with the female because the structure of the sperm cell is mainly a nucleus with a tail, while the egg cell has both nucleus and a large volume of cytoplasm containing other cellular organelles such as ribosomes and mitochondria. Debates in the 1930s about the relation between nucleus and cytoplasm—cast in terms of power relationships—involved metaphors of marriage and the "appropriate" relationship between husband and wife. Several different relationships were posited by the American and European scientists (all male) involved—domination of the nucleus over the cytoplasm, equal sharing of power and responsibility, and

domination of the cytoplasm over the nucleus—each corresponding to the personal and cultural attitude and experience of the individual scientists (Biology and Gender Study Group; S. Gilbert, unpublished).

[15] This distorted conflation is perhaps nowhere more evident than in the multibillion-dollar project to determine the complete DNA sequence of the human genome—all the genetic material in a human. As James Watson so clearly put it, the goal of this project is "to find out what being human is" (Roberts).

[16] One project under way since at least 1983 is the National Science Teachers Association's Scope, Sequence, and Coordination of Secondary School Science. For more information on the more than three hundred major policy studies on science and math education in the United States, write to Jay Shiro Tashiro, Math and Science Inst., Simon's Rock Coll., Great Barrington, MA 02130.

[17] It is fair to say that in the scholarship of higher education, it has been primarily educators (some of them scientists) in the new fields of the social study of science and women's studies who have challenged the traditional practices of science (the scientific method as a purely objective endeavor) that have tended to discourage scientists and science educators themselves from exploring not only the presence or absence of values and ideologies (such as sexism and racism) in the sciences but also the consequences for their students of societal values in science (see, for example, Harding, *Whose Science?* and *Science*; Keller; Knorr-Cetina and Mulkay; Restivo).

[18] Project 2061 is named for the next time that Comet Halley will return to our skies; the project started in 1985 when the comet was last seen. For a different assessment of the problem of scientific literacy and personnel shortfalls, see Tobias. That analysis is pertinent to some of the issues I raise with regard to who will do (and learn) science.

[19] Other specific aspects of science and technology are delineated that clearly reflect a commitment to a new kind of science curriculum, embracing many of the concerns of radical critics. That ideal curriculum would address: (1) the relation of science, mathematics, and technology to the social system in which they are embedded; in particular, technology understood as a product of social and economic forces, one that, in turn, affects human society in major, not always anticipated, ways; (2) the history of science and technology within the context of time and place; (3) science, mathematics, and technology as expressions "of both human ingenuity and human limitations" with broader dimensions, such as aesthetic, emotional, and ethical, than rationality or objectivity; (4) the fact and history of social barriers that have "led to the underrepresentation of women and minorities" in spite of the view that scientific progress depends on "the cumulative efforts of human beings with diverse interests, talents, and personalities"; (5) the insight that major changes occur in science, such as shifting boundaries of subdisciplines and different subject matter, and the need for a range of approaches (descriptive, experimental, and historical, for example); (6) the need "to identify and avoid bias." Other specifics empha-

size the impact of cultural settings and environmental factors—rather than genetics—on behavior and physical and mental health.

[20] I taught this course in 1984 as a visiting scholar at Wheaton College, after having been a regular biology professor there from 1975 to 1978 and then the director of the Balanced Curriculum Project from 1980 to 1983. The course was offered as an advanced special-topics course in the biology department through the open-minded encouragement of the new chair of biology, John Kricher. I have subsequently taught different versions of the course at SUNY Albany through the women's studies program, where the participants were primarily nonscience majors. Such courses serve equally important but usually quite different purposes for science majors and nonscience (even antiscience) students.

[21] Efforts in some biology courses to highlight individual voices in science are often limited to assigning James Watson's *Double Helix*. Here, an arrogant young personality with an extreme case of masculinist values (ruthless competition, the end justifies the means, women are entertainment or to be otherwise used) becomes a model of the successful and brilliant scientist. *The Double Helix* is, indeed, an interesting and valuable study of dominant ideologies in the practice of science. Watson's continued success as a scientist-administrator is seen in his appointment as the head of the Human Genome Project. That book should not be read or taught without Anne Sayre's book on Rosalind Franklin, the talented woman scientist from whom Watson and Francis Crick stole the critical data in the elucidation of the double helical structure of DNA and whom Watson demeans and misrepresents throughout (also, Hubbard).

[22] Only about 15% of all scientists and engineers are female, and less than 10% of the total are African American, Native American, Latino, and Asian men and women. However, those percentages are misleading, since they include the social sciences, with their significantly higher proportions of women and people of color. As recently as 1988, less than 10% of the doctorates in the physical sciences and engineering went to women (A. Anderson). The proportion of African Americans, Native Americans, and Latinos with doctorates in the natural sciences remains low. Asian Americans constitute a slightly higher (and increasing) proportion. While discrimination against Asians and Asian Americans is a significant problem, it appears to be of a lower magnitude and involve a different range of issues from the near-absence of blacks, Latinos, and tribal peoples.

[23] The students were given a week to read the article by Camilla Persson Benbow and Julian C. Stanley, published in the respected journal *Science*, claiming to show that differences in the proportions of young boys and girls with extraordinary math talent must be the result of inherent sex differences. Students also read commentary on the article by other scientists and by writers in the popular media. Wheaton's Balanced Curriculum Project in the psychology department used gender differences and societal beliefs as the major theme in the different sections of the introductory course; it also generated much

discussion and experience with critical analysis of scientific claims and societal values. See Spanier, Bloom, and Boroviak, as well as other feminist projects to transform the curriculum.

[24] A related argument is made by Sue Rosser (*Female-Friendly* 60, 68). Although little attention is given to the use of writing in transforming science courses, Rosser's books, *Teaching Science and Health from a Feminist Perspective* and *Female-Friendly Science: Applying Women's Studies Methods and Theories to Attract Students*, are rich sources for specific suggestions about curricular improvement for more (gender-, race-, class-) inclusive science courses.

[25] Serious science students are inculcated with the dominant beliefs in the sciences and also selected for their resonance to those beliefs. Thus the exceptional women and other underrepresented group members who enter and stay in the sciences are likely to share the dominant ideologies and values. Perceived as marginal, they may feel they have more to lose by taking a less popular stance or challenging the predominant attitudes. Those who are turned away by dominant attitudes are not present among scientists to be studied.

Advocacy and Neutrality: A Contradiction in the Discourse of Urban Planners

Louise Dunlap

The author is senior lecturer in writing and communication in the
Department of Urban Studies and Planning at MIT.
*I was glad to find a community of thinkers when writing across the disciplines
emerged about the same time I found myself teaching in urban planning. My
personal journey had taken me from a dissertation in medieval visionary wordplay
to this utilitarian, yet still visionary, new field—where language can lead to action
in the world. The planners liked my ideas about rhetoric and process, which
overlapped with some of theirs, and their interests in the environment and social
action were old ones of mine. After ten years I think I've lost some of my "outsider"
status, but the literature of writing across the disciplines has kept me in touch
with my full identity.*

This essay comes from ten years' experience teaching writing to graduate students in urban and regional planning, a field that attempts to
integrate the thinking of architects, economists, human service provid-
ers, environmentalists, and others into a professional practice that will
actively solve social problems. Although advocacy is intrinsic to most
conceptions of planning, the central problem in my students' work is
a deep reluctance to make assertions or to organize information into
critical arguments. Most students unconsciously self-censor their most
challenging thoughts and cloak what is left in obscure, "objective,"
actionless language—always seeming to prefer "neutral" or encyclopedic writing to the "critical" writing we say we want them to do.

What accounts for students' reluctance to assert? Most teachers understand the many factors that operate across the curriculum to inhibit
"voice" in academia—students are in a hurry, new to their subjects,
afraid to take risks. But I want to suggest a cause less discussed in

pedagogical circles: students' reluctance to assert is part of a pattern that affects the entire professional world they seek to enter. The models for writing in the planning field (and perhaps in others) are contradictory. My colleagues insist that good writing means writing that makes some kind of argument. I like to call it "critical writing," in resonance with the Greek root *krinein*, which means to "discern" or "discriminate." This root activity of scientific inquiry includes not only identification of separate issues (analysis) but judgments about which are most important. The weighting of points constitutes one's position, which may be argued with different degrees of advocacy. Despite the value that my colleagues place on writing, however, much of the writing they assign to students, and sometimes even compose themselves, is what I have come to call "neutral writing"—writing that attempts to present information without discriminating, writing that is somehow "objective" and positionless.

Good examples of "objective" and positionless writing are found in the genres of the environmental impact statement and the teaching case study. In the EIS, a team of consultants, often interdisciplinary, presents data on the anticipated effects of a proposal to build or develop. The audience is the most complicated imaginable—a government agency with power of decision over the project, other technical experts, and an often highly politicized general public. Most EISs are long and "encyclopedic," structured in categorized lists of all possible information relevant to alternative courses of action, without stating a position on them. This apparently neutral writing, of course, is not value-free (Susskind and Dunlap), yet its endless and positionless detail is a model for students as they imagine themselves doing "professional" writing. While planning instructors may ask them to write quite differently—for instance, to do a critical analysis of a case study—they usually don't assign model analyses for students to read. Instead, students read the case itself—again, an apparently neutral compendium of information on a planning situation. Such a case study may be the only writing by their professor that students read. The message is "do what we say, not what we do," and the confusion reinforces students' prior misconceptions.

But the mixed message about writing runs deeper than pedagogy, I think. It reflects a contradiction in what planners themselves value as writing, which itself reflects the conflicting natures of the institutions in which they work. The contradiction affects practice even beyond these institutions and affects urban planning classrooms that attempt to teach critical writing.

In what follows I examine the planning field in more detail and explore the struggle of one practitioner-academic to deal with the contradiction. I suggest a theory that explains the contradiction and tell the story of another practitioner who was able to transform the neutral writing in her workplace. I end with ideas about teaching in this field and some speculations about how typical the experience of planners may be.

The Planning Field and Its Discourse

In professional planning practice, designers or architects may work together with economists, statisticians, sociologists, geographers, engineers, natural scientists, historians, policy analysts, lawyers, and management specialists. Sometimes philosophers, transportation specialists, journalists, public health specialists, community organizers, anthropologists, and many others get in on the act. To a certain extent planners see themselves as the ones who "translate ideas" from the more technical disciplines into language accessible to everyone involved (Susskind and Dunlap 353).

About two-thirds of those who teach in the 155 planning departments in the United States have had their training in a discipline other than planning ("Recruitment" 7), and planning educators may fall anywhere on the broad continuum that connects scholarship with professional practice. Theory and academic research have very different priorities (and discourse modes) from the messy political flux of actual planning experience. There are also the distinctions between local, national, and international scenarios for planning and between work in the public and in the private sectors.

How do we define a discipline that includes all these fields of activity? As an even newer discipline than sociology or public administration, for example, planning has less internal agreement about identity. It is also less secure and established. Many of the social programs that launched the discipline—public housing, the war on poverty, and the funded research that went along with them—were decimated during the 1980s. Where will planning students work, and what do we need to teach to assure their effectiveness and influence? The newness of the field, its changing mandate, its eclectic disciplinary identity, its need to communicate with both academics and those immersed in practice, its possibly precarious future—all affect planners' conception of themselves and their discourse.

An Example from Practice: Struggling with the Contradictions

One colleague whose practice brings some of these questions into specific focus is Ralph Gakenheimer, one-time editor of the *Journal of the
American Planning Association* and professor of both urban studies
and civil engineering at MIT. Gakenheimer specializes in urban transportation, infrastructure, and urban development planning in both the
United States and the developing countries and is well connected in
these fields. He writes for an international community of experts in his
specialties and for consulting clients as well as for academic audiences.

Gakenheimer's situation is hardly typical, yet it is interesting for
several reasons. First, he writes a great deal (often up to 30 pages a
day on client reports) and addresses diverse audiences enmeshed in
the politics of decision making. He also has a strong sense of the
potential of language, more than other planners I've worked with, and
he struggles mightily with his writing, particularly with what I see as
the basic contradiction between neutral and critical.

I have been able to follow the struggle closely. Gakenheimer and I
have been in a department writing group for two years. He is interested
enough in my analysis of neutral writing to discuss the concept with
me frequently, to articulate the goals of neutral writing, and to describe
professional situations in which it has played a necessary role. But
what I call "critical" writing (a term he sees as too easily confused with
"judgmental") he claims to find difficult. Academic colleagues tell him
his usual prose is dense and ambiguous; writing that takes a clear
position on issues as complex as those he deals with requires not only
the will to take a position but a higher than usual degree of rewriting
and recrafting, which academic editors insist on. For a variety of reasons, Gakenheimer is not at home writing for audiences that require
this level of explicitness and clarity.

Critical Writing for an Academic Audience

To explore Gakenheimer's struggle, I am going to reproduce contrasting examples of his writing—one "critical" and one not. The first
is from an essay for academic readers that he was invited to write for
an anthology on teaching students from poor and developing countries.
I reproduce his entire introductory section because it gives a concrete
picture of the conflicting pressures and audience dynamics he faces in
his professional work and, at the same time, illustrates his ability, when
pushed, to do powerful critical thinking and critical writing for an
academic audience. At his editor's request, Gakenheimer restructured

this essay several times, throwing out over half of the original. Partly in jest, he claims that the current text is worth $1,000 a page at his consulting rates.

The Job of Transportation Education

The critical task in transportation education is deciding what to teach. Transportation problems are kaleidoscopic: viewed from slightly different angles they appear to be entirely different problems—inadequate street capacity, excessive use of private automobiles; misfitting technologies, such as low-speed nonmotorized vehicles on high-speed roads, or insufficient public discipline to keep parking from obstructing traffic flow; mud and grades that make ways impassable; service agency inadequacies that make public transport very inefficient; low personal incomes that limit mobility, and so on. Each perspective on the problem requires a different approach and different skills.

In the fragmented international professional community of transport planners different groups take different approaches. Some focus on increasing street capacity. They are often systems-oriented, predefining and assessing the problem as one of equilibrium between the demand and the supply facilities. Some groups aim at reducing the use of private automobiles by taxing them or restricting their use on certain streets. Some strive for greater system efficiency by sorting out the incompatible vehicles that use the same traffic ways, redesigning intersections, or by reducing obstructive parking, all through traffic engineering—the approach likely to make the greatest and lowest-cost short-run gains. Others focus on the institutional barriers—removing the mud and grades by improvements enabled through more adequate project financing and programming. They want to improve the public transport service by reorganizing chaotic transit agencies. Yet others see the transport problem as an undetachable element of the large economy. They advocate strategies to raise personal income as the key toward more transport access and a better life in general. There are many variations within each approach. Aggressive international interests represent each one.

In stable settings of public management the place of each of these approaches becomes conventionalized. The different approaches have levels of agreed applicability: they become the jobs of different agencies. But in institutional environments beset by uncertainty and frequent change, these approaches come and go with bewildering speed. Agency leadership may espouse one approach while a consultant advocating it is under contract, abandoning it for a different approach when the next consultant arrives. Advocates of several approaches may staff the same agency, the approach currently favored at any one time being a temporary outcome of agency politics.

This paper argues that transportation planners of the Third World, in contrast with those in the more settled pattern of First World planning, must be able to cope with widely different problem perceptions according to the moment and the situation. They must also know a wide range of techniques to deal with these different problem perceptions. This does not mean the planner should make facile choices of political convenience. While being flexible, the planner needs a firm commitment to the problem— a commitment that avoids token or cosmetic solutions in the face of its graveness, and doesn't lend itself to advocate sketchy general perspectives that cannot be of much use for practical policies.

Today's training programs seldom create this *flexible* yet *committed* professional identity. My teaching and practice suggest it is the key to significant problem penetration in the Third World. ("Comparison" 155–56)

As critical writing for an academic audience, this passage seems to me exemplary. Gakenheimer first describes the range of perspectives on Third World transportation problems with careful discernment. Then, in the second paragraph, he describes the related complexity of the fragmented group of transport professionals, and, in the third, he describes the complexity of their institutional settings. Having linked and weighted the issues, he twists all of them into a critical assertion in the short final paragraph. A clear pedagogical position emerges out of the confusion: professional training needs to emphasize both "flexibility" and "commitment." We look to the remainder of the essay to tell us how it can do so, and we are grateful for the crafting and the clarity of this opening, whatever its cost.

The Uses of Neutral Writing

By way of comparison, here is the introductory section from a piece Gakenheimer says is typical of the writing he does as a professional planner. He wrote the report from which this passage is taken for an international organization in Nairobi, which had sponsored a conference he was asked to convene among international experts on modal choice in transportation. While the conference focused on financial viability of transportation options (bus, rail, auto, etc.), the sponsoring organization asked (after the event) that the report focus on environmental concerns—sustainability—which the conference barely touched on. The switch in topic (and the divergence of values it signals) made it difficult for Gakenheimer to take any sort of position in the writing. He needed to satisfy the sponsoring organization (his client), yet at the same time, in his words, to "be respectful of persons who made the input," with most of whom he has ongoing professional connections. He makes tactful reference to this challenging task in a footnote I also include.

In form this introduction is similar to the one written for the academic audience: the initial paragraphs list a wide range of options, and a brief concluding paragraph narrows down their implications. But there are major differences in level of assertions, and, unlike the more critical piece, this one cannot be said to advocate either a line of thinking or an action.

Public Transit Mode Choice and
Sustainable Development in the Developing Countries[1]

The choice of mode for a new transit subsystem is a moment of utmost importance for a large city in the developing world. It is a choice that sets the reach of achievable transit network density and coverage of the city. It is a moment of determining the maximum level of transit corridors' passenger capacity—and the level of service in general. It is a commitment to a form of financing major capital and operating responsibilities—sources of revenue and amount of subsidy. It partly determines the extent of support possible to policies for sustaining environmental quality.

While negotiating the selection of a transit mode there are opportunities for leveraging coordinated action on dependent urban systems. A favorable mode choice can support plans for improved planning of the density and location of future urban development. It is a time for insisting on compatible roles for the existing urban transportation modes. That is, we may insist on pedestrianization or the restriction of downtown parking in exchange for new central city access, require feeder roles to the new subsystem for existing bus and paratransit services. It is a time when it may be possible to change conventions on who is responsible for financing public services, perhaps newly including non-user beneficiaries. It may be a moment for devolving decision making responsibility from national to metropolitan authorities. So far planners have sought few of these opportunities.

These opportunities must be interpreted in the context of two important understandings of the purpose of urban development: *economic productivity* and *environmental sustainability*.

[1] This report addresses—(*sponsoring organization's*) concern for public transit and sustainable development as informed by an expert-group meeting on mode choice. It is not a report on the expert-group meeting as such. The focus of _____'s concern evolved and matured during the preparation and execution of the meeting and was critically contemplated by the experts. Their views, cited here throughout, are fundamental to the current shape of the transit-suitable development concept and to thinking about the next steps.

This second introduction comes much closer to neutral writing. As in the first example, we are moved into the subject through carefully selected lists—in paragraph one, of implications facing a Third World city in selecting a public transit form; in paragraph two, of opportunities for the transit choice to influence other policy. In each list there is some allusion to environmental quality, the most important theme for the sponsoring organization and the least discussed theme of the conference (key words are "sustainability," "pedestrianization," etc.). In each, there are also references to the financing of transit, which was the actual focus of the conference. The two lists are related but not so tightly linked as in the first example, nor are items within each list closely linked.

What is most strikingly different in this second example, however, is the degree of assertiveness of the final short paragraph. While the earlier example ends with a fairly strong claim that planning education needs to develop "*flexible* yet *committed*" practitioners—two terms that had become clear in the previous discussion—this one ends by merely posing two relatively undeveloped concepts for further exploration. Gakenheimer's expression "must be interpreted" may *sound* strong, but the sentence does not argue, much less advocate, a position on what has preceded it. While "environmental sustainability" has been thematic (and is the key theme for the primary audience), "economic productivity" has been only vaguely alluded to. Perhaps a knowing reader would guess what the author is saying: Out of all the themes I am mentioning, there are two I am going to discuss—not because they are necessarily related but because I need to cover them for my two audiences.

"Irresolution"   This "neutral" mode of writing is the one in which Gakenheimer feels most at home. Here the struggle is not to craft a coherent position on information but to reflect a situation characterized by what he calls "a sense of irresolution." His word is interesting: it does not refer to himself as vacillating or wavering, but to a rhetorical situation in which dilemmas are not resolvable. Writing from within unresolvable tensions does not seem to slow Gakenheimer down or require multiple drafts so much as it assures that the writing will be unclear as to ultimate position. Gakenheimer defends the use of neutral writing in the many situations he encounters. His intention is not to take a middle position but to stop at the implications of evidence. To take a position would be "not commitment but posture." Assertive writing usually seems to him "a loud voice," which should not be mistaken for strength of character. "Indeed," he says, "it may reflect weakness of character, intolerance for ambiguity," since "in this field, few positions are 'right.' " Working so often in the presence of irresolution also makes it difficult to write at other times in the positioned mode. For Gakenheimer, "the irresolution creates complexities that ricochet back into one's whole writing style."

"Fast Writing" Other conditions in Gakenheimer's professional situation make this neutral writing his preferred mode. The need for speed is one of these conditions. Gakenheimer's professional writing life consists largely of what he terms "fast writing" (which he thinks we should teach students); he spends 90% of his time on a professional assignment on site, and he writes on his lap as he flies home from Cairo, Jakarta, or La Paz. This writing is often done "after there is no more budget" in a consulting job and is thus almost never rewritten. Careful structuring or crafting of such work, he says, "has a limited payoff," because clients and other readers don't read for enjoyment but to "mine it," to find what can be "used for ammunition" and what will need to be refuted.

Genres like the "Inception Report" A second condition is determined by what Gakenheimer's clients in professional practice expect and need. Gakenheimer readily admits that written products called for in consulting are "neutral"—for instance, the genre of the inception report. The inception report is submitted after a consultant has gained a contract. It is a reply to the terms-of-reference section in the contract— which is, itself, a model of apparent neutrality. The inception report presents an initial review of the problematic situation after a quick survey of alternatives and circumstances. "Any sense of predisposition" shown in the document, Gakenheimer says, will harm your standing with your client and all other parties to the situation. In such a report, a consultant, who has status as a truth sayer, seeks to define grounds for study that respect the limitations of sketchy information and also tries "to balance all the forces pressing in on the situation." In the unusual case in which there are grounds for assertion in an inception report, Gakenheimer says, "then by implication there is no need for a study" (personal interview).

Disciplinary Linguistic Habits Gakenheimer's training in civil engineering is also a factor in his struggles with the neutral style. Although some planning colleagues tell him he shouldn't, he actually admires the passive voice because it makes ideas "hard to track." He cannot fully repudiate his engineer's training that "the first person should never be used," that "logic" should carry your argument, not the "opinion" that takes over if "you enter the sentence as an individual." He also prefers to write with nouns, as in these lines excerpted from his transport education essay:

> For example, the current *focus* is *logistics*—the *use* of mathematical *algorithms* to increase the efficiency of *transport* systems in the *accomplishment* of prespecified *vehicle deployment requirements*. ("Comparison" 159; italics mine)

Almost every noun in this sentence (even those used as adjectives) hides an important verb, yet the thought seems well, even elegantly, packed together. Gakenheimer says such noun concepts are, for him, "too difficult to englobe in other words." As nouns, the concepts are ideas a reader can take or leave; as verbs, they might seem coercive, he feels. Often his passives are a witty response to the irresolution he so frequently deals with, as in the footnote to the transit study quoted above, in which he says that a sustainable environment "was critically contemplated by the experts."

How Representative Is Gakenheimer's Practice?

Disciplinary training, audience expectations, and perhaps a deep personal affinity for ambiguity have led Gakenheimer to the kind of professional writing in which he now excels. In the most complicated of disputes, he gives voice to the most complicated information without apparently taking a position on it. His writing may chronicle many dimensions of reality without prioritizing them, as critical writing does, to the chagrin of his more social-science-oriented planning colleagues. Whether to bridge the interdisciplinary gaps or in response to some inner leanings, Gakenheimer is now trying to shift gears in his writing practice, to take time to structure and craft positioned pieces of writing like the pedagogical essay. It will be interesting to see his positions on the deeply ambiguous world he studies and works in.

But Gakenheimer's work takes place in some of the most powerful circles of planning. Is his practice at all representative of the dilemmas of planners? I can recount almost endless examples of people in a wide range of planning-related jobs who felt vaguely uncomfortable with the perceived need to do neutral writing. Many of them were in entry-level positions; one, for instance, was a researcher for an environmental consulting firm who was asked to "objectively" write up "pure informa-tion" for an EIS without taking any position on it. (She had no idea where to begin.) Likewise, a housing specialist for a major Connecticut city, who was supposed to be an especially good writer, had the job of pasting "other cities' housing policies into our own reports," a practice her boss told her was "not plagiarism but research."

Although the products might resemble each other in form, however, neutral writing at Gakenheimer's level in the planning process is a much more highly skilled activity than the neutral writing in these other examples. The positionless writing often required of people in entry-level jobs lacks the controlling conceptualization from which Gakenheimer operates and has little power to shape outcomes. Yet the expert and the entry-level forms of neutral writing resemble each other enough to constitute a model that has come to exert considerable influence over my students. This model is so pervasive, so common across disciplinary lines, and so extremely seductive, that I have tried to discover a broader explanation for it.

Some Theorizing: Neutral and Critical Writing across the Professions

To understand the pervasiveness of the model and why Gakenheimer struggles with it, we need to look at the role writing and writers play in the economic system in general—across all the professions—be-cause this role constrains the way writing is done and thus the nature of the written discourse students and practitioners see and imitate. My approach is inspired by ideas from nonneoclassical economics—particularly studies of labor markets and the labor process (Braver-man; Harrison and Bluestone; Garson; Dunlap, "Professional Writing") that seem to resonate with the many personal stories I have listened to. Very briefly, there are two key concepts in this view of the writer's situation: a vast restructuring of the world economy, and the conse-quent reorganization of work processes in every industry and at every level.

Global Economic Restructuring

The first concept, the restructuring of the global economy, refers to the changing worldwide division of labor. Large multinational companies with the resources to do so are moving physical production processes—the factory assembly of raw materials into consumer goods—from the United States into less-developed countries. Sometimes parts of a single garment or car are assembled in several Third World countries, then brought back to the United States to be assembled into the final product.

The part of production that involves paperwork, however—the managerial activities of the companies involved in international relocation—remains here in the United States (or other developed countries). Because economic restructuring has dispersed and fragmented production, its managerial functions have had to become much more extensive. Whole industries, such as insurance, health care, advertising, banking and finance, legal, engineering, and architectural services, and many kinds of consulting, have sprung up to provide services not needed in the same way when production took place on a relatively small scale within a given community. In these new industries—and in the managerial wings of the more traditional production industries—writing plays a major role. Not only is writing important for internal communication, but in most of the service sector industries, the products are reports, policy, advice—all in written form. Thus writing has become an essential skill for people entering almost any profession in the new economy. Gakenheimer's writing is an example of the communication required in this new global process.

Redesign of Professional Work

Along with global restructuring comes the need (and opportunity) to restructure the process by which a given bit of work is done. A new division of labor at the international scale brings further divisions in the managerial work that remains. Here the Babbage principle generally rules: that tasks in any given endeavor should be organized for greatest efficiency. This approach, which is well known for bringing Taylorism and Fordism to the factory shop floor, has its analogue in professional work and certainly in the production of written work across the professions. With the exception of the few occupations in which work is still done individually—perhaps free-lance journalism, perhaps consulting by a single professional like Gakenheimer (although I would argue that both these examples are anachronistic)—writing is a team effort, with different individuals taking responsibility for various segments of (or themes in) a particular product. In addition,

production is usually managed hierarchically rather than collaboratively (which would mean egalitarian dialogue and decision making
among writers). I offer one illustration of how this management model
affects a writer's work. As I have recounted elsewhere, a student of
mine held the position of research analyst in a consulting firm that was
undertaking to evaluate compliance with a federal policy on discrimination against disabled employees ("Deskilling"). She was asked to
analyze data collected by others in the firm and to draft the standard
section of the evaluation explaining nonresponse to the survey her firm
had conducted. When she found a pattern in the lack of response that
revealed a flaw in the survey (and also shed light on the client's ongoing
problem with the term "disabled"), she was reprimanded and her draft
rewritten by her supervisor (with key ideas omitted and an infusion of
passive verbs).

In her firm, the task of critical analysis was structured into three
stages, each performed by a different person. The researcher gathered
the data, the analyst wrote a draft, but the supervisor, knowing both
the client's and the firm's needs best, made the ultimate decision about
what the report would say. Only the supervisor had the authority to do
critical writing (and in this case he decided that neutral writing would
be more appropriate). All subordinates—even those asked to draft the
report—were expected to do neutral writing. The student found this
demeaning and eventually quit her job. But how many do not?

The Contradictory Balance

I also hear stories about professional writing projects that run into
difficulty because supervisors are not able to find people who can do—
or are willing to do—critical writing. Stories such as Graham Smart's
at the National Bank of Canada—in which analysts joining the work
force with new PhDs in economics wrote neutral reports rather than
the kind of critical analysis their supervisors needed in order to set
policy—appear to point the finger at an educational system that turns
out neutral writers. Yet the many stories I hear from practice suggest
that on-the-job training, as illustrated by the student who worked for
the consulting firm just described, is as much to blame as is the educational system.

Wherever the mixed messages come from, they play an important
role in maintaining a contradictory dynamic in the management of
writing as a work process. As I have argued elsewhere, to make the
hierarchical system work, we need a number of people doing neutral
writing, yet we also need a few people doing critical writing ("Language" 74–75). If too few practice critical writing (especially outside

the higher-level policy positions in their firms), we will have too much critical thinking and thus instability in the hierarchy. However, if too few can do critical writing, and decision making therefore becomes concentrated among those few, the quality of the decisions will erode and the system will destabilize.

Continuing to restructure the economy and to maintain its hegemony requires an almost impossible balance between the right number of neutral and critical writers. The balance is constantly at risk. Inefficient writing practices become entrenched in bureaucratic custom, and neutral models are perpetuated through professional practice and the educational system. Yet if critical writing were universally and wholeheartedly taught, another imbalance in the system would arise.

Another Example from Practice: Transforming Neutral Writing

In planning practice it is sometimes possible for a relative newcomer to change entrenched neutral writing practices. Amy Schectman, who received her master's degree from our department in 1982 (with no particular training in professional writing), is emblematic. Schectman took a job in 1983 in the Department of Capital Planning and Operations for the Commonwealth of Massachusetts. This powerful department manages the state's property and capital, deciding what is needed to maintain all state-owned colleges, parks, hospitals, and so on, and working with the legislative branch of state government to achieve its goals. Schectman's boss was interested in improving communications in the department, and much of the work on this endeavor fell to her. A top priority was the annual budget memo. This important link went from her boss (the DCPO head) to the State Executive Office for Administration and Finance and from there to the Ways and Means Committee of the legislature, where it would be proposed as law.

Before Schectman's time, budget memos had always looked neutral. Budget recommendations left DCPO as a simple list of projects with price tags. DCPO would compile this list verbatim from the requests of various state departments without evaluating, prioritizing, or arguing for them. But Schectman's boss was claiming a more critical role for DCPO. Because the office was now recommending only the most important budget requests, examples from the budget memo files were inadequate writing models. Schectman needed to develop one that would reflect critical thinking in critical writing, a budget memo format that would advocate a particular set of budget decisions.

Over a period of several years, she developed a way of writing budget memos that is still in use, as of this writing. Schectman's memos avoid using any information not critical to the decision to be made, and they are as concise as possible, giving only the criteria used to evaluate requests and general categories. A short initial paragraph clearly identifies the position it will argue and a menu of what's to follow. In the remainder of the memo, every word goes to argue a critical position. The detailed list of requests that used to constitute the entire text of DCPO budget memos now follows the memo as an appendix. Having pioneered this and other writing models for DCPO, Schectman then began to train others in the department in critical, analytical writing. This effort led quickly to the realization that many professional staff members from various disciplinary backgrounds felt uncomfortable except when listing information. The new leadership at DCPO had instituted what labor economists call an "upskilling" of the work of writing. Staff members who had formerly done neutral writing were now being asked to represent information critically, to advocate, a more challenging skill. Now Schectman has moved back to academia, where she is a lecturer in our department, helping with internal communications and teaching professional practice skills, including writing.

Critical Writing in Planning Education

While grappling with self-definition over the past two decades, the planning field has been increasingly conscious of the importance of writing in its curriculum. In a survey conducted by the American Planning Association in 1978, writing was identified as the most important professional skill by 96.9% of responding practitioners. Many planning departments had begun to seek their own solutions to the "writing problem" several years before writing across the curriculum became current. My own department had tried having journalists or interested planning faculty members teach writing before it first borrowed me from the MIT writing program in 1980, then hired me full time to teach and consult with students and faculty. Since I joined its ranks, my department has continued to put major energy into revising its core curriculum, in which courses now in each year of our program and each subspecialty are designated as "writing-intensive." One of these, Quantitative Reasoning for Planners—which aims to help students build articulate arguments with numbers—has been widely discussed in the field (Schuster, "Quantatative"). At MIT, colleagues in a variety of subfields of planning have worked together in a faculty writing group and in several seminars on writing and learning. At the same time, my ideas on writing have been solicited and discussed at professional conferences and faculty seminars at other planning schools. In general, the field has benefited from writing-across-the-curriculum programs at various universities and from thoughtful attention to writing dilemmas by other social scientists (Becker) and by planning teachers and practitioners (Krieger).

A Second Wave

In the years I have known it, I have seen the planning field grow more attentive to writing—to its importance and to ways of teaching it successfully. What seems to be happening now is a second wave of attention. While I have been thinking about the contradiction surrounding neutral and critical writing, others have been looking closely at the characteristic discourse of the profession and what may be problematic about it. Lisa Peattie, an anthropologist who has been a respected member of the planning world for thirty years, argues that the representations of reality made in professional reports are too abstract and discipline-bound to shape the outcomes of planning. In a case from the 1960s, she studies two examples of American planners' reports that led to the creation of a new city in Venezuela. Architect-planners represented their vision in schematic designs, and economist-planners in numerical tables of projected employment. Although the neutral writing that framed both visions impressed government bureaucrats at the time, it was essentially misleading because it failed to question the clients' assumptions or to connect with larger crucial issues. The city that developed as a result became a nightmare from nearly every point of view (Peattie 111–52). Following Peattie's book and John Forester's *Planning in the Face of Power*, a number of planning theorists have begun to explore the discourse of the field using postmodernist, feminist, and other perspectives to analyze policies affecting the homeless (Liggett), a dispute over electricity rates (Throgmorton), communication more generally (Milroy; S. Mandelbaum), and specific development plans in Britain (Healey) and Canada (Tett and Wolfe).

With these critiques on the table, those of us who are interested in planners' representations, discourse, and professional education need to begin asking a new and more specific set of questions. Are there genres of writing or representation in the field that *do* encourage thoughtful outcomes? Are there effective interdisciplinary genres? How could we improve on these or create new ones? What do we learn from Gakenheimer's struggle with critical and neutral writing? How common are the situations of "irresolution" he faces? And how effective are the genres of writing professionals use in such situations? Are there styles other than Gakenheimer's that work? What distinguishes Schectman's situation from his and how common is her experience? Can change initiated by writers make institutions more accountable? At what level in a planning organization would the change need to come from?

Even to formulate these questions properly, we will need a more systematic understanding of the range of writing practices common in planning jobs. How do we find out what kinds of writing these jobs really require? What do employers actually mean by "good writing"? How do readers interpret critical or neutral planning documents? What forms does the contradiction between advocacy and neutrality take in the wide range of planning experience? And are there ways to exploit this contradiction? What do we make of Gakenheimer's struggle with it and how typical is his self-awareness? What guidelines will enable students (and colleagues, too) to decide when and how it is appropriate to advocate?

We must ask a new set of questions about curriculum as well. Should we, as Gakenheimer suggests, teach "fast writing"? Should we ask planning students to write inception reports? Should they learn to compose the classically fuzzy or open-ended terms of reference (which Gakenheimer assigns in one of his courses)? Or should we continue to stress the more time-consuming and crafted work they will not directly experience in his kind of practice? (I have suggested that Gakenheimer ask for a Schectman-style memo to accompany any terms-of-reference assignments he gives, explaining the strategy behind the fuzziness.) Is it effective to ask students to work through three drafts of a comparative, inductive argument built out of census data, as we do in our quantitative reasoning course (Schuster, "Statistically" 119–21)?

Looking Ahead

No matter what new ways we find to understand why planners use neutral writing, I don't expect to change my deep commitment to teaching critical writing. My years in the classroom helping students figure out what keeps them from doing this difficult work have shown me that this kind of writing is hard for them. Neutral writing is the path of least resistance, one taken at times by even the best of them. Few have had experience building a critical argument (much less in the language of numbers); most are too rushed by their other course work to take the time to learn to do so and are intimidated by their lack of familiarity with the material they are asked to analyze and by the community of readers they are writing for. (The best treatment of this latter problem I have seen is in Becker 26–42.) Unconscious self-censorship of critical thinking is an almost universal practice for graduate students (Dunlap, "Language" 69–71). However we understand the problem, we need to keep working against the internal and institutional pressures that inhibit students' critical voice.

But at the same time we should recognize that not all of their neutrality results from their powerlessness as students. The profession, itself, sanctions neutrality through the mixed models for writing that have been institutionalized in the field. Although we cannot reshape societal contradictions in our classrooms, we can educate students about their existence and empower them to make choices that may eventually— as in Schectman's case—lead to change. The most important thing we can do is to face the contradiction between neutrality and advocacy head on. Students (and practitioners, too) need to know the differences between neutral and critical writing and to see that, unless they can do the latter powerfully, they will never be effective through neutrality.

The pressures toward neutral writing, as well as the institutional contradictions that accompany them, affect those in planning, as they do other professionals. But most planners see themselves as change agents, advocates for the underrepresented in public decision making. Their underlying values give them incentives to speak out, to challenge, to provide critical analysis. Perhaps as we continue to study the issue, we will find that planners are the advance guard—experiencing a difficulty that will soon be hitting other professional disciplines in full force. If so, we may have some solutions for others as well as for ourselves.

Writing in the Disciplines:
A Prospect

Anne Herrington and Charles Moran

Anne Herrington is associate professor of English and director of the writing program at the University of Massachusetts, Amherst.

I have been involved with writing-across-the-curriculum efforts since 1976, when I worked with my colleagues at Johnson State College in Vermont to develop a program to integrate writing into courses in various disciplines. Since then, I have been drawn toward trying to understand more about how writing is actually used in specific classroom contexts. I know from my own experience and from colleagues and students that writing plays a powerful role in learning. What matters is how that role gets defined and by whom.

Charles Moran is professor of English at the University of Massachusetts, Amherst.

As past director of our university's writing program, I have been involved in writing-in-the-disciplines since we began to think about establishing such a program in 1980. Unindicted coconspirators include colleagues in my home department and in the school's sixty-five other departments. I feel most fortunate: I have been permitted, under this rubric, to think and write about teaching and have been forced to learn about other subjects and worlds of discourse not my own. I think of myself now not so much as a member of an English department but as a citizen of the university.

In his essay on the history of writing in the disciplines, David R. Russell finds the existence and the growth of this endeavor to be "surprising." An ADE survey conducted in 1986 found that 35% of American colleges and universities had established writing-in-the-disciplines programs (Fulwiler and Young); and in a survey conducted in 1987–88, Susan H. McLeod found that 38% of the responding institutions had installed such programs and that another 6% were actively planning to do so. Only 5 of the 1,113 responding institutions reported that they had had programs that had foundered. McLeod sees her survey as indicating "the resilience and staying power of WAC programs" ("Writing" 338). The findings of these two surveys are echoed in a study of the members of the American Association of Community and Junior Colleges, conducted by Barbara R. Stout and Joyce N. Magnotto in 1988. In this survey, "of the 400 schools that responded, approximately one-third had active WAC programs, one-third were planning to implement WAC within a year or two, and one-third reported no systematic WAC activities" (9).

How is it that this seemingly fragile, quasi-evangelical and quasi-populist movement has persisted and, at least arguably, prospered? Writing in the disciplines would seem to have at least two strikes against it: it is generally extradepartmental, or even antidepartmental, in its institutional location and purpose—and in postsecondary education the department is the locus of institutional power. Further, the movement's emphasis is on teaching, a low-status enterprise in the high-prestige, research-oriented universities, where teaching can be seen as a distraction and the most desirable positions have the smallest teaching load. And further, WAC is connected to the teaching of writing, itself a marginalized enterprise within the American academy (Russell, in this collection; Slevin). Yet writing in the disciplines has persisted, and expanded, despite what seem to be formidable odds. What reasons might we have to hope that writing in the disciplines will continue to persist and even flourish? We offer here several possible answers to this question, drawing on the research in the field and on our own experiences as teachers and administrators in programs of this nature.

Noted in this volume by Russell, fully described by Jacqueline Jones Royster, and attested to by the four faculty members in our interchange is the power of the writing-in-the-disciplines movement to energize teachers. A tour of the program descriptions in Toby Fulwiler and Art Young's collection, *Programs That Work*, confronts us again and again with the voices of teachers deeply engaged in their teaching: the professor of mathematics who uses electronic journals in his classes (236); the professor who initiated a collaborative writing project in his Chinese and Japanese art course and notes: "It did take some time to organize the groups and then hold the debates, but that was when they were practicing what art historians do: discussing ideas, working out problems. . . . Not only were they responsible for their learning, they were developing an educated point of view. And it was this work—this time of thinking—that led to the improvement in their papers. It was time well spent" (130–31). This commitment to teaching reverberates through much of the writing and research that has been generated by the writing-in-the-disciplines movement.

The commitment to teaching is an important but often submerged aspect of our profession. Many faculty members—perhaps most— came into the profession as teachers. Yes, the scholarly interest was there, but in most cases the initial impulse was to teach. We would expect to find variations in commitment to teaching as we move across disciplines and among institutions, and yet even the most research-oriented instructors will have been called to the discipline by mentors. The germ of the teacher is in all of us, and perhaps more powerfully so in those of us who have decided to spend our lives, one way or another, in school. At most institutions, however, there are few forums in which faculty members can talk about, and reflect on, their teaching. Historically, we teach alone: we are one of the few professions in which one does not habitually work with, or in the presence of, other professionals. In research universities, teaching is low status, and talk about teaching is relegated to schools of education. In two- and four-year postsecondary institutions in which research is not a high priority, teaching loads are high and departmental lines are firmly established. In these institutions, too, cross-disciplinary forums focused on teaching are rare.

It is against these obstacles that writing-in-the-disciplines programs attempt to provide a forum for talk about teaching—talk that is satisfying to the teacher who lurks within even the most research-oriented member of our profession. But the WAC movement has added what may be a crucial dimension to this talk: it encourages such talk across and among the academic disciplines. Lee Odell's essay in this collection describes a procedure that makes it possible for one teacher to discover another's criteria for "good thinking": a side-by-side comparison of "good" and "not-good" writing samples. This procedure, a species of contrastive analysis, may be even more valuable when it is conducted across disciplinary boundaries. So long as we stay "at home" in our own intellectual villages, our pedagogical goals and disciplinary criteria may seem inevitable, true, and therefore transparent. As we see from the interchange chapter, when we work with teachers from disciplines not our own, we see our own teaching in relief, standing out against the goals and strategies of other teachers in other disciplines. As we learn the grammar of our own language most easily through the study of a second, so we may learn the "grammar" of our own teaching most easily when we leave home and consider the teaching that takes place in other aspects of the academy.

Further, cross-disciplinary talk about teaching may be safer than the same talk within a discipline. Given institutional power structures, there may be in cross-disciplinary talk less competition, less to gain and to lose, because the speakers are in different academic units, judged by different personnel committees. Paradoxically, it may be easier for us to accept colleagues from other disciplines as coworkers than it is for us to accept members of our own departments.

It may be, too, that we are readier now than we have been before to see the academy as a set of sites, each local, for the construction of knowledge. One of the received assumptions of writing in the disciplines is that there are differences among disciplinary discourses—an assumption that makes it more difficult to call for system-wide "good writing" as an undifferentiated absolute. WAC thus encourages us to see the academy as a cultural democracy, and the disciplines as localities—as cultures within the larger culture. This view of the academy squares with the goals of interpretive anthropology, as Clifford Geertz outlines them: "To see others as sharing a nature with ourselves is the merest decency. But it is from the far more difficult achievement of seeing ourselves amongst others, as a local example of the forms human life has locally taken, a case among cases, a world among worlds, that the largeness of mind, without which objectivity is self-congratulation and tolerance a sham, comes" (*Local Knowledge* 16). Geertz's view resonates with what, in the world of English, we would consider a rhetorical perspective, one that sees the disciplines as discourse communities, each with its own preferred epistemological stance, preferred topoi, preferred modes of proof—local conventions that form locally accepted modes of thought and of discourse. Charles Bazerman asks us to conduct such rhetorical analyses. Bonnie Spanier's analysis of the language of the biological sciences demonstrates the epistemological and pedagogical importance of such analysis: in analyzing our discourse, we may uncover for critical examination tacit assumptions about ways of knowing, socially constructed views of gender roles, and ways of teaching and learning. Both perspectives—the perspective of the rhetorician and that of the interpretive anthropologist—evoke other aspects of contemporary thought: in computer science, where we now look for greater speed and efficiency from "distributed computing" and "parallel processing," in which many small, different units interact; in the life sciences, where we increasingly take an ecological approach toward the interactive life systems on spaceship earth; and in national and global politics, where we understand that we must see ourselves as a cultural democracy, an aggregate of disparate cultures living in a harmony that preserves difference and diversity.

A concern for teaching carries with it an implicit concern for learning. The development of writing in the disciplines has inevitably, therefore, illuminated not just the teacher but the situation of the student, the learner. Indeed, Nancy Martin sees the focus on learning and the role of language in learning as the heart of the writing-in-the-disciplines movement in Great Britain. Russell views this aspect of the movement as an emergence of elements in "progressive," child-centered education, citing Elaine Maimon's remark that at early writing-in-the-disciplines workshops, John Dewey was "the presiding ghost."

This concern for the "learning" that may or may not take place in the presence of teaching—and we refer you here to the essays by Judith A. Langer and by Joy Marsella, Thomas L. Hilgers, and Clemence McLaren—may come at a time that is propitious for American postsecondary education. Colleges and universities are losing their constituency, as the postwar baby boom has passed through the system, leaving a sharply diminished pool of applicants and an electorate in which fewer people feel that they have a direct and personal stake in higher education. The teaching and learning that take place in higher education, an area largely unexamined in the past, now undergo increasingly close and even hostile scrutiny. We note that small private colleges and universities have begun to emphasize their undergraduate curriculum with new energy. Stanford University is a recent example. And large public universities are retreating from the laissez-faire, "supermarket" approach to curriculum and are starting to pay attention to undergraduate education, at least to the extent of creating apparently coherent curriculum designs under the rubric "general education."

We guess that this new emphasis on the undergraduate curriculum is at least partly driven by market considerations: the increasing cost of postsecondary education carries with it an increase in what parents and students expect from that education. The price tag has soared in the past decade, at double the rate of inflation. Behind this escalation is the increasing cost of university-based research, whether expressed in terms of the cost of laboratory materials in the sciences or in terms of reduced teaching loads for those in the humanities. Who will pay for this research? Not the alumni and alumnae of private colleges, whose gifts contribute to the running these institutions; nor the state legislators, whose votes control the flow of public funds to the state systems of higher education. Both of these groups remember, and will support, the teaching and learning they experienced themselves; they are not likely to remember the faculty's research and are not likely, therefore, to support it. Signs of public resistance multiply: recently the federal government has begun to inquire into the mechanisms by which private colleges set their tuitions and into the ways in which research universities use the indirect costs—which can run as high as 71% of the granted funds; and still more recently the National Endowment for the Humanities released a report that was sharply critical of what it took to be the diversion of humanities' faculty effort from teaching to research (Watkins). In this political and economic frame, colleges and universities will probably continue to stress the teaching and learning that occur on their campuses. If teaching and learning are given appropriate value, writing in the disciplines is likely to remain a presence in our curricular landscape.

Still, this is a time of financial hardship for many institutions—particularly public institutions. It is a time when faculty members and students face pressures that make it difficult to nurture and maintain writing-in-the-disciplines programs: teaching loads of four and five courses per semester for full-time instructors; increasing reliance on part-time teachers for the delivery of instruction; at some colleges and universities, large lecture courses in which teaching assistants lead discussion sections; and students who must work thirty or forty hours a week to support themselves. Russell notes that WAC arose in a time when American higher education was expanding. If such expansion was a factor in the origin and development of writing in the disciplines, then the present contraction may be a factor in its demise. And Martin notes that the rise of writing to learn in the United Kingdom depended on, or was at least concurrent with, government support of educational research. If there is a relation between the priorities of government leaders and the viability of writing in the disciplines, then we may be in for hard times. Yet if we choose to remain in education even in hard times, then the healthiest course of action is to articulate our educational values and act on them in realistic ways, in the light of the constraints we face.

For many of us that means continuing to work with writing in the disciplines, believing that it carries with it the potential to bring about positive changes in the structures and values of higher education in the United States. Essentially, it challenges both institutions and individual faculty members to rethink the value they place on teaching and on pedagogically oriented research. Further, it challenges us to be more responsive to the students who enter our institutions. A reemphasis on the teaching and learning that occur in postsecondary institutions will itself foreground the conditions in which teachers work—and this foregrounding will make it more difficult for us all to accept the situation of the part-time faculty that now do so much of our teaching, the large classes that are becoming the norm in general education courses at public universities, and the high teaching loads that are becoming the norm at two-year colleges.[1]

In addition, the emphasis on teaching and learning will challenge institutions to support these activities in more substantial ways than they now do. If writing is to be used as a mode of teaching and of learning, there will be increased need for such units as writing centers and developmental programs for students who need additional support. The faculty's teaching requires its own support as well: a faculty-development program that will include time to revise curricula and encourage participation in ongoing discussions and workshops across disciplines. Essays in this collection demonstrate the range of issues that might be addressed in these discussions: integrating new classroom techniques, such as peer review, into our general practice; articulating for ourselves, and translating into our teaching, methods of inquiry that may be so internalized as to be tacit; helping students move through a problem, beginning with problem definition and proceeding to the finished text; introducing students to conventions of the discourse of particular professional forums in ways that will help them negotiate that discourse. Cross-disciplinary collaboration will also provide a forum in which we can consider how best to use the potential of the computer for enhancing—or changing absolutely—the teaching and learning environments we now have. The computer is, by its nature, a connector, and when we begin to connect, we find ourselves traveling, whether we like it or not, across the disciplines. Hypertext's branching environment soon carries us beyond our disciplinary boundaries, and computer-mediated conferencing makes a collaborative, project-based curriculum the preferred mode of activity (Harasim). Both hypertext and computer-mediated conferencing now proceed through language, a fact that suggests to us that computer technology and writing in the disciplines may complement each other powerfully. And the computer-mediated conference may be, as Marilyn M. Cooper and Cynthia L. Selfe have argued, a medium that encourages students to use language with more authority and thereby to become more active learners (867).

As essays in this book and in Fulwiler and Young's *Programs That Work* have made clear, writing across the disciplines requires such cross-disciplinary collaboration if faculty members are to get outside their own intellectual villages and thereby gain perspective on their goals, values, and teaching strategies. Unfortunately, in many institutions, support for teaching takes the form of the occasional professional development day or a marginal center for teaching. Writing in the disciplines makes it clear that such add-on, token support is not at all what we need (Fulwiler, "Reflections"; Young and Fulwiler; E. White). If we are to keep the concern for teaching where it belongs—with full-time faculty members in academic departments—such support for faculty teaching will be essential. Without such support, and considering that first-year writing instruction is already marginalized, it is probable that writing in the disciplines will, like the first-year writing course, become the work of part-time teachers, of graduate students, of tutorial programs, or of no one at all.

Implicit in the increased attention that we must give to teaching is a need for "research" institutions to include, in their definition of research, projects that undertake to examine the processes of teaching and learning. While scholarship on writing in the disciplines may count for those of us in rhetoric and composition, it is not likely to count for a professor of history or physics. Even within rhetoric and composition, some frown on work that is too heavily "pedagogical" or "applied." Critical of this limited view of scholarship that devalues teaching, a recent Carnegie Commission report, "Scholarship Reconsidered: Priorities of the Professoriate," calls for a broader definition of scholarship that would include both the application of knowledge and teaching itself (Leatherman 1).

Institutions that consider themselves primarily teaching schools face a somewhat different challenge: to provide research support for those teachers who wish to study their writing-in-the-disciplines programs and teaching projects. The participation of these teacher-scholars in professional forums—journals as well as conferences—is vital to the movement as we seek to understand the constituents of successful programs at a broad range of institutions, the relations between learning and certain types of and conditions for writing, and the experiences of students of diverse backgrounds as they try to accomplish the writing asked of them in specific classes.

Writing in the disciplines also challenges us, as teachers, to reflect critically on our teaching and our disciplinary values. Essays in this collection point the way for these reflections. Royster provides a model for faculty development that stresses the interactive nature of teaching, and James Britton calls us to take a "predisciplinary"—as opposed to a disciplinary—perspective when we consider issues of teaching. Bonnie Spanier, Louise Dunlap, and Charles Bazerman call for a critical examination of our disciplinary values and practices, both outside and within our classrooms. This critical perspective is difficult to achieve, for we are asked to rethink practices we may accept without question within our disciplinary worlds: do not use "I" in scientific writing, do not refer to personal examples or feelings to support a point, begin a research paper by citing relevant studies, avoid stating a position. These scholars ask us to reconsider the rationale for such practices in the light of alternative views of knowledge-making and communicating within a given discipline. As Spanier argues, writing in the disciplines invites such reconsideration because, through the writing our students do and the values we inscribe as we define and evaluate the writing, students are learning a way of knowing and communicating.

This examination should begin in our classrooms through the careful study of specific exchanges with our students. Because such close study and critical reflection lie at the heart of the enterprise of writing in the disciplines, we turn to a specific example of a teacher-student exchange. This exchange highlights an important challenge we face as readers of student writing: to understand discourse practices and values that may differ from our own.[2] The exchange occurred in a psychology course, where students were to conduct short experiments and write them up as research reports, following APA guidelines. For the first report, one student, Viet, wrote the following introduction.

Naturalistic Observation of Door Holding

Mother always told me to be a gentleman whenever encountering with the opposite sexes: young girls and ladies alike. Manhood is a big deal in my family. A manhood is to "hit the sack" early and wake up when the rooster cries, to work hard for any purpose and endure from any hardship, to have patience as well as kindness, and so on. And when he interacts with the opposite sex (female), he always gives her this most respect as would a knight in the Middle Age respect his lady.

Upon hearing my classmates who were going to do a study of naturalistic observation of door holding in order to determine which gender (male or female) would hold for whom, I was for sure that this study would not be much of a study, and believed that the males would appear most after the findings. In contract, most of the female classmates strongly believed that there would be no difference between both genders, claiming that female population does hold door for the opposite sex as well as male. Thus, this report is based on the study of naturalistic observation of door holding in order to determine whether or not holding door for the ladies is the men's job.

On the grading checksheet, Viet received a C for "statement of purpose for current study"; a C/D for "clarity of expression"; and a

C/D for "grammar, punctuation, spelling, etc." Wanting to understand how to improve his next report, Viet met with his teacher. Relating what the teacher told him, Viet said, "My past experience wasn't good enough because there's a lot of people may do the same experience and my own experience may not be significant because it just happen by chance. It's supposed to be other people experience. Like other people did research on it. It's not necessary what I feel." The teacher, in a later interview with a researcher, confirmed Viet's explanation, although she said such references to personal experience were acceptable for the first report, but not for subsequent ones. As the ratings indicate, Viet's teacher was also dissatisfied with his style and grammar, including, as she said, "using the first-person voice and talking about the class."

Viet wrote his second report the way he believed the teacher wanted him to.

Mnemonic Methods: Loci and Rote in Noise

The point of the study is to find out which mnemonic method, loci or rote, performs better result in noise and in quiet. Current study found that high imagery concepts were generally attained easier that low imagery concepts (Ketz and Paivio 1975). Thus, since rote memorization has a low to none image coding, and since method of loci has high image coding, concrete words recalled would be higher for method of loci and lower for rote memorization.

The experiment also tests the noise effect in memory performance by stimulating the half of the subjects with mid-rock music as a noise condition. According to Gisselbrecht-Simon's (1988) study, noise effect appears only through the unexpected recognition test, and not through the unexpected recall test; thus, the present study, which is based on the recall test, would likely have no noise effect on memory performances.

In this report, Viet makes no reference to himself or to his classmates; he cites published research; and, to us, he seems to write in a more opaque style, omitting "I" and interspersing phrases from the research with his own wording. When asked how he felt about writing this way, he commented, "At first I felt uncomfortable." Nevertheless, he proceeded, deciding, "Okay, this is what she wants. It's quicker to write their way than my own." For this second report, his ratings for the introduction included an A/B for "statement of purpose for current study" and an A for overall "clarity of expression."

* * *

What can we learn from this exchange? Clearly we can learn something about the discourse valued by the teacher and perhaps by her discipline. To a psychology teacher, the second report may indeed be much clearer in expression than the first report, while to two English composition teachers, it does not seem to be so. The exchange presents us—both psychology and English faculty members—with a challenge: to identify and understand differences among the discourse practices of our disciplines.

The exchange further demonstrates a challenge we face as readers of our students' writing: the need to read with empathy, so that we may see what is there as well as what is not there. Viet's teacher seemed to be reading his paper to see how it compared with her construct of what a psychological research report should look like: a piece that conforms to her understanding of APA style, what she called "a very specific, awkward style." Perhaps because of Viet's difficulty with English and his "personal" voice, the teacher's response to the writer emphasized how his "style" was inappropriate and different from the style she expected. Had the teacher read beyond the surface features of the text, she might have seen that in his first introduction, he did much that matched her expectations, including using the disjunction between his own beliefs and those of his classmates to establish a rationale for the study. Further, he explained himself clearly. Instead of recognizing his accomplishments, however, Viet's teacher emphasized the ways in which Viet's writing did not conform. As we have seen, Viet gave in and wrote what he thought was expected of him. Granted, he was learning to take on a new form of writing, but as a learner, he paid a price. For example, in his introduction, he stopped trying to make sense of what he was doing by putting it in his own words and chose the easier route of relying on phrases from the research he reviewed. Because she emphasized the disjunction between their discourses—hers and Viet's—the teacher made Viet's task formidable: Drop your old ways entirely and take on new ways, my ways.

Tom Fox argues that instead of stressing the disjunctions between new students' discourse practices and our own, we should learn to read our students' work for connections and build from them. To read interpretively for this recognition, he argues, will serve two aims: "(1) legitimate the cultural discourse students bring with them, and (2) challenge the notions (held by both the students and parts of the university) that those discourses are somehow inadequate to do university work." Fox is referring to basic writing courses, but he closes by arguing that this pedagogical work needs to be carried out by the university as a whole: "the Writing Across the Disciplines movement is a natural forum for such activity and many such programs seem increasingly concerned with issues of equity and political change" (82). Clearly, he and others (Spanier and Dunlap in this volume; Bizzell, "Cultural Criticism"; Elbow, "Reflections") are calling on us to reassess and be willing to change some of our disciplinary and personal values that define participation in our classrooms. Reading our own and our students' writing interpretively also challenges us to enter into a reciprocal relationship with our students: as they try to "read" us, we try to "read" them.

Viet stands for a challenge many of us now face and will face even more in the future if we are to turn our attention to the learner: students whose language, culture, class, and/or discourse practices may differ from those we value and expect. As Guadalupe Valdes argued at the 1991 Conference on College Composition and Communication, increasing numbers of our students are bilingual, with a language other than English as their home language, yet even those of us in composition studies have insufficient knowledge about the nature of language development for bilingual people and insufficient appreciation of the language accomplishments and difficulties of bilingual students writing in English. As a consequence, out of ignorance, many writing teachers and teachers in other disciplines place too much value on the correctness of idioms and surface features and may use mistakes in idioms and surface features as a basis for unfounded generalizations about literacy and intelligence. Charlotte Honda's comments in the interchange illustrate how participation in her college's writing-across-the-curriculum program helped change her views.

Differences between faculty members and students may extend beyond language. Marsha Z. Cummins, Jacqueline Stuchin-Paprin, and Judith A. Lamert describe the distance between faculty members and students at Bronx Community College in this way:

> Coming from the poorest area of New York City, Bronx Community College students are overwhelmingly female and minority, and nearly half are not native English speakers. More than 90 percent require some basic-skills work in language arts and mathematics. The faculty, by contrast, is predominantly white and male, with a median age of fifty-two. Because of the reward system, a substantial number of faculty members are involved in scholarly research and publishing. As a result, Bronx faculty share with other community college teachers . . . an ambivalence to-

ward the dual role of pursuing scholarship and teaching in a community college. (31–32)

Further, as Viet's writing illustrates, because of prior schooling and, in some instances, culture, many students' understanding of academic discourse practices—including what counts as knowledge and acceptable ways to present it—will not be what many teachers expect.

While the percentages may vary from one institution to another, the presence of students of diverse backgrounds will not—or, at least, *should not*—vary if we are to remain committed to a democratic, multicultural society that strives to remove barriers to education and participation based on race, language, class, and culture. Further, writing in the disciplines confronts us directly with the challenge of making our classrooms hospitable environments for teaching and learning for teachers and students of various cultures and backgrounds. In this respect, the history of the writing-across-the-disciplines program at Spelman College offers a model for us. Royster describes its evolution from a narrow focus on improvement in language skills to an "inquiry model for teaching and learning" that focuses on critical thinking skills and on the way students acquire knowledge and understanding in various disciplines. The aim of the Spelman program is to help teachers and students find their own "pathways to learning and empowerment." As Royster observes, that aim forces teachers to address "sensitive questions about classroom authority . . . about the need for faculty members to share control, to be more inclusive in defining the 'what' of learning, to enable diverse voices and experiences to find respect and appreciation in the classroom."

Royster's comments recall for us Mina Shaughnessy's 1976 article "Diving In," in which she presents a developmental scale for teachers of basic writing. It is based on her experiences teaching writing at the City University of New York during the early years of open admission, when a wide range of students, previously excluded from higher education, were admitted by virtue of holding a high school diploma. We think Shaughnessy's model applies now and applies to all teachers. In the first stage, "guarding the tower," teachers concentrate on "protecting the academy from the outsiders, those who do not seem to belong in the community of learners" (234). In the second stage, "converting the natives," teachers perceive the students as having the potential of "catching up," as "empty vessels ready to be filled with new knowledge" (235). As we see it, this stage would include those who view education as a passive process of initiation whose aim is to reproduce disciplinary cultures. Perhaps Viet's teacher was at this stage. The writing-across-the-disciplines program at Spelman seems to have moved on to the third stage in Shaughnessy's scale, "sounding the depths," in which teachers shift from seeing their students as empty vessels to viewing them as intelligent, capable people, although with different language experiences from their own. At this stage teachers become reflexive, turning "to the careful observation not only of [their] own students and their writing, but of [themselves] as writers and teachers" (236). She writes of the fourth stage, which she calls "Diving In," "that the teacher who has come this far must now make a decision that demands professional courage—the decision to remediate himself [or herself] to become a student of new disciplines and of his [or her] students themselves in order to perceive both their difficulties and their incipient excellence" (238). It is this attitude toward writing, learning, and teaching that is writing in the disciplines' greatest challenge and promise today, as it was in 1976: that we may integrate writing into our pedagogy in ways that are at once respectful of students and conducive to their learning—and to ours.

NOTES

[1] We cite two statistics to suggest the challenge. Commenting on the "undervalued state of teaching," Jane Peterson writes, "In 1988, the Commission on the Future of Community Colleges . . . reported that research universities allocate 38% of their budgets to instructional-related matters such as instruction, library services, and academic-support services; four-year schools allocate 42% of their budgets to instruction, and community colleges 61%. These spending patterns reveal the priorities within higher education" (26). Even with the higher percentage of support for instruction, community colleges face staffing problems. In *Programs That Work*, Joyce Magnotto and colleagues note that, at Prince George's Community College, "of critical importance are the more than four hundred part-time faculty whose other commitments make it difficult for them to attend WAC workshops—yet these faculty teach almost half our students" (Fulwiler and Young 78).

[2] This information is from a research study being conducted by Marcia Curtis, Elizabeth Bachrach Tan, and Anne Herrington at the University of Massachusetts, Amherst. They are studying the experiences of a linguistically and culturally diverse group of students as they do the writing asked of them in various college courses.

Works Cited

Abu-Lughod, Lila. *Veiled Sentiments: Honor and Poetry in a Bedouin Society.* Berkeley: U of California P, 1986.

Agonito, Rosemary. *History of Ideas on Woman: A Source Book.* New York: Putnam's, 1977.

Aikin, Wilford M. *The Story of the Eight-Year Study.* New York: Harper, 1942.

American Association for the Advancement of Science. *Science for All Americans: Summary; Project 2061.* Washington: AAAS, 1989.

Anderson, A. "Still a Soft Female Touch for Doctorates." *Nature* 340 (1989): 417.

Anderson, Worth, et al. "Cross-Curricular Underlife: A Collaborative Report on Ways with Academic Words." *College Composition and Communication* 41 (1990): 11–36.

Anson, Chris M. "The Classroom and the 'Real World' as Contexts: Re-examining the Goals of Writing Instruction." *Journal of the Midwest Modern Language Association* 20 (1987): 1–16.

———. "Toward a Multidimensional Model of Writing in the Academic Disciplines." *Advances in Writing Research.* Vol. 2 of *Writing in Academic Disciplines.* Ed. David A. Jolliffe. Norwood: Ablex, 1988. 1–33.

Applebee, Arthur N. *Literature Instruction in American Schools.* Albany: Center for the Learning and Teaching of Literature, 1990.

———. *A Study of Book-Length Works Taught in High School English Courses.* Albany: Center for the Learning and Teaching of Literature, 1989.

———. *Tradition and Reform in the Teaching of English: A History.* Urbana: NCTE, 1974.

———. *Writing in the Secondary School: English and the Content Areas.* NCTE Research Report 21. Urbana: NCTE, 1981.

Applebee, Arthur N., Russell Durst, and George Newell. "The Demands of School Writing." *Contexts for Learning to Write.* By Arthur Applebee et al. Norwood: Ablex, 1984. 55–77.

Axelrod, Rise B., and Charles R. Cooper. *Reading Critically, Writing Well: A Reader and Guide.* 2nd ed. New York: St. Martin's, 1990.

Ball, Stephen. "English for the English." *Social Histories of the Secondary Curriculum.* Ed. Goodson Ivor. Sussex: Palmer, 1985.

Barnes, Douglas, James Britton, and Harold Rosen. *Language, the Learner and the School.* Harmondsworth, Eng.: Penguin, 1969.

"Bay Area Writing Project/California Writing Project/National Writing Project: An Overview." Berkeley: Univ. of California School of Education, 1978. ERIC ED 184 123.

Bazerman, Charles. "Discourse Paths of Different Disciplines." MLA Convention. Los Angeles, 30 Dec. 1982.

———. *Shaping Written Knowledge: The Genre and Activity of the Experimental Article in Science.* Madison: U of Wisconsin P, 1988.

———. "What Written Knowledge Does: Three Examples of Academic Prose." *Philosophy of Social Science* 11 (1981): 361–87.

Beard, Charles A. *The Nature of the Social Sciences: In Relation to Objectives of Instruction.* New York: Scribner's, 1934.

Beauvoir, Simone de. *The Second Sex.* New York: Vintage, 1952.

Becher, Tony. *Academic Tribes and Territories.* Soc. for Research into Higher Education. Milton Keynes: Open UP, 1989.

Becker, Howard S. *Writing for Social Scientists: How to Start and Finish Your Thesis, Book, or Article.* Chicago: U of Chicago P, 1986.

Belanoff, Pat. "The Role of Journals in the Interpretive Community." Fulwiler, *Journal Book* 101–10.

Benbow, Camilla Persson, and Julian C. Stanley. "Sex Differences in Mathematical Ability: Fact or Artifact?" *Science* 210 (1980): 1262–64.

Bereiter, Carl, and Marlene Scardamalia. *The Psychology of Written Composition.* Hillsdale: Erlbaum, 1987.

Berkenkotter, Carol, Thomas N. Huckin, and John Ackerman. "Conventions, Conversations, and the Writer: Case Study of a Student in a Rhetoric Ph.D. Program." *Research in the Teaching of English* 22.2 (1988): 9–43.

Berlin, James A. *Rhetoric and Reality: Writing Instruction in American Colleges, 1900–1985.* Carbondale: Southern Illinois UP, 1987.

Berr, Henri, and Lucien Febvre. "History." *Encyclopedia of the Social Sciences.* Vol. 7. Ed. Edwin R. A. Seligman et al. New York: Macmillan, 1937. 357–68.

Berthoff, Ann E. "Dialectical Notebooks and the Audit of Meaning." Fulwiler, *Journal Book* 11–18.

Biology and Gender Study Group. "The Importance of Feminist Critique for Contemporary Cell Biology." *Hypatia* 3.1 (1988): 61–78.

Bird, Nancy K. "The Conference on College Composition and Communication: A Historical Study of Its Continuing Education and Professionalization Activities, 1947–1975." Diss. Virginia Polytechnic Inst., 1977.

Bizzell, Patricia. "Cognition, Convention, and Certainty: What We Need to Know about Writing." *PRE/TEXT* 3 (1982): 213–43.

———. " 'Cultural Criticism': A Social Approach to Studying Writing." *Rhetoric Review* 7 (1989): 224–30.

Blair, Catherine P. "Only One of the Voices: Dialogic Writing across the Curriculum." *College English* 50 (1988): 383–89.

Bleich, David. "The Subjective Paradigm in Science, Psychology, and Criticism." *New Literary History* 7 (1976): 313–46.

Bleier, Ruth. *Science and Gender: A Critique of Biology and Its Theories on Women.* New York: Pergamon, 1984.

Boys, Chris, et al. *Higher Education and the Preparation for Work.* Higher Education Policy Series 4. London: Kingsley, 1988.

Brandt, Deborah. "Toward an Understanding of Context in Composition." *Written Communication* 3 (1986): 139–57.

Braverman, Harry. *Labor and Monopoly Capital: The Degradation of Work in the Twentieth Century.* New York: Monthly Review, 1984.

Britton, James. "English Teaching: Retrospect and Prospect." *Prospect and Retrospect: Selected Essays of James Britton.* Ed. Gordon M. Pradl. London: Heinemann, 1982. 201–15.

———. *Language and Learning.* Harmondsworth, Eng.: Penguin, 1970.

———. "Language and the Nature of Learning: An Individual Perspective." *The Teaching of English.* Ed. James R. Squire et al. 76th Yearbook of the National Soc. for the Study of Education. Part 1. Chicago: U of Chicago P, 1977. 1–38.

———. "Literature." *The Arts and Current Trends in Education.* Ed. James Britton. London: Evans, 1963. 34–61.

———. "Shaping at the Point of Utterance." *Reinventing the Rhetorical Tradition.* Ed. Aviva Freedman and Ian Pringle. Conway: L and S, for the Canadian Council of Teachers of English, 1980. 61–65.

———. "Viewpoints: The Distinction between Participant and Spectator Role Language in Research and Practice." *Research in the Teaching of English* 18 (1984): 320–31.

Britton, James, and Merron Chorny. "Current Issues and Future Directions." *Handbook of Research on Teaching the English Language Arts.* Ed. James Squire et al. Philadelphia: Macmillan, 1990. 1–55.

Britton, James, Tony Burgess, Nancy Martin, Alex McLeod, and Harold Rosen. *The Development of Writing Abilities (11–18).* London: Macmillan, 1975.

Broadhead, Glenn, and Richard C. Freed. *The Variables of Composition: Process and Product in a Business Setting.* Carbondale: Southern Illinois UP, 1985.

Bruffee, Kenneth A. "The Brooklyn Plan: Attaining Intellectual Growth through Peer-Group Tutoring." *Liberal Education* 64 (1978): 447–68.

———. "Collaborative Learning and the 'Conversation of Mankind.'" *College English* 46 (1984): 635–52.

———. "Social Construction, Language, and the Authority of Knowledge: A Bibliographical Essay." *College English* 48 (1986): 773–90.

Bruner, Jerome S. *The Process of Education.* Westminster: Random, 1963.

Bureau of the Census. *Historical Atlas of the U. S.* Washington: GPO, 1975.

Calfee, Robert C., and Robert Curley. "Structures of Prose in Content Areas." *Understanding Reading Comprehension.* Ed. James Flood. Newark: Int. Reading Assn. 1984. 161–80.

Carr, Edward Hallett. *What Is History?* New York: Knopf, 1961.

Central Advisory Council for Education (Eng.). *Children and their Primary Schools* (The Plowden Report). London: HMSO, 1967.

Chapman, David, and Gary Tate. "A Survey of Doctoral Programs in Rhetoric and Composition." *Rhetoric Review* (1987): 124–83.

Chickering, Arthur W., and Zelda F. Gamson. *Seven Principles for Good Practice in Undergraduate Education.* Racine: Johnson Foundation, 1987.

Clark, Burton, and Martin Trow. "The Organizational Context." *College Peer Groups.* Ed. Theodore M. Newcomb and Everett K. Wilson. Chicago: Aldine, 1966. 17–70.

Clifford, Geraldine Joncich, and James W. Guthrie. *Ed School: A Brief for Professional Education.* Chicago: U of Chicago P, 1988.

Clifford, James. "On Ethnographic Authority." *Representations* 1.2 (1983): 118–46.

Clifford, James, and George Marcus. *Writing Culture: The Poetics and Politics of Ethnography.* Berkeley: U of California P, 1986.

Coles, William. *The Plural I: The Teaching of Writing.* New York: Holt, 1978.

Committee on Composition and Rhetoric. "Report of the Committee on Composition and Rhetoric." No. 28. 1892. *Reports of the Visiting Committees of the Board of Overseers of Harvard College.* Cambridge: Harvard Coll., 1902.

Conkin, Paul K. "Causation Revisited." *History and Theory* 13 (1977): 1–20.

Cook, Caldwell. *The Play Way.* London, 1917.

Cook, Thomas D., and Donald T. Campbell. *Quasi-experimentation: Design and Analysis Issues for Field Settings.* Chicago: Rand McNally Coll., 1979.

Cooper, Charles R. "Holistic Evaluation of Writing." Cooper and Odell 3–31.

Cooper, Charles R., and Lee Odell, eds. *Evaluating Writing: Describing, Measuring, Judging.* Urbana, NCTE, 1977.

Cooper, Marilyn M., and Cynthia L. Selfe. "Computer Conferences and Learning: Authority, Resistance, and Internally Persuasive Discourse." *College English* 52 (1990): 847–69.

Corbett, Edward P. J. *Classical Rhetoric for the Modern Student.* New York: Oxford UP, 1971.

Crapanzano, Victor. *Tuhami: Portrait of a Moroccan.* Chicago: U of Chicago P, 1980.

Cremin, Lawrence A. *The Transformation of the School: Progressivism in American Education.* New York: Vantage, 1961.

Cummins, Marsha Z., Jacqueline Stuchin-Paprin, and Judith A. Lambert. "A Solution to Student-Faculty Mismatch." Stanley and Ambron 31–36.

Daly, John A., and Anne Hexamer. "Statistical Power in Research in English Education." *Research in the Teaching of English* 17 (1983): 157–64.

Daniels, Harvey. *Famous Last Words: The American Language Crisis Reconsidered.* Carbondale: Southern Illinois UP, 1983.

Darnell, James, Harvey Lodish, and David Baltimore. *Molecular Cell Biology.* 1986. New York: Scientific American, 1990.

Day, Robert A. *How to Write and Publish a Scientific Paper.* Phoenix: Oryx, 1988.

Dean, Terry. "Multicultural Classrooms, Monocultural Teachers." *College Composition and Communication* 40 (1989): 23–37.

Dept. of Education and Science (Great Britain). *A Language for Life* (The Bullock Report). London: HMSO, 1975.

"The Development of the Communication Skills Program at Central College, Pella, Iowa." Pella: Central Coll. Archives, 1985.

Dewey, John. "Progressive Organization of Subject Matter." *John Dewey: The Later Works, 1925–1953.* Ed. Jo Ann Boydston. Vol. 13. Carbondale: Southern Illinois UP, 1988. 48–62.

Dewey, John, et al. *Art and Education.* 2nd ed. Merion: Barnes Foundation, 1947.

Dixon, John. *Growth through English.* London: Oxford UP, 1967.

Douglas, Wallace W. "Notes toward an Ideology of Composition." *ADE Bulletin* 43 (1974): 24–33.

Dowst, Kenneth. "Cognition and Composing." *Freshman English News* 11 (1983): 1–14.

Dray, William H. "Mandelbaum on Historical Narrative." *History and Theory* 8 (1969): 287–94.

Dumont, Jean-Paul. *The Head-Man and I.* Austin: U of Texas P, 1978.

———. *Under the Rainbow.* Austin: U of Texas P, 1976.

Dunfee, Maxine. *Social Studies for the Real World.* Columbus: Merrill, 1978.

Dunlap, Louise. "The Deskilling of Writing in the Professional Workplace." Pennsylvania State Conference on Rhetoric and Composition. College Park, July 1985.

———. "Language and Power: Teaching Writing to Third World Students." Sanyal 57–81.

———. "Professional Writing and the Economics of Work." Interdisciplinary Approaches to Technical Communication. Conference on College Composition and Communication. Seattle, 17 Mar. 1989.

Eisenstadt, Abraham Seldin. *The Craft of American History.* Vol. 1. New York: Harper, 1966.

Elbow, Peter. "Reflections on Academic Discourse: How It Relates to Freshmen and Colleagues." *College English* 53 (1991): 135–55.

———. *Writing without Teachers.* New York: Oxford UP, 1973.

Emig, Janet. "The Uses of the Unconscious in Composing." *College Composition and Communication* 15 (1964): 6–11.

———. "Writing as a Mode of Learning." *College Composition and Communication* 28 (1977): 122–28.

Fabian, Johannes. *Time and the Other: How Anthropology Makes Its Object.* New York: Columbia UP, 1983.

Fairbank, John King. *The Great Chinese Revolution, 1800–1985.* New York: Harper, 1986.

Festinger, Leon. *Cognitive Dissonance*. Stanford: Stanford UP, 1957.

Fetterley, Judith. *The Resisting Reader: A Feminist Approach to American Fiction*. Bloomington: Indiana UP, 1978.

Feyerabend, Paul K. *Against Method: Outlines of an Anarchistic Theory of Knowledge*. London: New Left, 1975.

Fleck, Ludwig. *Genesis and Development of a Scientific Fact*. Chicago: U of Chicago P, 1979.

Flower, Linda S. "The Role of Task Representation in Reading-to-Write." *Technical Report No. 6*. Berkeley: Center for the Study of Writing, 1987.

Forester, John. *Planning in the Face of Power*. Berkeley: U of California P, 1989.

Fox, Tom. "Basic Writing as Cultural Conflict." *Journal of Education* 172 (1990): 65–83.

Fulkerson, Richard. "Four Philosophies of Composition." *College Composition and Communication* 30 (1979): 343–48.

Fulwiler, Toby. "How Well Does Writing across the Curriculum Work?" *College English* 46 (1984): 113–25.

———, ed. *The Journal Book*. Portsmouth: Boynton/Cook, 1987.

———. "Reflections: How Well Does Writing across the Curriculum Work?" *Writing across the Disciplines: Research into Practice*. Ed. Art Young and Toby Fulwiler. Upper Montclair: Boynton/Cook, 1986. 235–46.

Fulwiler, Toby, and Art Young, eds. *Programs That Work: Models and Methods for Writing across the Curriculum*. Portsmouth: Boynton, 1990.

Gakenheimer, Ralph. "Comparison and Choice in Urban Transportation." Sanyal 155–71.

———. Interview by Louise Dunlap. 3 Oct. 1990.

———. "Public Transit Mode Choice and Sustainable Development in the Developing Countries." Unpublished essay, 1990.

Gardiner, Patrick. "Causation in History." *Dictionary of the History of Ideas: Studies of Selected Pivotal Ideas*. Vol. 1. Ed. Philip P. Wiener. New York: Scribner's, 1973. 279–86.

Garson, Barbara. *The Electronic Sweatshop: How Computers Are Transforming the Office of the Future into the Factory of the Past*. New York: Simon, 1988.

Geertz, Clifford. *Local Knowledge: Further Essays in Interpretive Anthropology*. New York: Basic, 1983.

———. *Works and Lives: The Anthropologist as Author*. Stanford: Stanford UP, 1988.

Gere, Anne R. *Writing Groups: History, Theory, and Implications*. Carbondale: Southern Illinois UP, 1987.

Gibson, Walker. *Seeing and Writing: Fifteen Exercises in Composing Experience*. New York: McKay, 1959.

Gilbert, G. Nigel, and Michael Mulkay. *Opening Pandora's Box*. Cambridge: Cambridge UP, 1984.

Gould, Stephen Jay. *The Mismeasure of Man*. New York: Norton, 1981.

Greenbaum, Leonard A. "A Tradition of Complaint." *College English* 31 (1969): 174–78.

Griffin, C. Williams. "Programs for Writing across the Curriculum: A Report." *College Composition and Communication* 36 (1985): 398–403.

———, ed. *Teaching Writing in All Disciplines*. New Directions for Teaching and Learning 12. San Francisco: Jossey-Bass, 1982.

Harasim, Linda. "On-line Education: A New Domain." *Mindweave*. Ed. Robin Mason and Antony Kaye. New York: Pergamon, 1989. 50–73.

Haraway, Donna. *Primate Visions: Gender, Race, and Nature in the World of Modern Science*. New York: Routledge, 1989.

Harding, Sandra. *Whose Science? Whose Knowledge? Thinking from Women's Lives*. Ithaca: Cornell UP, 1991.

———. *The Science Question in Feminism*. Ithaca: Cornell UP, 1986.

Harding, Sandra, and Merrill Hintikka, eds. *Discovering Reality: Feminist Perspectives on Epistemology, Metaphysics, Methodology, and Philosophy of Science*. Dordrecht: Reidel, 1983.

Harrison, Bennett, and Barry Bluestone. *The Great U-Turn: Corporate Restructuring and the Polarizing of America*. New York: Basic, 1988.

Healey, Patsy. "The Communicative Work of Development Plans." ACSP/AESOP International Congress. Oxford, 10 July 1991.

Herrington, Anne. "Writing in Academic Settings: A Study of the Contexts for Writing in Two College Chemical Engineering Courses." *Research in the Teaching of English* 19 (1985): 331–61.

Hillocks, George, Jr. *Research on Written Composition*. Urbana: NCTE, 1986.

Hubbard, Ruth. "The Double Helix: A Study of Science in Context." *The Politics of Women's Biology*. New Brunswick: Rutgers UP, 1990. 48–66.

Hubbard, Ruth, M. S. Henifin, and Barbara Fried, eds. *Biological Woman: The Convenient Myth*. Cambridge: Schenkman, 1982.

Hubbard, Ruth, and Marian Lowe, eds. *Genes and Gender II: Pitfalls in Research on Sex and Gender*. New York: Gordian, 1979.

Hurd, Paul DeHart. *Biological Education in American Secondary Schools, 1890–1960*. Washington: American Inst. of Biological Sciences, 1961.

———. *New Directions in Teaching Secondary School Science*. Chicago: Rand, 1969.

Jenks, Christopher, and David Riesman. *Academic Revolution*. Garden City: Doubleday, 1968.

Jensen, Verner. "Writing in College Physics." Fulwiler, *Journal Book* 330–36.

Jolliffe, David, ed. *Writing in Academic Disciplines*. Norwood: Ablex, 1988.

Kandel, Issac A. *Examinations and Their Substitutes in the United States*. New York: Carnegie Foundation for the Advancement of Teaching, 1936.

Kaufer, David S., and Cheryl Geisler. "Novelty in Academic Writing." *Written Communication* 6 (1989): 286–311.

Keller, Evelyn Fox. *Reflections on Gender and Science*. New Haven: Yale UP, 1984.

Kelly, George. "Behaviour as an Experiment." *Perspectives in Personal Construct Theory.* Ed. D. Bannister. London: Academic, 1970. 255–69.

——. "Man's Construction of His Alternatives." *Clinical Psychology and Personality: The Selected Papers of George Kelly.* Ed. Brendan Maher. New York: Wiley, 1989. 66–93.

King, Arthur R., Jr., and John A. Brownell. *The Curriculum and the Disciplines of Knowledge.* New York: Wiley, 1966.

Kintgen, Eugene, Barry M. Kroll, and Mike Rose, eds. *Perspectives on Literacy.* Carbondale: Southern Illinois UP, 1988.

Klaus, Carl H., and Nancy Jones. *Courses for Change in Writing.* Upper Montclair: Boynton/Cook, 1984.

Kneupper, Charles. "Dramatistic Invention: The Pentad as Heuristic Procedure." *Rhetoric Society Quarterly* 9 (1979): 130–36.

Knorr-Cetina, Karen, and Michael Mulkay, eds. *Science Observed: Perspectives on the Social Study of Science.* Beverly Hills: Sage, 1983.

Kohl, Herbert R. *The Open Classroom: A Practical Guide to a New Way of Teaching.* New York: Random, 1969.

Koshland, Daniel. Editorial. *Science* 6 Jan. 1989: 9.

Krieger, Martin. "The Inner Game of Writing." *Journal of Policy Analysis and Management* 7 (1988): 408–16.

Kuhn, Thomas S. *The Structure of Scientific Revolutions.* 1962. Chicago: U of Chicago P, 1970.

Langer, Judith A. "Literacy Instruction in American Schools: Problems and Perspectives." *American Journal of Education* 93 (1984): 107–32.

——. *The Process of Understanding Literature.* Report Series 2.1. Albany: Center for the Learning and Teaching of Literature, 1989. Rpt. and rev. "The Process of Literary Understanding: Reading for Literary and Informative Purposes." *Research in the Teaching of English* 24.3 (1990): 229–60.

Langer, Judith A., and Arthur N. Applebee. *How Writing Shapes Thinking.* Urbana: NCTE, 1987.

——. *Writing and Learning in the Secondary School.* Final report to the Natl. Inst. of Education. Stanford, 1986.

Langer, Susanne K. "The Growing Center of Knowledge." *Philosophical Sketches.* Baltimore: Johns Hopkins UP, 1962. 143–82.

Larsen, Erling. "Carleton College." *Options for the Teaching of English: The Undergraduate Curriculum.* Ed. Elizabeth Wooton Cowan. New York: MLA, 1975. 7–11.

Latour, Bruno. *Science in Action.* Cambridge: Harvard UP, 1987.

Latour, Bruno, and Steve Woolgar. *Laboratory Life: The Social Construction of Scientific Facts.* Beverly Hills: Sage, 1979.

Lauer, Janice M., and J. William Asher. *Composition Research: Empirical Designs.* New York: Oxford UP, 1988.

Leatherman, Courtney. "Definition of Faculty Scholarship Must Be Expanded to Include Teaching, Carnegie Foundation Says." *Chronicle of Higher Education* 5 Dec. 1990: 1+.

Lewontin, R. C., Steven Rose, and Leon J. Kamin. *Not in Our Genes: Biology, Ideology, and Human Nature.* New York: Pantheon, 1984.

Liggett, Helen. "Where They Don't Have to Take You In: The Representation of Homelessness in Public Policy." *Journal of Planning Education and Research* 10 (1991): 201–08.

Lindberg, Gary. "The Journal Conference: From Dialectic to Dialog." Fulwiler, *Journal Book* 119–28.

Lorence, J. L. "The Critical Analysis of Documentary Evidence: Basic Skills in the History Classroom." *Teaching History: A Journal of Methods* 8.2 (1983): 77–84.

Lothian, John. *Adam Smith: Lectures in Rhetoric and Belles Lettres.* Edinburgh: Nelson, 1963.

Lunsford, Andrea, and Lisa Ede. *Singular Texts/Plural Authors: Perspectives on Collaborative Writing.* Carbondale: Southern Illinois UP, 1990.

Luria, A. R., and F. Yudovich. *Speech and the Development of Mental Processes in the Child.* London: Staples, 1959.

Lyons, Robert. "Mina Shaughnessy." *Traditions of Inquiry.* Ed. John Brereton. New York: Oxford UP, 1985. 171–89.

Macrorie, Ken. *Searching Writing: A Contextbook.* Upper Montclair: Boynton, 1980.

———. *Uptaught.* Rochelle Park: Hayden, 1970.

Maimon, Elaine. "Writing, Learning, and Thinking at Beaver College." Address. College English Assn. Convention. Savannah, ERIC 1979. ED 175 054.

Mandelbaum, Maurice H. *The Problem of Historical Knowledge.* New York: Liveright, 1938.

Mandelbaum, Seymour. "Telling Stories." *Journal of Planning Education and Research* 10 (1991): 209–14.

Manning, Kenneth. *Black Apollo: The Life and Work of Ernest Everett Just.* Oxford: Oxford UP, 1983.

Marcus, George. "Rhetoric and the Ethnographic Genre in Anthropological Research." *Current Anthropology* 21 (1980): 507–10.

Marcus, George, and Dick Cushman. "Ethnographies as Texts." *Annual Review of Anthropology* 11 (1982): 25–69.

Marshall, James D. "The Effects of Writing on Students' Understanding of Literary Texts." *Research in the Teaching of English* 21 (1987): 30–63.

Martin, Emily. *The Woman in the Body: A Cultural Analysis of Reproduction.* New York: Beacon, 1987.

Martin, Nancy, Pat D'Arcy, Bryan Newton, and Robert Parker. *Writing and Learning across the Curriculum, 11–16.* London: Ward Lock, 1976.

Mascia-Lees, Frances, Patricia Sharpe, and Colleen Ballerino-Cohen. "The Postmodernist Turn in Anthropology: Cautions from a Feminist Perspective." *Signs* 15 (1989): 7–33.

McCarthy, Lucille P. "A Stranger in Strange Lands: A College Student Writing across the Curriculum." *Research in the Teaching of English* 21.3 (1987): 233–65.

McCarthy, Lucille Parkinson, and Barbara E. Fassler Walvoord. "Models for Collaborative Research in Writing across the Curriculum." McLeod, *Strengthening* 77–90.

McCloskey, Donald N. *The Rhetoric of Economics*. Madison: U of Wisconsin P, 1986.

McLeod, Susan H. *Strengthening Programs for Writing across the Curriculum*. San Francisco: Jossey-Bass, 1988.

———. "Writing across the Curriculum: The Second Stage, and Beyond." *College Composition and Communication* 40 (1989): 337–43.

Miller, Carolyn R., and Jack Selzer. "Special Topics of Argument in Engineering Reports." Odell and Goswami 309–41.

Miller, George. *Spontaneous Apprentices: Children and Language*. San Francisco: Seabury, 1977.

Milroy, Beth Moore. "Into Postmodern Weightlessness." *Journal of Planning Education and Research* 10 (1991): 181–87.

Muller, Herbert J. *The Uses of English*. New York: Holt, 1967.

Myers, Greg. "The Social Construction of Two Biologists' Proposals." *Written Communication* 2 (1985): 219–45.

———. *Writing Biology*. Madison: U of Wisconsin P, 1990.

NCTE's Position on the Teaching of English: Assumptions and Practices. Urbana: NCTE, 1990.

Neel, Jasper P., ed. *Options for the Teaching of English: Freshman Composition*. New York: MLA, 1978.

Newell, George E. "Learning from Writing in Two Content Areas: A Case Study/Protocol Analysis." *Research in the Teaching of English* 18 (1984): 265–87.

North, Stephen S. "Writing in Philosophy Class: Three Case Studies." *Research in the Teaching of English* 20.3 (1986): 225–62.

Odell, Lee. "Beyond the Text." Odell and Goswami 249–80.

———. "Defining and Assessing Competence in Writing." *The Nature and Measurement of Competency in English*. Ed. Charles R. Cooper. Urbana: NCTE, 1981. 95–136.

———. "The Process of Writing and the Process of Learning." *College Composition and Communication* 31 (1980): 42–50.

———. "Written Products and the Writing Process." *The Writer's Mind*. Ed. Janice N. Hays, Phyllis H. Roth, Jon R. Ramsey, and Robert D. Foulke. Urbana: NCTE, 1983. 53–65.

Odell, Lee, and Dixie Goswami, eds. *Writing in Non-academic Settings*. New York: Guilford, 1985.

Osborne, Martha Lee, ed. *Women in Western Thought*. New York: Random, 1979.

Pastra-Landis, Styliani. "Changes within the Disciplines: Chemistry II." Spanier, Bloom, and Boroviak 207–09.

Peattie, Lisa. *Planning: Rethinking Ciudad Guayana*. Ann Arbor: U of Michigan P, 1987.

Perrin, Porter G. "The Remedial Racket." *English Journal* 22 (1933): 382–88.

Peterson, Jane. "Valuing Teaching: Assumptions, Problems, and Possibilities." *College Composition and Communication* 42 (1991): 25–33.

Piaget, Jean. *The Language and Thought of the Child.* 3rd ed. London: Routledge, 1959.

———. *Play, Dreams and Imitation in Childhood.* London: Routledge, 1962.

Piché, Gene. "Class and Culture in the Development of High School English Curriculum, 1800–1900." *Research in the Teaching of English* 11 (1977): 17–25.

Polanyi, Michael. "Life's Irreducible Structure." *Science* 160 (1968): 1308–12.

———. *Personal Knowledge: Toward a Post-critical Philosophy.* London: Routledge, 1958.

Porter, James W. "Intertextuality and the Discourse Community." *Rhetoric Review* 5 (1986): 34–47.

Postman, Neil, and Charles Weingartner. *Teaching as a Subversive Activity.* New York: Dell, 1969.

Purves, Alan C., and William C. Purves. "Viewpoints: Cultures, Text Models, and the Activity of Writing." *Research in the Teaching of English* 20 (1986): 174–97.

Rabinow, Paul. *Reflections on Fieldwork in Morocco.* Berkeley: U of California P, 1977.

Rader, Ralph W., chair. "Report of the Committee on Prose Improvement, 1964–65." Papers of the Prose Improvement Committee. Berkeley: Dept. of English, Univ. of California, 1965.

"The Recruitment and Retention of Faculty Women and Faculty of Color in Planning Education: Survey Results." *Associated Collegiate Schools of Planning Update.* Spec. issue (1990).

Restivo, Sal. "Modern Science as a Social Problem." *Social Problems* 35 (1988): 206–25.

Rice, John A. *Mathematical Statistics and Data Analysis.* Pacific Grove: Wadsworth and Brooks/Cole, 1988.

Rich, Adrienne. "Taking Women Students Seriously." *On Lies, Secrets, and Silences.* New York: Norton, 1979.

Roberts, Leslie. "Genome Project Underway, at Last." *Science* 13 Jan. 1989: 167.

Roland, Robert C. "The Influence of Purpose on the Field of Argument." *Journal of the American Forensic Association* 18 (1982): 228–44.

Rosaldo, Renato. "Where Objectivity Lies: The Rhetoric of Anthropology." *The Rhetoric of the Human Sciences.* Ed. John Nelson, Allan Megill, and Donald McCloskey. Madison: U of Wisconsin P, 1987.

Rose, Mike. "The Language of Exclusion: Writing Instruction at the University." *College English* 47 (1985): 341–59.

Rosser, Sue V. *Female-Friendly Science: Applying Women's Studies Methods and Theories to Attract Students.* New York: Pergamon, 1990.

———. *Teaching Science and Health from a Feminist Perspective.* New York: Pergamon, 1986.

Rudolph, Fredrick. *Curriculum: A History of the American Undergraduate Course of Study since 1636.* San Francisco: Jossey-Bass, 1978.

Russell, David R. "The Cooperation Movement: Writing and Mass Education, 1890–1930." *Research in the Teaching of English* 23 (1989): 399–423.

———. "Romantics on Writing: Liberal Culture and the Abolition of Composition Courses." *Rhetoric Review* 6 (1988): 132–48.

———. "Writing across the Curriculum and the Communications Movement: Some Lessons from the Past." *College Composition and Communication* 38 (1987): 184–94.

———. *Writing in the Academic Disciplines, 1870–1990: A Curricular History.* Carbondale: Southern Illinois UP, 1991.

Sanyal, Bishwapriya, ed. *Breaking the Boundaries: A One-World Approach to Planning Education.* New York: Plenum, 1990.

Sayre, Anne. *Rosalind Franklin and DNA.* New York: Norton, 1975.

Schectman, Amy. Interview by Louise Dunlap. 26 Jan. 1990.

Schuster, J. Mark Davidson. "Quantitative Reasoning in the Planning Curriculum." *Journal of Planning Education and Research* 6 (1986): 30–36.

———. "Statistically Significant Differences? Students from Developing Areas and the Developing Area of Quantitative Reasoning." Sanyal 107–24.

Schwab, Joseph. "The Practical: A Language for Curriculum." *School Review* 78 (1969): 1–23.

Scott, Fred Newton. "English Composition as a Mode of Behavior." *English Journal* 11 (1922): 463–73.

Scott, Jerrie C. "Maintaining the Cultural Integrity of Literacy Programs." *Louisiana Literacy Forum 1990 Proceedings.* Baton Rouge: Louisiana Endowment for the Humanities, 1990. 107–17.

Scott, Jerrie C., Willis Davis, and Albertina Walker. "A Picture Is Worth a Thousand Words: The Visual Print Connection." *Dialogue: Arts in the Midwest* Nov.–Dec. 1989: 19–21.

Shaughnessy, Mina. "Diving In: An Introduction to Basic Writing." *College Composition and Communication* 27 (1976): 234–39.

Shaver, James P., O. L. Davis, Jr., and Suzanne W. Helburn. "The Status of Social Studies Education: Impressions from Three NSF Studies." *Social Education* 43 (1979): 150–53.

Shayer, David. *The Teaching of English in Schools 1900–1970* London: Routledge, 1972.

Sherif, Muzafer, and Carolyn W. Sherif, eds. *Interdisciplinary Relationships in the Social Sciences.* Chicago: Aldine, 1969.

Shugrue, Michael F. *English in a Decade of Change.* New York: Pegasus, 1968.

Slevin, James. "Depoliticizing and Politicizing Rhetoric and Composition." *The Politics of Writing Instruction.* Ed. Richard Bullock and John Trimbur. Portsmouth: Boynton/Cook, 1991.

Smart, Graham. "Writing to Discover and Structure Meaning in the World of Business." *Carleton Papers in Applied Language Studies* 2 (1985): 33–44.

Smith, Eugene R., Ralph Tyler, and the Evaluation Staff. *Appraising and Recording Student Progress.* New York: Harper, 1942.

Smith, Myrna J. "Bruner on Writing." *College Composition and Communication* 28 (1977): 129–33.

Smith, Ron. "Composition Requirements: A Report on a Nationwide Survey of Four-Year Colleges and Universities." *College Composition and Communication* 25 (1974): 138–48.

Spanier, Bonnie. *Gender and Ideology in Science: A Study of Molecular Biology.* Bloomington: Indiana UP, forthcoming.

———. "Gender and Ideology in Science: A Study of Molecular Biology." *National Women's Studies Association Journal* 3.2 (1991): 167–98.

———. "Transforming the College Biology Curriculum: Themes, Strategies, and Resources." *Ideas and Resources for Integrating Women's Studies into the Curriculum.* Vol. 1. Ed. Myra Dinnerstein and Betty Schmitz. Tucson: Southwest Inst. for Research on Women, 1986. 38–54.

Spanier, Bonnie, Alex Bloom, and Darlene Boroviak, eds. *Toward a Balanced Curriculum.* Cambridge: Schenkman, 1984.

Stanley, Linda C., and Joanna Ambron, eds. *Writing across the Curriculum in Community Colleges.* San Francisco: Jossey-Bass, 1991.

Steffens, Henry. "Journals in the Teaching of History." Fulwiler, *Journal Book* 219–26.

Stewart, Donald. "The Status of Composition and Rhetoric in American Colleges, 1880–1902: An MLA Perspective." *College English* 47 (1975): 734–46.

Stout, Barbara R., and Joyce N. Magnotto. "Building on Realities: WAC Programs at Community Colleges." Stanley and Ambron 9–13.

Strauss, Mary Jo. "Feminist Education in Science, Mathematics, and Technology." *Women's Studies Quarterly* 11.3 (1983): 23–25.

Strenski, Ellen. "Disciplines and Communities, 'Armies' and 'Monasteries,' and the Teaching of Composition." *Rhetoric Review* 8 (1989): 137–44.

Strunk, William, and E. B. White. *The Elements of Style.* New York: Macmillan, 1979.

Summerfield, Geoffrey. "Not in Utopia: Reflections on Journal-Writing." Fulwiler, *Journal Book* 33–40.

Susskind, Lawrence E., and Louise Dunlap. "The Importance of Nonobjective Judgments in Environmental Impact Assessments." *Environmental Impact Assessment Review* 2 (1981): 335–66.

Sutton, Marilyn. "The Writing Adjunct Program at the Small College of California State College, Dominguez Hills." Neel 104–09.

Tavris, Carol, and Carole Wade. *The Longest War: Sex Differences in Perspective.* 2nd. ed. New York: Harcourt, 1984.

Tchudi, Stephen. "The Hidden Agendas in Writing across the Curriculum." *English Journal* 75 (1986): 22–25.

Tett, Alison, and Jeanne M. Wolfe. "Discourse Analysis and City Plans." *Journal of Planning Education and Research* 10 (1991): 195–200.

Thaiss, Christopher. "A Journal in the Arts." Fulwiler, *Journal Book* 246–53.

Throgmorton, J. A. "Planning as Persuasive Storytelling: 'Negotiating' an Electric Power Rate 'Settlement' in Illinois." ACSP/AESOP International Congress. Oxford, 10 July 1991.

Tobias, Sheila. *They're Not Dumb, They're Different: Stalking the Second Tier.* Tucson: Research Corp., 1990.

Toulmin, Stephen, Richard Rieke, and Allan Janik. *An Introduction to Reasoning.* 2nd ed. New York: Macmillan, 1984.

Tyler, Stephen. *The Unspeakable.* Madison: U of Wisconsin P, 1987.

Valdes, Guadalupe. "Language Issues in Writing: The Problem of Compartmentalization of Interest Areas in CCCC." CCCC. Boston, 22 Mar. 1991.

van Maanen, John. *Tales of the Field: On Writing Ethnography.* Chicago: U of Chicago P, 1988.

Vygotsky, Lev. *Thought and Language.* Cambridge: MIT Press, 1962.

Walvoord, Barbara E. Fassler. "The Interdepartmental Composition Program at Central College." Neel 84–89.

Watkins, Beverly T. " 'Practices Gone Wrong' Pervade Education, Humanities-Fund Chief Says." *Chronicle of Higher Education* 14 Nov. 1990: 1–22.

Watson, James D. *The Double Helix.* New York: Atheneum, 1969.

Watson, James D., et al. *Molecular Biology of the Gene.* 4th ed. Menlo Park: Benjamin/Cummings, 1987.

Weeks, Ruth Mary, comp. *A Correlated Curriculum.* NCTE Educational Monograph 5. New York: Appleton, 1936.

White, Edward. "The Damage of Innovations Set Adrift." *AAHE Bulletin* 43 (1990): 3–5.

White, Hayden. *The Content of the Form: Narrative Discourse and Historical Presentation.* Baltimore: Johns Hopkins UP, 1987.

White, James Boyd. *Heracles' Bow: Essays on the Rhetoric and Poetics of the Law.* Madison: U of Wisconsin P, 1986.

"Why Johnny Can't Write." *Newsweek* 9 Dec. 1975: 58–65.

Wilcox, Thomas W. *Anatomy of Freshman English.* San Francisco: Jossey-Bass, 1973.

Wilson, Edward O. *On Human Nature.* Cambridge: Harvard UP, 1978.

Wozniack, John Michael. *English Composition in Eastern Colleges, 1850–1940.* Washington: UP of America, 1978.

Wright, Grace S. *Core Curriculum Development: Problems and Practices.* US Office of Education Bulletin 5. Washington: GPO, 1952.

Yager, Robert E. "The Importance of Terminology in Teaching K–12 Science." *Journal of Research in Science Teaching* 20 (1983): 577–88.

Yates, JoAnne. *Control through Communication: The Rise of System in American Management.* Baltimore: Johns Hopkins UP, 1989.

Young, Art. "Teaching Writing across the University: The Michigan Tech Experience." Address. College English Assn. Convention. Savannah, Mar. 1979. ED 176 928.

Young, Art, and Toby Fulwiler. "The Enemies of Writing across the Curriculum." Fulwiler and Young 287–94.

Young, Richard, Alton Becker, and Kenneth Pike. *Rhetoric: Discovery and Change.* New York: Harcourt, 1970.

Zappert, L., and K. Stanbury. "In the Pipeline: A Comparative Analysis of Men and Women in Graduate Programs in Science, Engineering, and Medicine at Stanford University." Working Paper 20. Palo Alto: Inst. for Research on Women and Gender, Stanford Univ., 1984.

Index